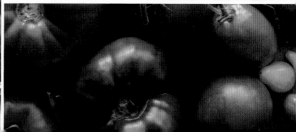

# Better Homes & Gardens®

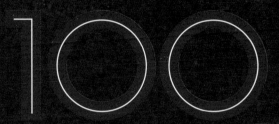

# 100
# RECIPES
# YOU'LL
# MAKE
# FOREVER

## PERFECTED IN OUR
## TEST KITCHEN FOR
## SUCCESS IN YOURS

HOUGHTON MIFFLIN HARCOURT

BOSTON · NEW YORK · 2017

**BETTER HOMES AND GARDENS® 100 RECIPES YOU'LL MAKE FOREVER**

**Editor:** Jan Miller

**Project Editor:** Lisa Kingsley, Waterbury Publications, Inc.

**Contributing Editor:** Tricia Bergman, Waterbury Publications, Inc.

**Contributing Copy Editor and Proofreader:** Carrie Truesdell, Gretchen Kauffman

**Test Kitchen Director:** Lynn Blanchard

**Test Kitchen Product Supervisor:** Colleen Weeden

**Test Kitchen Home Economists:** Sarah Brekke, Linda Brewer, Kelsey Bulat, Carla Christian, Juli Hale, Sammy Mila

**Contributing Photographers:** Jason Donnelly, Jacob Fox, Andy Lyons

**Contributing Stylists:** Greg Luna, Dianna Nolin, Charlie Worthington

**Administrative Assistants:** Barb Allen, Marlene Todd

**BETTER HOMES AND GARDENS®**

**Editor in Chief:** Stephen Orr

**Creative Director:** Jennifer D. Madara

**Editorial Director, Special Interest Publications:** Jennifer Dorland Darling

**Senior Art Director, Special Interest Publications:** Stephanie Hunter

**HOUGHTON MIFFLIN HARCOURT**

**Editorial Director:** Cindy Kitchel

**Executive Editor, Brands:** Anne Ficklen

**Editorial Associate:** Molly Aronica

**Managing Editor:** Marina Padakis Lowry

**Art Director:** Tai Blanche

**Production Director:** Tom Hyland

**WATERBURY PUBLICATIONS, INC.**

**Design Director:** Ken Carlson

**Associate Design Director:** Doug Samuelson

**Production Assistant:** Mindy Samuelson

Names: Better Homes and Gardens Books (Firm), author.
Title: 100 recipes you'll make forever perfected in our test kitchen for success in yours.
Other titles: Better homes and gardens.
Description: Boston : Houghton Mifflin Harcourt, [2017] | "Better homes and gardens." | Includes bibliographical references and index.
Identifiers: LCCN 2017019216 (print) | LCCN 2017018471 (ebook) | ISBN 9780544974265 (ebook) | ISBN 9780544977228 (paper over board : alk. paper)
Subjects: LCSH: Cooking, American. | LCGFT: Cookbooks.
Classification: LCC TX715 (print) | LCC TX715 .A11245 2017 (ebook) | DDC 641.5973—dc23
LC record available at https://lccn.loc.gov/2017019216

Book design by Waterbury Publications, Inc., Des Moines, Iowa.

Printed in China.

SCP 10 9 8 7 6 5 4 3 2 1

Our seal assures you that every recipe in *Better Homes and Gardens® 100 Recipes You'll Make Forever* has been tested in the Better Homes and Gardens® Test Kitchen. This means that each recipe is practical and reliable and meets our high standards of taste appeal. We guarantee your satisfaction with this book for as long as you own it.

**Pictured on front cover:**
Balsamic BBQ Sauce, page 240; Make-It-Mine Vegetable Stir-Fry (with beef), page 180; Potato Cinnamon Rolls, page 70

# CONTENTS

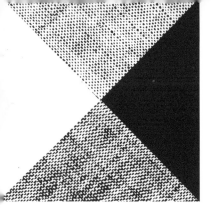

# WELCOME TO OUR TEST KITCHEN

Back in 1928, the editors of *Better Homes and Gardens®* opened the state-of-the-art Better Homes and Gardens Testing-Tasting Kitchen to create and evaluate recipes to be published. It was the first "in-house" test kitchen of its kind, located steps from the editorial offices of the magazine in downtown Des Moines. "It was a modern workshop as near as possible in size and equipment to what you would find in a real home," *BH&G* editors wrote in a 1929 feature.

It's been almost 90 years since our first culinary specialist tied on an apron. Today we're called the BH&G Test Kitchen, and 60,000-plus recipes have passed our standards to be printed in our magazines and cookbooks, including our famed Red Plaid Cookbook—officially known as the *Better Homes and Gardens® New Cook Book.*

Our kitchen has been remodeled and updated many times, but one thing remains: We fail so you don't. We

**THE TEST KITCHEN SEAL ASSURES YOU THAT EVERY RECIPE TESTED IN THE BETTER HOMES AND GARDENS® TEST KITCHEN IS PRACTICAL AND RELIABLE, AND MEETS OUR HIGH STANDARDS OF TASTE APPEAL.**

anticipate any difficult spots home cooks might encounter so we can make our recipes foolproof. We're not a chef's kitchen outfitted with top-of-the-line professional equipment—we make every effort to use the same everyday tools and appliances that you use at home. And we're not a group of classically trained chefs in white coats. Our backgrounds vary—among us are registered dietitians, culinary-school grads, and home economists. We cook all day, but we still go home and cook for our families. We may test and taste eight chocolate cakes (someone has to do it!) to come up with the very best one. It's the same cake we make for our own families.

Bottom line: We do everything we can in *our* kitchen to make sure every recipe is delicious, practical, and reliable in *your* kitchen.

We made *100 Recipes You'll Make Forever* so that you'll have a foolproof collection of the very best recipes, tested and retested, to make sure you get perfect results every time. Want to make cookies that are crunchy on the outside but chewy inside? Or roasted vegetables that are seared just right? Those answers and more are in the pages of this book. It's a stellar collection that includes the best versions of classics as well as modern favorites. Rigorous testing, tasting, and tweaking—plus our favorite tips and techniques—ensures not only that a recipe will work the first time you make it, but that you'll make it again and again.

So welcome to our Test Kitchen! We know you'll enjoy making these recipes as much as we enjoyed the process of perfecting them. Happy cooking!

**PART OF OUR COOKING LEGACY AT *BETTER HOMES AND GARDENS* IS THE FAMED RED PLAID *NEW COOK BOOK* (CURRENTLY IN ITS 16TH EDITION). THIS BOOK IS AT THE HEART OF EVERYTHING WE DO IN THE TEST KITCHEN. EVERY NEW KITCHEN DISCOVERY WE MAKE IS ADDED TO THIS BOOK. EVERY NEW FLAVOR AND TWIST ON THE CLASSICS LANDS IN ITS PAGES.**

# APPETIZERS & SNACKS

# 001  BAKED ROOT VEGETABLE CHIPS

TASTING COMMENTS:  *For maximum crunch we used a two-step baking process—similar to the double-frying method for french fries—for these veggie chips. Baking, letting them stand, then baking again also brings out the best in their earthy flavor.—CW*

**PREP** 15 MINUTES   **BAKE** 14 MINUTES AT 375°F   **STAND** 5 MINUTES   **COOL** 5 MINUTES

**Nonstick cooking spray**

**2 sweet potatoes, purple beets, or golden beets,\* peeled**

**¼ tsp. salt**

**¼ tsp. black pepper**

1. Preheat oven to 375°F. Lightly coat two large baking sheets with cooking spray.

2. Use a mandoline to slice vegetables ¹⁄₁₆ inch thick. If using beets, place slices between layers of paper towels and press firmly to remove excess liquid. Arrange slices in a single layer on prepared baking sheets. Spray tops of vegetables with cooking spray; sprinkle with salt and pepper.

3. Bake 10 minutes. Remove and let stand 5 minutes. Return baking sheets to oven. Bake 4 to 8 minutes more; check for doneness every minute after 4 minutes. Chips are done when centers no longer look wet. Cool chips on paper towels 5 minutes to crisp. Store cooled chips in an airtight container up to 24 hours. If necessary, recrisp chips in a 325°F oven 3 to 4 minutes.

**\*TIP** For a change, try a combination of these vegetables. To avoid burning, check the doneness frequently and remove each type of chip when done.

PER SERVING  *56 cal., 0 g fat, 0 mg chol., 181 mg sodium, 13 g carb., 2 g fiber, 3 g sugars, 1 g pro.*

*Root vegetables are low in moisture compared to other veggies, so they're perfect for making baked chips. You can use all of one type, but we like to use a combination for a more colorful mix!*

*Most of a sweet potato's moisture is trapped in the interior. The key to crisp chips is to properly cook paper-thin slices of veggies. A chip that is undercooked or sliced too thick will be limp. That's why we love the mandoline!*

## TESTING NOTES

1. Use a mandoline to slice the veggies ¹⁄₁₆ inch thick. Small, thin pieces have a lot of surface area and will quickly lose moisture in the oven. Low moisture means crispy chips.

2. Sandwich slices between paper towels; press to remove as much liquid as possible. You want the interiors of the sliced veggies, as they cook, to be dry by the time the crust forms on the exteriors.

3. Lay sliced veggies in a single layer on a baking sheet. After baking for the last 4 minutes, watch these closely. After the sugars caramelize and crisp, the chips may brown more rapidly.

# 002  PEPPERED KALE CHIPS

TASTING COMMENTS: *Kale transforms from bitter and tough to soft and sweet with just a few minutes of oil massage. After a short stay in the oven, the chips will practically dissolve in your mouth.—CC*

**PREP** 10 MINUTES  **BAKE** 22 MINUTES AT 300°F

- 1 **bunch fresh kale (12 oz.)**
- 1 **Tbsp. olive oil**
- ¼ **tsp. salt**
- ¼ **tsp. coarsely ground black pepper**
- ⅛ **tsp. cayenne pepper (optional)**

**1.** Preheat oven to 300°F. Line two large baking sheets with parchment paper; set aside.

**2.** Remove and discard thick stems from kale. Tear leaves into bite-size pieces. Rinse and dry kale pieces in a salad spinner or pat dry with paper towels.

**3.** In a large bowl combine kale, oil, salt, black pepper, and, if desired, cayenne pepper; use your hands to massage oil and seasonings into the kale. Arrange kale in a single layer on prepared baking sheets. Bake 20 minutes. Stir gently. Bake 2 to 4 minutes more or until completely dry and crisp (check chips frequently to prevent burning).

**MAKE-AHEAD DIRECTIONS** Make chips up to 24 hours in advance and store in an airtight container. If necessary, recrisp chips in a 300°F oven 5 minutes.

PER SERVING *73 cal., 4 g fat (1 g sat. fat), 0 mg chol., 182 mg sodium, 9 g carb., 2 g fiber, 2 g sugars, 3 g pro.*

## TESTING NOTES

1. Think about potato chips and tear your leaves into similar-size pieces. Holding each leaf at the base of the stem, tear the leafy portions away from the thick stem.

2. Rinse the torn leaves and use a salad spinner to completely dry them. If you don't have a spinner, dry the leaves between paper towels. If the kale is wet, the oil won't adhere and your chips won't crisp.

After baking 20 minutes, stir the kale chips and return to the oven for 2 to 4 minutes.

They should be crispy, brittle, and browned—but not burned. They actually crisp up even more as they cool, so you have to be patient before digging in!

3. Use your hands to massage the oil and spices onto the leaves. This helps to break down the cellulose structure of the kale and bring out its flavor. The leaves will darken and wilt slightly.

4. Spread kale on a parchment-lined baking sheet in a single layer. An overcrowded baking sheet will keep the leaves from browning evenly—leaves on the bottom might be soggy.

# 003   HUMMUS

TASTING COMMENTS:   *we always let hummus stand at room temperature for 30 minutes before serving to allow its beany, garlicky, toasty flavor and creamy texture to fully express itself.—JH*

**START TO FINISH** 15 MINUTES

- 1 15- to 16-oz. can garbanzo beans (chickpeas), rinsed and drained
- 1 clove garlic, minced
- ¼ cup tahini (sesame seed paste)
- ¼ cup lemon juice
- ¼ cup olive oil
- ½ tsp. salt
- ¼ tsp. paprika
- Stir-ins (such as ¼ cup sliced green onions; ¼ cup crumbled feta cheese; ⅓ cup chopped ripe olives or Kalamata olives; ⅓ cup chopped roasted red sweet peppers; ¼ cup basil pesto; 2 to 3 chopped chipotle peppers;* and/or 1 Tbsp. snipped fresh dill weed) (optional)
- 1 Tbsp. snipped fresh parsley
- 2 to 3 tsp. olive oil (optional)
- 2 Tbsp. pine nuts, toasted** (optional)
- Toasted pita wedges and/or cut-up vegetables

*Tahini is a creamy, thick paste made from ground sesame seeds. Look for it at larger grocery stores in the Asian foods section.*

**1.** In a blender or food processor combine the first seven ingredients (through paprika). Cover and blend or process 1 minute or until smooth.

**2.** If desired, add one or more of the optional stir-ins. Sprinkle with parsley. If desired, drizzle with additional oil and top with pine nuts. Serve at room temperature with pita wedges and/or vegetables.

**\*TIP** Chile peppers contain oils that can irritate your skin and eyes. Wear plastic or rubber gloves when working with them.

**\*\*TIP** To toast nuts, spread them in a single layer in a shallow baking pan. Bake in a 350°F oven 5 to 10 minutes or until golden brown, shaking pan once or twice.

PER SERVING *97 cal., 6 g fat (1 g sat. fat), 0 mg chol., 176 mg sodium, 8 g carb., 2 g fiber, 2 g sugars, 2 g pro.*

**BEET HUMMUS** In a blender or food processor combine one 15-oz. can cannellini beans (white kidney beans), rinsed and drained; ¼ cup tahini; 2 Tbsp. lemon juice; one 8-oz. pkg. refrigerated cooked whole baby beets or one 15-oz. can small whole beets, drained; 1 Tbsp. prepared horseradish; 2 cloves garlic, minced; and ½ tsp. salt. Cover and blend or process until nearly smooth. With machine running, add ¼ cup olive oil in a slow stream until combined. If desired, cover and chill up to 24 hours. If desired, top with chopped hard-cooked egg and/or snipped fresh parsley.

**CARROT HUMMUS** In a covered small saucepan cook 1 cup chopped carrots in a small amount of boiling water 6 to 8 minutes or until tender; drain. In a blender or food processor combine cooked carrots; one 15-oz. can garbanzo beans (chickpeas), rinsed and drained; ¼ cup tahini; 2 Tbsp. lemon juice; 2 cloves garlic, quartered; ½ tsp. ground cumin; and ¼ tsp. salt. Cover and blend or process until smooth. If necessary, stir in enough water, 1 Tbsp. at a time, to reach dipping consistency. Stir in 1 Tbsp. snipped fresh parsley.

**ROASTED RED PEPPER HUMMUS** Preheat oven to 425°F. Cut 2 red sweet peppers in half lengthwise; remove stems, seeds, and membranes. Place pepper halves, cut sides down, on a foil-lined baking sheet. Add 4 unpeeled garlic cloves. Roast 20 to 25 minutes or until peppers are charred and very tender. Bring foil up around peppers and garlic; fold edges together to enclose. Let stand 15 minutes or until cool enough to handle. Use a sharp knife to loosen edges of the pepper skins; pull off the skins in strips and discard. Peel garlic. In a blender or food processor combine roasted peppers and garlic; one 15-oz. can garbanzo beans (chickpeas), rinsed and drained; ¼ cup sliced green onions; ¼ cup tahini; 2 Tbsp. lemon juice; ½ tsp. salt; ¼ tsp. paprika; and, if desired, a dash crushed red pepper. Cover and blend or process until smooth. With machine running, add ⅓ cup olive oil in a slow stream until blended.

Beet Hummus

Carrot Hummus

Roasted Red Pepper Hummus

# 004    ASIAGO-ARTICHOKE DIP

TASTING COMMENTS:    *We've tasted a lot of artichoke dips in our Test Kitchen over the years! This is one of the creamiest baked artichoke dips ever. The secret is just a little flour stirred into the sour cream before baking. We couldn't stop eating at taste panel!—LB*

**PREP** 20 MINUTES    **BAKE** 30 MINUTES AT 350°F    **COOL** 15 MINUTES

1 14-oz. can artichoke hearts, rinsed and drained

2 oz. thinly sliced prosciutto or 2 slices bacon

1 cup arugula or fresh spinach, chopped

1 8-oz. carton sour cream

3 Tbsp. all-purpose flour

½ cup mayonnaise

½ cup bottled roasted red sweet peppers, drained and finely chopped

¾ cup finely shredded Asiago or Parmesan cheese (3 oz.)

¼ cup thinly sliced green onions

Thinly sliced prosciutto or bacon, cut up and crisp-cooked (optional)

Assorted crackers, pita chips, flatbread, and/or toasted baguette slices

*we like either prosciutto or bacon in this dip. Because prosciutto is so thinly sliced, it has a crisper and more delicate texture when cooked than American bacon. which one you use is up to your preference and what you might have on hand.*

**1.** Preheat oven to 350°F. Place artichoke hearts in a fine-mesh sieve; press with paper towels to remove liquid. Chop artichoke hearts. Set aside.

**2.** Stack 2 oz. prosciutto or 2 bacon slices; cut crosswise into thin strips and separate pieces as much as possible. In a medium skillet cook and stir prosciutto or bacon over medium heat 2 minutes or until browned and slightly crisp. Add arugula; cook and stir 1 minute. Set aside.

**3.** In a large bowl stir together sour cream and flour until combined. Stir in mayonnaise and roasted peppers. Stir in ½ cup of the cheese, the green onions, artichokes, and arugula mixture. Transfer to an ungreased 9-inch pie plate. Sprinkle with remaining ¼ cup cheese (if desired, set aside 1 Tbsp. cheese for serving).

**4.** Bake, uncovered, 30 minutes or until edges are lightly browned and dip is hot in center. Cool 15 minutes. If desired, sprinkle with additional prosciutto or bacon and reserved cheese. Serve dip with crackers, chips, flatbread, and/or baguette slices.

PER SERVING *157 cal., 14 g fat (5 g sat. fat), 26 mg chol., 324 mg sodium, 4 g carb., 1 g fiber, 1 g sugars, 4 g pro.*

**LIGHT ASIAGO-ARTICHOKE DIP**
Prepare Asiago-Artichoke Dip as directed, except omit prosciutto. Increase arugula to 2 cups and add it in Step 3. Substitute light sour cream for the sour cream and reduced-fat mayonnaise for the mayonnaise. Omit the ¼ cup finely shredded Asiago cheese sprinkled on top. Serve with assorted vegetable dippers.

PER SERVING *96 cal, 7 g fat (3 g sat. fat), 15 mg chol., 324 mg sodium, 6 g carb, 1 g fiber, 1 g sugars, 2 g pro.*

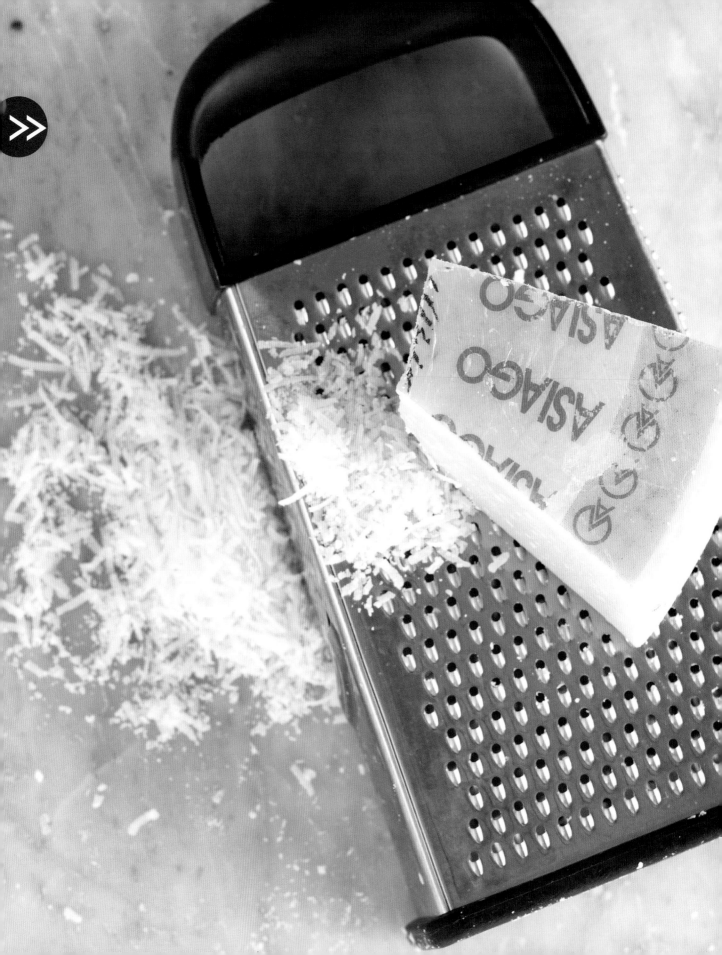

# TESTING NOTES

1. Aged Asiago, a cow's-milk cheese from Italy, has a sharp, tangy flavor and texture similar to Parmesan. For best results in the dip, buy a chunk and shred it yourself. Skip the packaged shredded variety.
←

2. To prevent the dip from becoming watery, drain the artichokes thoroughly before using. Place the rinsed artichokes in a large fine-mesh sieve or colander placed over a bowl. Use paper towels to gently press artichokes, removing as much excess moisture as possible.

↑

3. Make sure you thoroughly mix the flour into the sour cream before you add the remaining dip ingredients. The flour-sour cream mixture binds the dip together during baking and gives it a smooth, creamy texture and appearance.

4. Prosciutto is not easy to cut into small pieces before cooking. Briefly cooking prosciutto before cutting into strips makes the job so much easier. To cook, place whole slices in a skillet over medium heat and cook 2 minutes, turning once. Remove from the pan and let cool until easy to handle. It will crisp as it cools. Then to make cutting really easy, use kitchen shears to cut into bite-size strips.
↓

**SKIP THE OVEN AND SERVE IT COLD!**
*Prepare dip as directed through Step 2. Let arugula mixture cool 15 minutes before proceeding with Step 3. Omit flour. Combine sour cream, mayonnaise, roasted peppers, ½ cup of the cheese, the green onions, artichokes, and arugula mixture. Cover and chill at least 1 hour or up to 24 hours. If dip thickens when chilled, stir in 1 to 2 Tbsp. milk. Sprinkle with only 1 Tbsp. cheese before serving. Garnish with an additional 1 Tbsp. thinly sliced green onion.*

We love crisp, sturdy baguette slices for scooping this dip. Cut an 8-inch baguette into 36 slices. Arrange slices on two large baking sheets. Brush one side of each slice with olive oil. Broil, one pan at a time, 3 to 4 inches from the heat 2 to 3 minutes or until toasted, turning once.

## 005  DEVILED EGGS

TASTING COMMENTS: *Delicious deviled eggs are easy to make if you start with perfectly boiled hard-cooked eggs. The secret is simple: Fresh is not best. Use eggs that are a week old for easiest peeling.—SM*

**START TO FINISH** 25 MINUTES

6 hard-cooked eggs*
¼ cup mayonnaise or salad dressing
1 tsp. prepared mustard
1 tsp. vinegar
Salt (optional)
Black pepper (optional)
Paprika or fresh parsley leaves (optional)

*Size matters, color doesn't! Eggs come in medium, large, and extra-large sizes. We use large eggs in testing, so the timing in this recipe works best for large eggs. If you use extra-large eggs, let the eggs stand in the boiled water 18 minutes instead of 15 minutes.*

**1.** Cut eggs in half lengthwise and remove yolks. Set whites aside. Place yolks in a small bowl; mash with a fork. Stir in mayonnaise, mustard, and vinegar. If desired, season to taste with salt and pepper.

**2.** Spoon or pipe the yolk mixture into egg halves. Cover; chill at least 1 hour or up to 24 hours. If desired, sprinkle with paprika or parsley.

**\*TIP** To hard-cook the eggs, place eggs in a single layer in a large saucepan. Add enough cold water to cover eggs by 1 inch. Bring to a full rolling boil over high heat; remove from heat. Cover and let stand 15 minutes; drain. Place eggs in ice water to cool. Drain and peel.

PER SERVING *72 cal., 6 g fat (1 g sat. fat), 109 mg chol., 62 mg sodium, 0 g carb., 0 g fiber, 0 g sugars, 3 g pro.*

**BACON AND BASIL EGGS** Prepare Deviled Eggs as directed, except stir 2 slices crisp-cooked and crumbled bacon; 2 Tbsp. chopped tomato; and 1 Tbsp. snipped fresh basil into the yolk mixture. If desired, top with additional crisp-cooked bacon.

**SMOKED SALMON EGGS** Prepare Deviled Eggs as directed, except stir 1 Tbsp. snipped fresh chives into the yolk mixture. Top each egg with strips of lox-style smoked salmon, sour cream, and additional snipped chives.

**MEXICAN-STYLE EGGS** Prepare Deviled Eggs as directed, except substitute Mexican-style sour cream dip for mayonnaise and stir ¼ cup chopped avocado and 1 Tbsp. snipped fresh cilantro into the yolk mixture. If desired, top with additional cilantro, avocado, and chopped fresh jalapeño chile pepper (tip, page 18).

**GREEK-STYLE EGGS** Prepare Deviled Eggs as directed, except stir 2 Tbsp. crumbled feta cheese, 1 Tbsp. finely chopped pitted Kalamata olives, and 2 tsp. snipped fresh oregano into the yolk mixture. If desired, top with additional chopped olives, crumbled feta cheese, and snipped oregano.

**BLUE CHEESE, APPLE, AND WALNUT EGGS** Prepare Deviled Eggs as directed, except stir ¼ cup chopped apple, 1 Tbsp. crumbled blue cheese, and 1 Tbsp. chopped toasted walnuts into the yolk mixture.

If you are particular about how smooth your filling is, push the yolk through a fine-mesh sieve. The sieve creates a very fine-texture yolk to stir into your remaining filling ingredients. If you like a chunkier filling, use a fork to mash to the desired texture.

Deviled Eggs

Mexican-Style
Eggs

Bacon and
Basil Eggs

Blue Cheese, Apple,
and Walnut Eggs

Smoked
Salmon Eggs

Greek-Style
Eggs

MAKES: *16 servings*   TESTED BY: *Sarah B.*

# 006   **CHUNKY GUACAMOLE**

TASTING COMMENTS: *The key to great guacamole is perfectly ripe avocados. We buy ours when they're firm so they don't bruise on the way from the store—then we let them ripen at for a couple of days before using.—SB*

*Some like it hot—to varying degrees! For kicked-up guacamole, stir in one or more of the following: 1 fresh jalapeño chile pepper, seeded and finely chopped; 1 canned chipotle chile pepper in adobo sauce, finely chopped; ¼ tsp. ancho chile powder; or ⅛ tsp. cayenne pepper.*

**START TO FINISH** 20 MINUTES

- ⅔ cup finely chopped and seeded roma tomatoes
- ¼ cup sliced green onions
- 1 to 2 cloves garlic, minced
- 2 Tbsp. lime juice
- 1 Tbsp. olive oil
- ¼ tsp. salt
- ⅛ tsp. black pepper
- 2 ripe avocados, halved, seeded, peeled, and coarsely mashed
- Tortilla chips

**1.** In a medium bowl combine first seven ingredients (through pepper). Gently stir in avocados.

**2.** Serve immediately or cover the surface with plastic wrap and chill up to 1 hour. Serve guacamole with tortilla chips.

PER SERVING  *48 cal., 5 g fat (1 g sat. fat), 0 mg chol, 39 mg sodium, 3 g carb., 1 g fiber, 0 g sugars, 1 g pro.*

*Ancho chile powder*

*Fresh jalapeño pepper*

*Cayenne pepper*

*Chipotle chile pepper*

**RIPENESS IS KEY**  *Ripe avocados are heavy for their size and feel soft under gentle palm pressure. (Don't press them with your finger or they'll bruise.) Avoid avocados that have dark spots on the skin or feel overly soft. If you have hard, underripe avocados, speed-ripen by placing them in a closed paper bag at room temperature up to 5 days. Once an avocado is ripe, you can store it in the refrigerator up to 2 days.*

## TESTING NOTES

1. To remove seeds from roma tomatoes, cut them into quarters. Use a spoon or your fingers to scoop out and discard the seeds.

2. To remove the avocado seed, cut the avocado lengthwise around the seed. Twist the two halves to separate. If the seed does not loosen from the flesh, use a small spoon to remove the seed from the avocado.

3. For an easy, clean way to mash, place avocado flesh, garlic, lime juice, olive oil, salt, and pepper in a plastic bag. Seal and use your hands to mash everything together. Snip a hole in one corner and squeeze mashed avocado mixture into a bowl with tomatoes and onion. Or place in the refrigerator until ready to use (up to 8 hours).

4. If you're not planning to serve guacamole immediately after you make it, place plastic wrap directly on the surface to prevent it from discoloring. Store in the refrigerator and serve within 8 hours.

MAKES: *24 servings*   TESTED BY: *Kelsey B.*

# 007   ROASTED SALSA ROJA

TASTING COMMENTS:   *We test tomato recipes even in the dead of winter. If you are worried about the flavor of your tomatoes, roasting brings out their best! A hot oven concentrates and caramelizes their natural sugars, adding depth and intensity to homemade salsa.—KB*

**PREP** 30 MINUTES   **BROIL** 14 MINUTES   **COOL** 10 MINUTES

- 3 tomatoes (about 1½ lb. total), cored and each cut into eighths
- 5 cloves garlic, peeled
- 1 fresh jalapeño chile pepper, stemmed, halved, and seeded (tip, page 18)
- 2 to 3 Tbsp. vegetable oil
- 1 cup snipped fresh cilantro
- ⅓ cup chopped onion
- ¼ to ⅓ cup lime juice
- ½ tsp. sugar
- 1 tsp. salt

*Add lime juice gradually to give your salsa a tangy bite without adding too much additional liquid. I taste as I go to get it just right.*

**1.** Preheat broiler. In a large bowl combine tomatoes, garlic, and chile pepper; toss with just enough of the oil to coat. Spoon into a 15×10-inch baking pan.

**2.** Broil 5 to 6 inches from heat 8 minutes. Turn vegetables. Broil 6 to 8 minutes more or until edges of vegetables begin to darken. Transfer pan to a wire rack; cool 10 minutes.

**3.** Transfer roasted vegetables and their cooking juices to a food processor; pulse until coarsely chopped. Add cilantro, onion, lime juice, and sugar; pulse until salsa is desired consistency. Season to taste with salt. Serve immediately or cover and chill up to 3 days.

PER SERVING *19 cal., 1 g fat, (0 g sat. fat), 0 mg chol., 76 mg sodium, 2 g carb., 1 g fiber, 1 g sugars, 0 g pro.*

**CHOOSE YOUR TOMATO** *Use whatever fresh summer tomatoes you have on hand—regardless of their size and variety, you can't go wrong with this recipe. Remember: Tomatoes do not like the refrigerator. Always store tomatoes at room temperature. Cool temps change their flavor and make them mealy.*

## TESTING NOTES

1. To core a tomato, use a small sharp paring knife to cut a small circle around the stem. Using the tip of the knife, remove and discard the core.

2. If you like your salsa extra hot, leave in some of the chile pepper's seeds and membranes—they are the hottest parts. If mild is more your style, remove them altogether.

3. Roasting vegetables in a very hot oven brings out their natural sweetness and gives them a brown, almost crispy exterior while keeping the insides moist and tender. Place vegetables in a single layer and don't crowd them. For easier cleanup, line the pan with foil.

# 008  SALSA VERDE

TASTING COMMENTS: *The best way to experience the addictive, sour tanginess of tomatillos is in a really good salsa verde. And we think the secret to really good salsa verde is getting the balance of chiles and tomatillos just right. We love it with tortilla chips but also on grilled chicken, fish, and shrimp.—CW*

**PREP** 20 MINUTES  **BROIL** 7 MINUTES  **STAND** 10 MINUTES

- 12 oz. fresh tomatillos, husks removed, rinsed, and drained
- 1 fresh poblano chile pepper
- 1 fresh serrano chile pepper
- 2 cloves garlic, minced
- ½ tsp. salt
- ¼ tsp. sugar
- 2 Tbsp. chopped onion
- 2 Tbsp. snipped fresh cilantro

*If you can't find fresh tomatillos, substitute one 11-oz. can tomatillos, rinsed and drained, and decrease the salt to ¼ tsp. Don't broil the canned tomatillos, but do broil the chile peppers for a bit of charring, which is not only pretty but adds flavor, too!*

1. Preheat broiler. Arrange tomatillos and chile peppers on a foil-lined broiler pan. Broil 7 to 8 minutes or until charred, turning tomatillos and peppers once or twice. Enclose tomatillos and peppers in the foil. Let stand 10 minutes. Using a sharp knife, loosen edges of skins on peppers; gently pull off skins in strips and discard.

2. In a food processor combine tomatillos, chile peppers, garlic, salt, and sugar. Pulse until chopped. Stir in onion and cilantro. Add water, 1 Tbsp. at a time, until desired consistency.

PER SERVING *7 cal., 0 g fat., 0 mg chol., 49 mg sodium, 1 g carb., 0 g fiber, 1 g sugars, 0 g pro.*

**TOMATILLOS** *Tomatillos are small green fruits that belong to the same family as tomatoes, but they have a tart, citrusy flavor. Look for fresh tomatillos that are firm, bright green, and unblemished. Remove the inedible papery skin and rinse off the sticky outer coating before use. Store at room temperature up to 5 days or refrigerate up to 2 weeks.*

*Store peppers, covered, in the refrigerator up to 5 days.*

## TESTING NOTES

1. Salsa verde gets its flavor and heat from two different chile peppers. Poblano peppers are larger and one of the more mild varieties of hot peppers. Serrano peppers are much smaller but pack quite a bit more heat.

2. When choosing any variety of pepper, look for those that are glossy and have bright color; avoid any that are shriveled, bruised, or have soft spots.

3. After roasting, use a small sharp paring knife to loosen edges of the pepper skins; gently pull off the skins in strips and discard.

4. After removing the skin, slice off and discard the stem. Cut the pepper into strips. If desired, use a spoon to scrape out the seeds (leave some or all of the seeds if you want additional heat).

MAKES: *12 servings*   TESTED BY: *Carla C.*

# 009   **CALIFORNIA SUSHI ROLLS**

**TASTING COMMENTS:** *Great sushi features fresh ingredients wrapped up nice and tight in pieces that don't fall apart. The trick is "sticky" rice that's easy to shape. Short grain rice releases more starch than medium or long grain rice, which is why it's used for sushi.—CC*

**START TO FINISH** 30 MINUTES

- 2 **8-inch square sheets nori (seaweed)**
- 1 **recipe Sticky Rice**
  **Desired fillings (such as small carrot, zucchini, or cucumber sticks; avocado slices; canned crabmeat; smoked salmon [lox-style]; and/or small cooked shrimp, peeled and deveined)**
- 1 **recipe Honey-Ginger Sauce**

*Nori is made by shredding seaweed and pressing it into thin but sturdy sheets—much like the process of making paper—that keep the sushi pieces neat and tidy. If you can't find nori in the Asian foods section at your supermarket, look at a whole-foods store or Asian market.*

**1.** Lay nori on a sushi mat lined with plastic wrap; with damp fingers, spread 1 cup of the Sticky Rice over each sheet to within 1 inch of one edge. Arrange desired vegetable or seafood fillings crosswise just off the center of the rice.

**2.** Roll seaweed toward the 1-inch unfilled edge. (For a tight, even roll, place your hands under the edge of the mat closest to you. While carefully lifting the edge of the nori, roll it away from you.) Press unfilled edge over top, brushing with water to seal if necessary.

**3.** Cut each roll into six pieces; arrange on a platter. If desired, cover and chill up to 4 hours. Serve with Honey-Ginger Sauce for dipping.

**PER SERVING** *73 cal., 0 g fat., 1 mg chol., 293 mg sodium, 17 g carb., 1 g fiber, 8 g sugars, 1 g pro.*

**STICKY RICE** In a fine-mesh sieve wash ½ cup short grain rice under cold running water, rubbing grains together with your fingers. In a small saucepan combine rinsed rice and ¾ cup cold water. Bring to boiling; reduce heat. Simmer, covered, 15 minutes (rice should be sticky). Remove from heat. In a small bowl stir together 2 tsp. rice vinegar, 1 tsp. sugar, and ½ tsp. salt. Stir vinegar mixture into rice in saucepan; cover and cool about 45 minutes or until room temperature. (Rice can be covered and chilled up to 3 days.)

**HONEY-GINGER SAUCE** In a small saucepan combine ⅓ cup honey; ¼ cup water; 2 Tbsp. plum sauce; 2 Tbsp. soy sauce; and 1- to 2-inch piece fresh ginger, peeled and thinly sliced. Bring to boiling, stirring frequently; reduce heat. Simmer, uncovered, 15 to 20 minutes or until slightly thickened, stirring occasionally. Strain into a small bowl; cool. Cover and chill.

*Placing the fillings closer to one edge makes an even layer of rice around the fillings in each piece.*

## TESTING NOTES

1. Press small handfuls of the rice evenly over the nori. Dip your fingers in water to keep the rice from sticking to you.

2. Just off-center and opposite the unfilled edge of the nori, arrange the filling ingredients crosswise on rice.

**3.** Use the sushi mat to lift and roll the nori toward the unfilled edge. Roll as tightly as you can. Wet the edge of the nori with water for a good seal.

**4.** Use a good sharp knife to cut the rolls into even pieces. A sharp knife will slice down easily through the nori and the fillings. A dull knife will result in squashed or flattened pieces of sushi.

# BREAKFAST
# & BRUNCH

TESTED BY: *Colleen W.*

# 010   COOKING EGGS

TASTING COMMENTS: *For hard-cooked eggs with perfect sunny-yellow yolks (and no gray ring), cook them gently in just-boiled water off the heat.—CW*

## HARD-COOKED EGGS

**START TO FINISH** 25 MINUTES   **MAKES** 6 SERVINGS

**6 large eggs***
**Cold water**

**1.** Place eggs in a single layer in a large saucepan (do not stack eggs). Add enough cold water to cover the eggs by 1 inch. Bring to a rapid boil over high heat (water will have large, rapidly breaking bubbles). Remove from heat, cover, and let stand 15 minutes;* drain.

**2.** Run cold water over eggs or place them in ice water until cool enough to handle; drain.

**3.** To peel eggs, gently tap each egg on the countertop. Roll the egg between the palms of your hands. Peel off eggshell, starting at the large end.

***TIP** If you use extra-large eggs, let eggs stand in the boiled water 18 minutes.

PER SERVING *78 cal., 5 g fat (2 g sat. fat), 212 mg chol., 62 mg sodium, 1 g carb., 0 g fiber, 0 g sugars, 6 g pro.*

## TESTING NOTES

↑
1. The eggs should be in a single layer, not stacked. After the water comes to a rapid boil, immediately remove from heat. Cooking the eggs too long is what creates the gray ring around the edge of the yolk. Cover the pot to retain the heat and let it stand for 15 minutes.

↑
2. After the 15 minutes are up, drain the eggs and place them in a bowl of ice water. Let them cool until they are easy to handle.

↑
3. Slightly crack the eggs and roll between the palms of your hands or against the countertop. This will help to preserve the shape of the egg inside, making it easier to peel off the shell.

↑
4. If you are using 7- to 10-day-old eggs, peeling should be easy. Starting at the large end, gently peel off the shell. Peeling eggs under running water also helps the shell come off more easily. Use a sharp paring knife to cut eggs in half.

## POACHED EGGS

**START TO FINISH** 10 MINUTES
**MAKES** 4 SERVINGS

- 4 cups water
- 1 Tbsp. vinegar
- 4 eggs
  Salt and black pepper

**1.** Add the water to a large skillet; add vinegar. Bring to boiling; reduce heat to simmering (bubbles should begin to break the surface of the water).

**2.** Break an egg into a cup and slip egg into water. Repeat with remaining eggs, allowing each egg equal space in the water.

**3.** Simmer eggs, uncovered, 3 to 5 minutes or until whites are set and yolks begin to thicken but are not hard. Remove eggs. Season to taste with salt and pepper.

### PAN-POACHED EGGS
Lightly grease cups of an egg-poaching pan. Place cups into pan over boiling water; reduce heat to simmering. Break an egg into a custard cup. Slide egg into a poaching cup. Repeat with remaining eggs. Cover; cook 4 to 6 minutes or until the whites are set and yolks begin to thicken but are not hard. Run a knife around edges to loosen eggs.

### MAKE-AHEAD DIRECTIONS
Prepare as directed. Place cooked eggs in a bowl of cold water. Cover and chill up to 1 hour. To reheat eggs, in a saucepan bring water to simmering. Using a slotted spoon, slip eggs into the simmering water and heat about 2 minutes.

PER SERVING *73 cal., 5 g fat (2 g sat. fat), 212 mg chol., 273 mg sodium, 1 g carb., 0 g fiber, 0 g sugars, 6 g pro.*

## TESTING NOTES

↑
1. Hold the lip of the cup close to the simmering vinegar mixture to slip the egg in so it doesn't break. The vinegar helps the egg quickly firm up.

↑
2. When the eggs are cooked, use a slotted spoon to remove them from the skillet so the liquid drains away.

**POACHER** *Although a special pan is not essential to achieving the perfect poached egg, it makes the job easier and the eggs more uniformly shaped.*

## FRIED EGGS

**START TO FINISH** 10 MINUTES
**MAKES** 4 SERVINGS

- 2 tsp. butter or margarine or nonstick cooking spray
- 4 eggs
  Salt (optional)
  Black pepper (optional)

**1.** In a large skillet melt butter over medium heat. (Or coat an unheated skillet with nonstick cooking spray.) Break eggs into skillet. If desired, sprinkle with salt and pepper. Reduce heat to low; cook eggs 3 to 4 minutes or until whites are completely set and yolks start to thicken.

**2.** For fried eggs over-easy or over-hard, turn the eggs and cook 30 seconds more (over-easy) or 1 minute more (over-hard).

### STEAM-BASTED FRIED EGGS
Prepare as directed, except when egg edges turn white, add 1 Tbsp. water to skillet. Cover skillet and cook eggs 3 to 4 minutes or until yolks begin to thicken but are not hard.

PER SERVING *88 cal., 7 g fat (3 g sat. fat), 217 mg chol., 84 mg sodium, 0 g carb., 0 g fiber, 0 g sugars, 6 g pro.*

## TESTING NOTES

↑
1. Make sure the skillet is hot. Swirl the butter to coat bottom of pan.

↑
2. For over-easy or over-hard eggs, gently turn the eggs over after the whites have almost completely set.

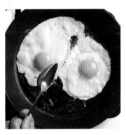

↑
3. For prettier eggs, cook the tops with steam; do not turn eggs. Add 1 Tbsp. water to the skillet. Cover the skillet.

↑
4. A glass lid lets you see when the yolks are set but still a little runny.

# SCRAMBLED EGGS

**START TO FINISH** 10 MINUTES
**MAKES** 3 SERVINGS

*Vigorously whisking the egg mixture incorporates air and helps give the scrambled eggs a light and fluffy texture.*

6 eggs
⅓ cup milk or half-and-half
¼ tsp. salt
Dash black pepper
1 Tbsp. butter or margarine

**1.** In a medium bowl whisk together eggs, milk, salt, and pepper. In a large skillet melt butter over medium heat; pour in egg mixture. Cook over medium heat, without stirring, until mixture begins to set on bottom and around edges.

**2.** With a spatula or large spoon, lift and fold the partially cooked eggs so the uncooked portion flows underneath. Continue cooking over medium 2 to 3 minutes or until eggs are cooked through but still glossy and moist. Immediately remove from heat.

PER SERVING *191 cal., 14 g fat (6 g sat. fat), 435 mg chol., 372 mg sodium, 2 g carb., 0 g fiber, 0 g sugars, 14 g pro.*

### MEAT-LOVER'S SCRAMBLED EGGS

Prepare as directed, except omit butter. In the skillet cook and stir 3 slices bacon, chopped, and 4 oz. bulk pork sausage over medium heat until bacon is crisp and sausage is browned. Drain, reserving 1 Tbsp. drippings in skillet. Set meat aside. Cook egg mixture in drippings. Sprinkle with bacon, sausage, and ⅓ cup chopped cooked ham or Polish sausage. Continue cooking as directed.

### CHEESE-AND-ONION SCRAMBLED EGGS

Prepare as directed, except cook 2 Tbsp. sliced green onion in the butter 30 seconds; add egg mixture and continue as directed. After eggs begin to set, fold in ½ cup shredded cheddar, mozzarella, or Monterey Jack cheese with jalapeño peppers (2 oz.).

### MUSHROOM SCRAMBLED EGGS

Prepare as directed, except increase the butter to 2 Tbsp. Cook 1½ cups sliced fresh mushrooms and 1 Tbsp. chopped onion in the butter. Add 1 Tbsp. snipped fresh parsley, ½ tsp. dry mustard, and ¼ tsp. Worcestershire sauce to beaten egg mixture. Add egg mixture to skillet and continue as directed.

### LOW-FAT SCRAMBLED EGGS

Prepare as directed, except substitute 3 whole eggs and 5 egg whites for the 6 whole eggs. Substitute fat-free milk for the milk. Omit the butter and coat a nonstick skillet with nonstick cooking spray before cooking the egg mixture as directed.

### DENVER SCRAMBLED EGGS

Prepare as directed, except omit salt and increase butter to 2 Tbsp. In the skillet cook 1 cup sliced fresh mushrooms, ⅓ cup diced cooked ham, ¼ cup chopped onion, and 2 Tbsp. finely chopped green sweet pepper in the butter. Add egg mixture to skillet and continue as directed.

**EGG MATH** *One medium egg contains about 3 Tbsp. volume, large eggs about 3½ Tbsp. volume, and extra-large eggs about 4 Tbsp. volume. The Test Kitchen uses large eggs when testing all recipes.*

**PUT IT TO USE!** *If you need breakfast on the run, make your scrambled eggs portable with these easy ideas.*

**BURRITOS** Simply roll up scrambled eggs, a little shredded cheese, and salsa in a flour tortilla. This makes a great breakfast to go!

**PIZZA** Start with a purchased pizza crust and top with scrambled eggs and your favorite toppings. Bake according to package directions.

## TESTING NOTES

1. After you pour the eggs into the heated skillet, let them sit 20 to 30 seconds or until the eggs begin to set on the bottom. Resist the urge to stir! Let ribbons of cooked egg begin to form before you put your spatula to work.

2. Lift and fold the cooked egg toward the center, allowing uncooked egg to flow under the spatula. Repeat lifting and folding until eggs are just set and still appear slightly wet.

MAKES: *1 serving* TESTED BY: *Carla C.*

# 011 FRENCH OMELET

TASTING COMMENTS: *Make it easy on yourself! We always use a small nonstick skillet with flared sides to make omelets. The proteins in eggs bind to cooking surfaces, making them stick. Omelets slide out of a nonstick pan. —CC*

**START TO FINISH** 10 MINUTES

2 eggs
2 Tbsp. cold water
⅛ tsp. salt
Dash black pepper
1 Tbsp. butter or margarine

*Adding 1 Tbsp. of cold water per egg creates steam when the eggs are cooking, which makes for fluffier omelets.*

**1.** In a small bowl combine eggs, the water, salt, and pepper. Beat with a fork until combined but not frothy. Heat a small nonstick skillet with flared sides over medium-high heat until skillet is hot.

**2.** Melt butter in skillet. Add egg mixture to skillet; reduce heat to medium. Immediately begin stirring gently but continuously until egg mixture resembles small pieces of cooked egg surrounded by liquid egg. Stop stirring. Cook 30 to 60 seconds more or until egg is set and shiny.

**3.** With a spatula lift and fold omelet edge about a third of the way toward the center. Fold opposite side toward center and transfer to a warm plate. If making more than one omelet, keep warm while preparing additional omelets.

PER SERVING *216 cal., 17 g fat (8 g sat. fat), 244 mg chol., 559 mg sodium, 1 g carb., 0 g fiber, 0 g sugars, 14 g pro.*

**FILLED FRENCH OMELET** Prepare one of the fillings, opposite, before making omelet. For one omelet, if using fresh vegetables (⅓ to ½ cup chopped or sliced mushrooms, onion, sweet pepper, or potatoes), cook vegetables in 1 tsp. butter or vegetable oil in a skillet. If desired, add ⅛ to ¼ tsp. herb to egg mixture. Use 2 to 3 Tbsp. shredded cheese and ⅓ to ½ cup cooked meat. Spoon filling across the center of omelet before Step 2. If desired, sprinkle omelet with additional cheese.

**LOWER-CHOLESTEROL OMELET** Prepare as directed, except substitute 2 egg whites for one of the whole eggs.

## TESTING NOTES

1. Immediately reduce the heat to medium after adding the egg mixture to the skillet to avoid overbrowning the bottom of the omelet.

2. Although a triple fold is the most common way to finish an omelet, you can place the filling on one half and fold the other half over the top of it.

3. A rubber spatula is a good tool to use when making omelets—rather than a turner—because it is flexible and soft and won't tear the egg.

**POTATO-BACON** Cook frozen diced hash brown potatoes and chopped bacon in oil. Add to omelet; add shredded cheddar cheese.

**SHRIMP-AVOCADO** Fill with whole or chopped cooked shrimp, sliced avocado, and fresh cilantro sprigs.

**DENVER** Cook chopped green and/or red sweet pepper, onion, and basil in butter; stir in chopped cooked ham.

**ASPARAGUS-HAM** Add dill to eggs; fill with chopped cooked asparagus, cooked ham or prosciutto, and finely shredded Parmesan.

**BEAN-FILLED** Fill with black beans, salsa, and shredded Monterey Jack cheese.

**CHEESE-MUSHROOM** Cook sliced fresh mushrooms in butter; add to omelet. Add shredded cheddar cheese.

**ITALIAN** Fill with cooked Italian sausage, chopped roasted red sweet peppers, and torn provolone cheese.

**SPINACH-FETA** Fill with shredded fresh spinach and crumbled feta cheese.

MAKES: *6 servings*   TESTED BY: *Julie H.*

# 012   SHAKSHUKA

TASTING COMMENTS: *One of the things that makes this dish so tasty is the balance of the acidity in the highly seasoned tomato sauce and the richness of the egg yolks—and vice versa.—JH*

**HANDS ON** 15 MINUTES   **TOTAL TIME** 45 MINUTES

- 2 Tbsp. olive oil
- 1 cup chopped onion
- 1 large red sweet pepper, seeded and chopped
- 1 jalapeño chile pepper, stemmed, seeded, and chopped (tip, page 18)
- 3 cloves garlic, sliced
- 1 tsp. ground cumin
- 1 tsp. sweet paprika
- 1 tsp. ground turmeric
- ½ tsp. kosher salt
- ¼ tsp. black pepper
- 1 28-oz. can whole plum tomatoes with juices, coarsely chopped
- 6 eggs
  Feta cheese, crumbled
  Fresh cilantro and/or oregano

*Jalapeños vary widely in their heat level. If you don't like a lot of heat, your safest bet is removing all of the seeds— the hottest part of the pepper.*

1. In a large deep skillet heat oil over medium heat. Add the next nine ingredients (through black pepper). Cook and stir 10 minutes or until vegetables are soft but not browned. Stir in undrained tomatoes. Bring to boiling; reduce heat. Simmer, uncovered, 10 minutes or until slightly thickened, stirring occasionally.

2. Crack eggs, one at a time, into a small dish and carefully pour into sauce. Cover; reduce heat. Cook 5 to 10 minutes or until whites are set and yolks are desired doneness. Top with feta and cilantro and/or oregano.

PER SERVING *174 cal., 11 g fat (3 g sat. fat), 192 mg chol., 478 mg sodium, 11 g carb., 4 g fiber, 6 g sugars, 9 g pro.*

**SHAK-WHAT?** *Shakshuka (shahk-SHOO-kah) is the quintessential Israeli breakfast (the equivalent of our eggs, bacon, and toast). At its most basic, the dish is eggs cooked on top of a rich simmering tomato sauce with onions, peppers, and a cumin spice mixture. You can skew the sauce in any direction your mood (or fridge) dictates. Brown mushrooms with the peppers or throw a handful of spinach into the sauce before adding the eggs.*

*Paprika, cumin, and turmeric are commonly used in Middle Eastern cooking. The highly aromatic spices infuse foods with warmth and pungency.*

## TESTING NOTES

1. As when poaching eggs, crack the eggs, one at a time, into a small dish or ramekin.

2. Carefully pour the individual eggs into the simmering tomato sauce, allowing each an equal amount of space. Pouring from a small dish allows you to get the lip close to the surface of the sauce so the egg yolk is less likely to break.

# 013 PERFECT HASH BROWNS

TASTING COMMENTS: *Russets are the best potato for these hash browns. Their high starch/low moisture content creates a fluffy interior and a crisp exterior.—LB*

**PREP** 20 MINUTES **COOK** 20 MINUTES

1¼ lb. russet potatoes
¼ tsp. salt
⅛ tsp. black pepper
1 to 2 Tbsp. olive oil
1 Tbsp. butter
Paprika (optional)

*This combo is ideal for frying. Butter gives great flavor, but the milk solids burn at a high temperature. Combining it with oil protects the milk solids and allows a higher frying temperature— which ensures delicious, crispy potatoes.*

**1.** Peel potatoes. Coarsely shred potatoes using a handheld shredder or a food processor with a coarse shredding blade.

**2.** Place shredded potatoes in a large bowl. Add enough cool water to cover; stir well. Drain in a colander set in a sink. Repeat rinsing and draining two or three times or until water runs clear. Press out as much water as you can with a rubber spatula. Line a salad spinner with paper towels; add potatoes and spin.* Repeat, if necessary, until potatoes are dry. Transfer potatoes to a large bowl. Sprinkle potatoes with salt and pepper, tossing to combine.

**3.** In a large nonstick skillet** heat 1 Tbsp. of the oil and the butter over medium-high heat until butter foams. Add potatoes to the skillet; spread into an even layer. Gently press with the back of a spatula to form a cake. Reduce heat to medium. Cook, without stirring, 12 minutes or until the bottom is golden brown and crisp.

**4.** Invert a baking sheet or plate over the top of the skillet. Carefully invert skillet with the baking sheet or plate to transfer the potatoes to the baking sheet or plate. If needed, add the remaining 1 Tbsp. oil to the skillet. Using the baking sheet or plate, slide potatoes back into the skillet, uncooked side down. Cook, without stirring, 8 minutes more or until the bottom is golden brown. If desired, sprinkle with paprika.

**MAKE-AHEAD DIRECTIONS** Shred potatoes as directed in Step 1. Place in a bowl of cool water. Refrigerate overnight. Rinse and continue with Steps 2 through 4 as directed.

***TIP** For better browning, dry shredded potatoes well before cooking using a salad spinner or press potatoes with paper towels.

****TIP** A skillet with flared sides works best.

PER SERVING *110 cal., 4 g fat (2 g sat. fat), 5 mg chol., 120 mg sodium, 17 g carb., 1 g fiber, 1 g sugars, 2 g pro.*

## TESTING NOTES

1. Once the butter is foamy, you know the oil and butter are hot. Sprinkle your dried shredded potatoes in an even layer in the bottom of your skillet. Gently press with the back of a spatula to slightly compress the potatoes to form a cake.

2. After cooking about 12 minutes, carefully lift up a section of the potatoes to peek underneath. If they are golden brown, they're ready to flip.

3. Invert a baking sheet to cover the surface of the skillet. Invert them together so the potatoes end up on the baking sheet. Gently slide the potatoes from the baking sheet back into the skillet to cook the other side.

## HASH BROWN-CRUSTED QUICHE

**PREP** 30 MINUTES **COOK** 25 MINUTES
**BAKE** 50 MINUTES AT 325°F
**STAND** 10 MINUTES **MAKES** 8 SERVINGS

- 1¼ lb. russet potatoes
- ¼ tsp. salt
- ⅛ tsp. black pepper
- 1 to 2 Tbsp. olive oil
- 1 Tbsp. butter
- 4 slices bacon
- 1¼ cups coarsely shredded zucchini (1 medium)
- ½ cup chopped red onion (1 medium)
- 4 eggs, lightly beaten
- 1 cup half-and-half or light cream
- ¼ tsp. crushed red pepper
- 1 cup shredded Swiss cheese (4 oz.)
- 1 Tbsp. all-purpose flour

**1.** Preheat oven to 325°F. Lightly grease a 9-inch pie pan or plate. Prepare potatoes as directed in Perfect Hash Browns (page 44) through Step 3. Invert hash browns onto a baking sheet. Use the baking sheet to transfer hash browns to prepared pie pan, pressing them into the bottom and up the sides of pan.

**2.** In a large skillet cook bacon until crisp. Drain, reserving 1 Tbsp. of the drippings. Crumble bacon; set aside. Cook zucchini and onion in the reserved drippings over medium heat 3 to 5 minutes or until tender but not browned.

**3.** In a large bowl combine eggs, half-and-half, an additional ¼ tsp. salt, and the crushed red pepper. Stir in bacon and zucchini mixture. In a small bowl combine shredded cheese and flour. Add to egg mixture; mix well.

**4.** Pour egg mixture into the hash brown-lined pie pan. Bake 50 to 55 minutes or until a knife inserted near the center comes out clean. Let stand 10 minutes before serving.

**PER SERVING** *324 cal., 22 g fat (9 g sat. fat), 133 mg chol., 412 mg sodium, 20 g carb., 3 g fiber, 2 g sugars, 12 g pro.*

## HASH BROWNS O'BRIEN

**PREP** 20 MINUTES
**COOK** 25 MINUTES **MAKES** 6 SERVINGS

- 1¼ lb. russet potatoes
- ¼ tsp. salt
- ⅛ tsp. black pepper
- 1 to 2 Tbsp. olive oil
- 1 Tbsp. butter
- ½ cup chopped red onion (1 small)
- ½ cup chopped red sweet pepper (1 small)
- ½ cup chopped green sweet pepper (1 small)
- 2 cloves garlic, minced
- 1 Tbsp. snipped fresh sage

**1.** Prepare potatoes as directed in Perfect Hash Browns (page 44) through Step 2. In a large nonstick skillet heat 1 Tbsp. of the oil and the butter over medium heat until butter foams. Add onion, sweet peppers, and garlic. Cook about 5 minutes or until tender.

**2.** Add potatoes and sage to skillet, stirring to combine; spread into an even layer. Gently press with the back of a spatula to form a cake. Cook, without stirring, about 12 minutes or until the bottom is golden brown and crisp.

**3.** Invert a plate over the top of the skillet. Carefully invert the skillet to transfer the potatoes to the plate. If needed, add the remaining 1 Tbsp. oil to the skillet. Using the plate, slide the potatoes back into the skillet, uncooked side down. Cook, without stirring, 8 to 12 minutes more or until the bottom is golden brown.

**SOUTHWEST HASH BROWNS O'BRIEN**
Prepare as directed, except substitute ¼ cup chopped fresh Anaheim or poblano chile pepper (tip, page 18) for the green sweet pepper.

**PER SERVING** *123 cal., 4 g fat (2 g sat. fat), 5 mg chol., 121 mg sodium, 20 g carb., 2 g fiber, 2 g sugars, 2 g pro.*

# 014  STUFFED FRENCH TOAST

TASTING COMMENTS: *For Stuffed French Toast perfection—golden and crisp on the outside, soft and melty on the inside—the right bread is essential. We tested this recipe with French bread, challah, Hawaiian bread, and Texas toast. The French bread and challah were definitely our favorites!—CW*

**PREP** 20 MINUTES·  **CHILL** 2 HOURS  **COOK** 4 MINUTES

4 1½-inch-thick slices French bread or challah bread

½ of an 8-oz. pkg. cream cheese, softened

2 Tbsp. sugar

½ tsp. vanilla

4 eggs

1 cup milk

2 Tbsp. honey or sugar

1 tsp. vanilla

Maple syrup or Salted Caramel Sauce

*Mascarpone is a soft, rich Italian cheese that tastes like a cross between whipped butter and cream cheese. It can be used in place of cream cheese in any variation of this stuffed French toast.*

**1.** Cut a 3-inch pocket about 2 inches deep in the top-crust side of each bread slice, cutting to but not all the way through the other side. For filling, in a medium bowl beat cream cheese with a mixer on medium to high 30 seconds. Add 2 Tbsp. sugar and the ½ tsp. vanilla. Beat until smooth. Spoon cream cheese filling into pocket of bread slices. Place slices in a 2-qt. rectangular baking dish; set aside.

**2.** In a medium bowl whisk together eggs, milk, honey, and the 1 tsp. vanilla. Slowly pour the egg mixture over bread slices. Using the back of a wide spatula, press bread down lightly to soak with egg mixture. Cover and chill at least 2 hours or up to 24 hours, turning bread slices once or twice.

**3.** Heat a lightly greased griddle over medium heat. Cook bread slices on hot griddle 4 to 6 minutes or until golden brown, turning once. Serve with syrup or Salted Caramel Sauce.

PER SERVING *403 cal., 16 g fat (8 g sat. fat), 222 mg chol., 358 mg sodium, 51 g carb., 1 g fiber, 32 g sugars, 14 g pro.*

**SALTED CARAMEL SAUCE** In a heavy medium saucepan stir together ¾ cup packed brown sugar, ½ cup heavy cream, ½ cup butter, and 2 Tbsp. light-color corn syrup. Bring to boiling over medium-high heat, whisking occasionally; reduce heat to medium. Boil gently 3 minutes. Remove from heat. Stir in 1 tsp. vanilla and ½ tsp. sea salt. Pour into a small bowl. Cool to room temperature. If desired, cover and chill up to 24 hours. (If chilled, let stand at room temperature 1 hour before serving.) If desired, stir in 1 thinly sliced banana. If desired, serve with chopped toasted pecans. Makes 1⅓ cups (or 1¾ cups with banana).

**BAKED FRENCH TOAST** Prepare Stuffed French Toast as directed through Step 2. Preheat oven to 350°F. Line a 15×10-inch baking pan with parchment paper. Arrange bread slices in prepared pan. Bake, uncovered, 30 to 35 minutes or until golden brown, turning once. Serve with syrup or Salted Caramel Sauce.

**MASCARPONE-STUFFED FRENCH TOAST** Prepare Stuffed French

### MASCARPONE-STUFFED FRENCH
TOAST Prepare Stuffed French Toast as directed, except in the filling substitute ½ cup mascarpone cheese for the cream cheese, reduce sugar to 1 Tbsp., and add ¼ cup chopped toasted pecans. In the egg mixture substitute brown sugar for the 2 Tbsp. honey or sugar and add ½ tsp. ground cinnamon.

### BANANA-STUFFED FRENCH TOAST Prepare
Stuffed French Toast as directed, except in a small skillet melt 1 Tbsp. butter over medium heat. Add 1 small banana, sliced, and 2 tsp. sugar to the melted butter. Cook and stir 30 to 60 seconds to soften the banana. Remove from heat. Stir in ¼ cup chopped toasted pecans. Cool slightly. Stir into cream cheese mixture before spooning into bread slices.

### STRAWBERRY-STUFFED FRENCH
TOAST Prepare Stuffed French Toast as directed, except stir ½ cup chopped fresh strawberries into the cream cheese mixture.

### BACON-STUFFED FRENCH TOAST Prepare
Stuffed French Toast as directed, except crisp-cook 3 slices bacon; crumble bacon and stir into the cream cheese mixture.

## TESTING NOTES

↑

1. Holding a bread slice firmly on a cutting board, use a small sharp knife to carefully cut a pocket about 3 inches across and 2 inches deep into the top crust of the bread slices, taking care not to cut through the bottom crust. It is important to start with bread slices that are wide enough—1½ inches is ideal—to form a pocket with thick sides so the filling doesn't ooze out.

↑

2. Use a teaspoon or small rubber spatula to fill the bread pockets evenly with the cream cheese mixture. Take care not to overstuff the pockets or the filling may seep out during soaking and cooking.

3. Gently pour the egg mixture over bread slices, making sure each one gets thoroughly coated. Lightly press down on the slices with a wide spatula to help the egg mixture soak into the bread, but avoid pressing so hard that the filling begins to come out. For even tenderness, it's important to carefully flip the slices over once or twice during chilling so the egg mixture is evenly distributed.

↓

4. Cook French toast slices on a griddle over medium heat just until golden brown, carefully turning once with a spatula halfway through cooking. Watch carefully because the slices may go from nicely brown to too dark quickly. If you're cooking for a crowd, bake this dish for convenience. Expect the egg mixture to puff up during baking and deflate as it cools.

↓

**BREAD BASICS** *French bread and challah are our favorite choices for this recipe because they're substantial enough to stand up to overnight soaking in an egg mixture and dense enough to hold a rich cream cheese filling intact. Be sure to buy it the day before you need it—day-old bread soaks up the egg mixture better than fresh bread. You'll be glad you did!*

*French bread (above) is made with just flour, yeast, water, and salt, making it the lighter alternative (if you can call it that!) for this recipe. Challah (top) contains both eggs and oil, which makes this rich dish even richer!*

MAKES: *9 servings*   TESTED BY: *Sarah B.*

# 015   FRUIT COFFEE CAKE

TASTING COMMENTS: *Simply knowing when to stop is the secret to this best-ever, most-tender coffee cake. From cutting in the butter to stirring the batter to cooking the filling, follow our cues for the quitting point for all three steps to achieve coffee cake success. —SB*

**PREP** 35 MINUTES   **BAKE** 40 MINUTES AT 350°F

*Mixing cornstarch with sugar allows the grains to disperse evenly, which prevents lumps. Cornstarch begins to thicken (the starch grains begin to swell) just under the boiling point, but in the presence of sugar, it takes a higher temp to swell the starch. So be sure to simmer the fruit filling for the full 2 minutes to make the most of the thickening power.*

1½ to 2 cups blueberries or raspberries; sliced, peeled apricots or peaches; or chopped, peeled apples or pears
¼ cup water
¼ cup sugar
2 Tbsp. cornstarch
1½ cups all-purpose flour
¾ cup sugar
½ tsp. baking powder
¼ tsp. baking soda
¼ cup butter, cut up
1 egg, lightly beaten
½ cup buttermilk or sour milk (tip, page 53)
½ tsp. vanilla
¼ cup all-purpose flour
¼ cup sugar
2 Tbsp. butter

**1.** For filling, in a medium saucepan combine fruit and the water. Bring to boiling; reduce heat. If using raspberries, remove from heat. For other fruits, cover and simmer 5 minutes or until fruit is tender. In a small bowl combine ¼ cup sugar and the cornstarch; stir into fruit. Cook and stir over medium heat until mixture is thickened and bubbly. Cook and stir 2 minutes; set aside.

**2.** Preheat oven to 350°F. In a medium bowl combine the next four ingredients (through baking soda). Using a pastry blender or two knives, cut in the ¼ cup butter until mixture resembles coarse crumbs. Make a well in the center of the flour mixture; set aside.

**3.** In another bowl combine egg, buttermilk, and vanilla. Add egg mixture all at once to flour mixture. Stir just until moistened (batter should be lumpy). Spread half the batter into an ungreased 8×8-inch baking pan. Carefully spread filling over batter. Drop remaining batter in small mounds onto filling.

**4.** For topping, in a small bowl stir together the ¼ cup flour and ¼ cup sugar. Using a pastry blender or two knives, cut in the 2 Tbsp. butter until mixture resembles coarse crumbs. Sprinkle over coffee cake. Bake 40 to 45 minutes or until topping is golden brown. Serve warm.

PER SERVING *298 cal., 9 g fat (5 g sat. fat), 44 mg chol., 126 mg sodium, 52 g carb., 1 g fiber, 31 g sugars, 4 g pro.*

**RHUBARB-STRAWBERRY COFFEE CAKE** Prepare as directed, except substitute ¾ cup fresh or frozen cut-up rhubarb and ¾ cup frozen unsweetened whole strawberries for fruit. Continue as directed.

## TESTING NOTES

1. Cornstarch is the starch of choice for this fruit filling. After cooking, it becomes somewhat opaque instead of cloudy and stays soft without becoming gluelike or breaking down after baking.

2. Most of the fruit choices need to simmer for 5 minutes in water until tender before adding the cornstarch and sugar—except raspberries. They will fall apart! If you choose raspberries, bring them to boiling as directed in Step 1, then add the cornstarch-sugar mixture and continue to cook as directed.

↑

3. The crumb of this coffee cake is rich and tender because of the butter that is gently cut into the flour mixture. Using a pastry blender or two knives, cut butter into the dry ingredients just until the butter is the size of small pebbles.

↑

4. Once you've added the wet ingredients to the dry ingredients, stir the batter just until moistened. The batter will be lumpy. Don't stir out the lumps. If you overmix the batter, you will begin to lose the little pieces of butter that hinder gluten development. As the cake bakes, the butter melts—turning to steam—helping to leaven your coffee cake.

5. A small offset spatula is the perfect tool for preparing this cake. Because it is bent at the just-right angle, it makes an easy job of spreading the batter and the fruit filling evenly into those hard-to-reach corners.
↓

6. Use spoons to drop the rest of the batter in small mounds on top of the filling. Don't worry about spreading—the rich batter will expand and bake together in the oven.
↓

**MAKE IT SEASONAL!** *This coffee cake calls for fresh fruit, so take advantage of peak-season pickings in the grocery store, farmers market, or your backyard. Look for berries, peaches, and apricots all summer long. Turn to apples and pears in the fall and winter months.*

**MAKE IT BIGGER!** *To serve 18, double the recipe and use a 13×9-inch pan. Preheat oven to 350°F. Bake 45 to 50 minutes or until topping is golden brown.*

*No buttermilk at home? No problem! To make ½ cup sour milk, place 1½ tsp. lemon juice or vinegar in a glass measuring cup. Add enough milk to make ½ cup total liquid; stir. Let stand 5 minutes before using.*

# 016 QUINOA-PUMPKIN SEED GRANOLA

TASTING COMMENTS: *The high sugar content of dried fruit causes it to burn when baked—which makes it hard to get the granola crunchy before the fruit burns. The solution was to stir in the dried fruit after the granola was baked.—KB*

**PREP** 20 MINUTES   **BAKE** 20 MINUTES AT 350°F   **COOL** 15 MINUTES

¾ **cup uncooked quinoa, rinsed and well drained**

½ **cup raw pumpkin seeds (pepitas)**

½ **cup whole and/or slivered almonds**

¼ **cup flaxseeds**

¼ **cup honey**

2 **Tbsp. canola oil**

1 **tsp. ground cinnamon**

½ **tsp. coarse salt**

¾ **cup dried cherries, cranberries, golden raisins, and/or snipped dried apricots**

*Granola needs a little oil to help hold it together and keep it crisp as it bakes and cools.*

**1.** Preheat oven to 350°F. In a large bowl combine quinoa, pumpkin seeds, almonds, and flaxseeds. Microwave honey 20 seconds. Add oil, cinnamon, and salt to honey; whisk to combine. Pour honey mixture over quinoa mixture; toss to coat. Spread in a 15×10-inch baking pan.

**2.** Bake, uncovered, 20 minutes or until golden brown, stirring twice. Stir in dried fruit. Cool in pan 15 minutes. Spread on a large piece of foil. Cool completely. Store in an airtight container up to 2 weeks in the refrigerator.

PER SERVING *191 cal., 11 g fat (1 g sat. fat), 0 mg chol., 94 mg sodium, 22 g carb., 3 g fiber, 11 g sugars, 6 g pro.*

**QUINOA** *Rinse quinoa before using! In its natural state, quinoa is coated with bitter-tasting saponins. Most processed quinoa has this coating removed, but it's best to rinse anyway.*

**FLAX** *While you may get more of the beneficial nutrients from ground flaxseeds, we liked the texture of the whole seeds in this recipe.*

**HONEY** *Switch up the flavor of your granola with a different variety of honey. Try clover, orange blossom, buckwheat, wildflower, or blueberry.*

**PUMPKIN SEEDS (PEPITAS)** *If pumpkin seeds aren't a favorite, substitute pistachios,*

## TESTING NOTES

In cookie recipes, use an equal amount of granola in place of rolled oats. Break up any larger granola clusters before measuring and adding to the cookie dough.

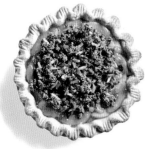
For streusel topping, in a medium bowl combine 1/4 cup packed brown sugar and 3 Tbsp. all-purpose flour. Using a pastry blender, cut in 2 Tbsp. butter until mixture resembles coarse crumbs. Stir in 1/2 cup crumbled granola. Sprinkle over unbaked pie filling. Bake as directed.

For fruit and yogurt parfaits, layer granola with your favorite flavor of low-fat Greek yogurt in a clear glass or bowl. Top with fresh raspberries, blueberries, blackberries, and/or sliced strawberries.

# 017  BUTTERMILK PANCAKES

TASTING COMMENTS:  *Don't be worried by lumps in your pancake batter—no matter what kind you're making. Treating the batter gently results in pancakes that are super tender with a crisp edge.—SM*

**START TO FINISH** 25 MINUTES

1³⁄₄ cups all-purpose flour

2 Tbsp. granulated sugar

2 tsp. baking powder

½ tsp. baking soda

¼ tsp. salt

1 egg, lightly beaten

1½ cups buttermilk or sour milk (tip, page 53)

3 Tbsp. vegetable oil

Desired fruit options (optional)*

Butter (optional)

Desired syrup (optional)

**1.** In a large bowl stir together the first five ingredients (through salt). In another bowl use a fork to combine egg, buttermilk, and oil. Add egg mixture all at once to flour mixture. Stir just until moistened (batter should be slightly lumpy). If desired, stir in desired fruit.

**2.** For standard-size pancakes, pour about ¼ cup batter onto a hot, lightly greased griddle or heavy skillet. Spread batter if necessary. For dollar-size pancakes, use about 1 Tbsp. batter. Cook over medium heat 1 to 2 minutes on each side or until pancakes are golden brown; turn over when surfaces are bubbly and edges are slightly dry. Serve warm. If desired, top with butter and additional syrup.

**PANCAKES** Prepare as directed, except substitute milk for buttermilk, increase baking powder to 1 Tbsp., and omit baking soda.

**WHOLE WHEAT PANCAKES** Prepare as directed, except substitute whole wheat flour for all-purpose flour and packed brown sugar for granulated sugar.

**BUCKWHEAT PANCAKES** Prepare as directed, except use ³⁄₄ cup all-purpose flour and add 1 cup buckwheat flour.

**CORNMEAL PANCAKES** Prepare as directed, except use 1¼ cups all-purpose flour and add ½ cup cornmeal.

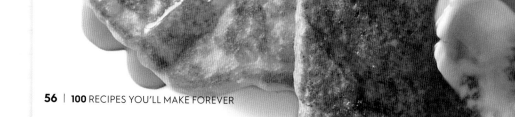

PER SERVING *123 cal., 4 g fat (1 g sat. fat), 19 mg chol., 179 mg sodium, 18 g carb., 0 g fiber, 0 g sugars, 3 g pro.*

**\*FRUIT OPTIONS** If desired, stir one of the following fruits into the pancake batter before pouring batter onto griddle: ½ cup chopped fresh apple, apricot, peach, nectarine, or pear; ½ cup fresh or frozen blueberries; or ¼ cup chopped dried apple, pear, apricot, raisins, currants, dates, cranberries, blueberries, cherries, or mixed fruit.

## TESTING NOTES

↑
1. When stirring the wet ingredients into flour mixture, the batter should be slightly lumpy. Do not overmix or the pancakes will be tough.

↑
2. Pour batter onto a hot griddle or skillet using a scoop or ¼-cup measuring cup.

↑
3. The pancakes are ready to turn when the top surfaces are bubbly and the edges look slightly dry.

**MAPLE-BLUEBERRY SYRUP**
*In a medium saucepan combine 2 cups fresh or frozen blueberries, 1 cup pure maple syrup, and 2 tsp. lemon juice. Bring to boiling; reduce heat. Simmer, uncovered, 15 to 20 minutes or until blueberries are softened, stirring occasionally. Use a potato masher to thoroughly mash blueberries. Set a fine-mesh sieve or a strainer lined with 100%-cotton cheesecloth over a medium bowl. Strain blueberry mixture through sieve. Discard solids. Serve warm. Pour any remaining syrup into an airtight storage container. Cover and refrigerate up to 1 week.*

MAKES: *16 servings*   TESTED BY: *Juli H.*

# 018   CAKE DONUTS

TASTING COMMENTS: *In our effort to make the very best cake donut, we spent a lot of time tasting donuts warm from the fryer and then cool to be sure we liked them as much. We did!—JH*

**PREP** 45 MINUTES   **CHILL** 2 HOURS   **COOK** 2 MINUTES PER BATCH

- 4 cups all-purpose flour
- 2 tsp. baking powder
- ¼ tsp. salt
- 2 eggs
- 1¼ cups granulated sugar
- 1 tsp. vanilla
- ⅔ cup milk
- ¼ cup butter, melted
- Vegetable oil or shortening for deep-fat frying
- Powdered sugar, granulated sugar, Chocolate Glaze, or Powdered Sugar Icing (recipe, page 258)

**1.** In a medium bowl combine flour, baking powder, and salt; set aside. In a large bowl combine eggs, the 1¼ cups granulated sugar, and the vanilla; beat with a mixer on medium 3 minutes or until thick. In a small bowl combine milk and melted butter.

**2.** Add flour mixture and milk mixture alternately to egg mixture, beating on low after each addition just until combined. Cover; chill dough 2 to 4 hours.

**3.** On a well-floured surface roll dough to ½-inch thickness (do not stir in additional flour). Cut dough with a floured 2½-inch donut cutter, dipping cutter into flour between cuts. Reroll dough as necessary.

**4.** Pour 3 inches of vegetable oil in a 3-qt. saucepan. Fry two or three donuts at a time in hot oil (365°F) 2 to 3 minutes or until donuts are golden brown, turning once. Remove with a slotted spoon and drain on paper towels. Repeat with remaining dough. Cool donuts slightly. Coat with powdered sugar or granulated sugar. Or dip tops in Chocolate Glaze or Powdered Sugar Icing.

PER DONUT AND DONUT HOLE WITH POWDERED SUGAR *342 cal., 18 g fat (3 g sat. fat), 35 mg chol., 100 mg sodium, 42 g carb., 1 g fiber, 0 g sugars, 4 g pro.*

**SPICED DONUTS** Prepare as directed, except add 1 tsp. ground cinnamon, ½ tsp. ground ginger, and ⅛ tsp. ground cloves to the flour mixture. Coat warm donuts in a mixture of ⅔ cup granulated sugar and ½ tsp. ground cinnamon.

**CHOCOLATE GLAZE** In a small saucepan melt 3 oz. unsweetened chocolate and 3 Tbsp. butter over low heat. Remove from heat. Stir in 3 cups powdered sugar, 1½ tsp. vanilla, and enough warm water (4 to 5 Tbsp.) until glaze coats the back of a spoon.

*Remove donut holes from the cutter; do not reroll. Fry them with donuts for tasty bites.*

## TESTING NOTES

1. Roll out dough on a generously floured surface so dough doesn't stick.

2. Dip cutter into flour between cuts to prevent dough from sticking to the cutter.

3. Use a slotted spoon to turn and remove donuts; allow excess oil to drain into pan before moving donuts to paper towels.

4. If glazing donuts, dip tops halfway in glaze. Allow to dry on a wire rack.

1 cup sugar + 1 tsp. ground cinnamon

powdered sugar

*Powdered Sugar Icing p. 258*

*Chocolate Glaze p. 58*

**SHAKE, DIP, EAT!** *The finishing touch on these donuts can be powdered sugar, plain granulated sugar, cinnamon sugar, or Chocolate Glaze or Powdered Sugar Icing sprinkled with jimmies. When tossing in sugar, make sure the donuts are still warm—just 30 seconds to 1 minute out of the hot oil—so the sugar sticks.*

# 019   BANANA BREAD

TASTING COMMENTS:   *We discovered that roasting the bananas turns the natural sugars in the fruit into a caramelly syrup, which adds rich flavor to banana bread. There's no need to mash, either—the roasted bananas blend right into the batter.—CW*

**PREP** 25 MINUTES   **ROAST** 15 MINUTES AT 350°F   **BAKE** 55 MINUTES AT 350°F   **COOL** 10 MINUTES
**STAND** OVERNIGHT

5 whole bananas

2 cups all-purpose flour

1½ tsp. baking powder

½ tsp. baking soda

½ tsp. ground cinnamon

¼ tsp. salt

¼ tsp. ground nutmeg

⅛ tsp. ground ginger

2 eggs, lightly beaten

1 cup granulated sugar

½ cup vegetable oil or melted butter

¼ cup chopped walnuts

1 recipe Streusel-Nut Topping (optional)

*Ripe bananas —those that are soft to the touch with brown spots on the peel—are usually called on for banana bread. But when you roast bananas first, it doesn't matter how ripe they are before baking.*

**1.** Preheat oven to 350°F. Line a 15×10-inch baking pan with foil; arrange bananas in the pan. Prick banana skins with a fork at 1-inch intervals. Roast 15 minutes. Cool bananas on baking pan. Grease bottom and ½ inch up the sides of one 9×5×3-inch or two 7½×3½×2-inch loaf pans. Set pan(s) aside.

**2.** In a large bowl combine the next seven ingredients (through ginger). Make a well in the center of flour mixture; set aside.

**3.** In a medium bowl stir together eggs, sugar, and oil; set aside. Using a small sharp knife, split banana peels. Measure 1½ cups of the roasted bananas (gently press roasted bananas into a measuring cup). Stir into egg mixture. Add egg mixture all at once to flour mixture. Stir just until moistened (batter should be lumpy). Fold in walnuts. Spoon batter into prepared pan(s). If desired, sprinkle Streusel-Nut Topping over batter.

**4.** Bake 55 to 60 minutes for the 9×5-inch pan or 45 to 55 minutes for

the 7½×3½ loaves or until a toothpick inserted near center(s) comes out clean. If necessary to prevent overbrowning, cover loosely with foil the last 15 minutes of baking. Cool in pan(s) on a wire rack 10 minutes. Remove from pan(s). Cool completely on rack. Wrap and store overnight before slicing. (The bread's texture will be more evenly moist and less crumbly after standing.)

PER SERVING *220 cal., 9 g fat (1 g sat. fat), 23 mg chol., 119 mg sodium, 33 g carb., 2 g fiber, 17 g sugars, 3 g pro.*

**STREUSEL-NUT TOPPING** In a small bowl combine 3 Tbsp. packed brown sugar and 2 Tbsp. all-purpose flour. Using a pastry blender, cut in 4 tsp. butter by repeatedly pushing down through the butter until mixture resembles coarse crumbs (rotate the pastry blender and bowl to cut in uniformly). Stir in ¼ cup chopped walnuts.

## TESTING NOTES

1. After roasting, the bananas become dark and ugly but wonderfully sweet! Roasting caramelizes their natural sugars, giving them a rich sweetness and making them soft enough to stir into the batter without mashing.

2. Grease the bottom of the pan and just ½ inch up the sides for a uniform loaf with a slightly rounded top. If you grease all the way up the sides of the pan, the loaf will have a flat top.

**PB&J BANANA BREAD** Use 9×5-inch pan. Add ¼ cup peanut butter with bananas; replace walnuts with ¼ cup chopped dry-roasted peanuts. Swirl ¼ cup strawberry preserves in batter in pan. If using Streusel-Nut Topping, replace walnuts with ¼ cup chopped dry-roasted peanuts. Bake 70 minutes. After bread stands, microwave 2 Tbsp. strawberry preserves 15 seconds or until melted, snipping any large pieces of fruit. Drizzle melted preserves over top of bread.

**BLUEBERRY-COCONUT BANANA BREAD** Toss ½ cup fresh or frozen blueberries in 1 Tbsp. all-purpose flour; fold into the batter with the walnuts. Sprinkle an additional ¼ cup fresh or frozen blueberries on top of batter in pan(s). If using the Streusel-Nut Topping, add ¼ cup flaked coconut.

**DARK CHOCOLATE-RASPBERRY BANANA BREAD** Stir ½ cup dark chocolate pieces into the batter with walnuts. Swirl ¼ cup raspberry preserves into batter in pan(s). After baked bread stands, combine ⅓ cup dark chocolate pieces and ½ tsp. shortening. Microwave on 70% power 20 seconds; stir. Microwave until smooth, stirring every 15 seconds. Drizzle over bread. Microwave ¼ cup raspberry preserves on high 20 to 30 seconds or until melted, snipping any large pieces of fruit. Drizzle preserves on bread.

**MANGO-GINGER BANANA BREAD** Use 9×5-inch pan. Omit cinnamon and nutmeg, increase ginger to 1 tsp., and substitute ¼ cup snipped pitted dates for the chopped walnuts. Toss ½ cup chopped fresh mango with 1 Tbsp. all-purpose flour; fold into the batter with the dates. If using the Streusel-Nut Topping, omit walnuts and add ¼ cup chopped pistachio nuts and 1 Tbsp. chopped crystallized ginger. Bake 70 minutes or until a toothpick inserted near center comes out clean.

# 020 FLAKY BISCUITS

TASTING COMMENTS: *Fat creates a tender texture and helps to form the flaky layers in rolled biscuits. Butter delivers flavor. We tested with butter and a mix of butter and shortening. Because shortening is lower in water than butter, it creates more-distinct layers. —LB*

**PREP** 15 MINUTES   **BAKE** 10 MINUTES AT 450°F

3 cups all-purpose flour

1 Tbsp. baking powder

1 Tbsp. sugar

1 tsp. salt

¾ tsp. cream of tartar

¾ cup butter or ½ cup butter and ¼ cup shortening

1 cup milk

Milk for brushing (optional)

*Double-acting baking powder creates carbon dioxide bubbles that "lift" baked goods in two ways: once when it's combined with a liquid and again when it's exposed to heat.*

1. Preheat oven to 450°F. In a large bowl combine flour, baking powder, sugar, salt, and cream of tartar.* Using a pastry blender, cut in butter until mixture resembles coarse crumbs. Make a well in center of flour mixture. Add the 1 cup milk. Using a fork, stir just until mixture is moistened.

2. Turn dough out onto a lightly floured surface. Knead dough by folding and gently pressing it just until dough holds together. Pat or lightly roll dough until ¾ inch thick.** Cut dough with a floured 2½-inch biscuit cutter; reroll scraps as necessary and dip cutter into flour between cuts.

3. Place dough circles 1 inch apart on an ungreased baking sheet. If desired, brush with additional milk. Bake 10 to 14 minutes or until golden.

*TIP If baking powder or cream of tartar appears lumpy, sift it through a fine-mesh sieve.

**TIP Alternately, roll dough into a circle; cut into wedges. Or roll into a rectangle; cut into strips or squares.

PER SERVING *231 cal., 12 g fat (7 g sat. fat), 32 mg chol., 427 mg sodium, 26 g carb., 1 g fiber, 2 g sugars, 4 g pro.*

**DROP BISCUITS** Prepare as directed through Step 1, except increase milk to 1¼ cups. Drop dough into 12 mounds onto a greased baking sheet. Bake as directed.

**BUTTERMILK BISCUITS** Prepare as directed, except for rolled-dough biscuits, substitute 1¼ cups buttermilk or sour milk (tip, page 53) for the 1 cup milk. For drop biscuits, substitute 1½ cups buttermilk or sour milk for the 1¼ cups milk.

**GREEK** Stir in ½ cup crumbled feta cheese, ⅓ cup chopped pitted Kalamata olives, and ⅓ cup snipped dried tomatoes (not oil-packed) with the flour-butter mixture.

**CHILE CHEESE** Stir 2 Tbsp. chopped chipotle peppers in adobo sauce (tip, page 18) and 1 cup shredded cheddar cheese into the milk.

**WHITE CHEDDAR AND PROSCIUTTO** Stir in ⅓ cup sliced green onions, ¾ cup shredded white cheddar cheese, and 2 Tbsp. chopped prosciutto with the flour-butter mixture.

**GARLIC AND HERB** Stir 3 or 4 cloves roasted garlic, minced, and 1 Tbsp. snipped fresh thyme into the milk.

**BACON AND BLUE CHEESE** Stir in 2 slices cooked, crumbled bacon and ½ cup crumbled blue cheese with the flour-butter mixture.

**PEPPER 'N' PARMESAN** Stir in 2 tsp. cracked black pepper and 1 cup finely shredded Parmesan cheese with the flour-butter mixture. Sprinkle cut biscuits with additional Parmesan.

**CHOCOLATE CHIP-ORANGE** Stir in ⅓ cup miniature semisweet chocolate pieces and 2 tsp. orange zest with the flour-butter mixture. Sprinkle cut biscuits with additional sugar.

**SUGAR AND CINNAMON** Increase sugar in biscuits to 2 Tbsp. Stir in ⅓ cup raisins and 1 tsp. ground cinnamon with the flour-butter mixture. Sprinkle tops of cut biscuits with a mixture of 2 tsp. sugar and ½ tsp. ground cinnamon.

Greek

Chile Cheese

White Cheddar
and Prosciutto

Garlic and Herb

Bacon and Blue Cheese

Pepper 'n' Parmesan

Chocolate Chip-Orange

Sugar and Cinnamon

MAKES: *12 servings*   TESTED BY: *Carla C.*

# 021   DOUBLE-BLUEBERRY MUFFINS

TASTING COMMENTS: *After we perfected blueberry muffins, we considered what other flavors we might like. The result: Double-Raspberry, Orange-Chocolate, and White Chocolate-Cherry variations. —CC*

**PREP** 15 MINUTES   **BAKE** 20 MINUTES AT 375°F   **COOL** 15 MINUTES

- 2 cups all-purpose flour
- ¾ cup sugar
- 2½ tsp. baking powder
- ¼ tsp. salt
- 2 eggs, lightly beaten
- ¾ cup buttermilk, sour milk, or milk
- 6 Tbsp. butter, melted
- 1 cup fresh or frozen blueberries
- ¼ cup blueberry preserves
- 2 Tbsp. sugar
- 1 tsp. orange zest
- 1 tsp. lemon zest
- 2 Tbsp. butter, melted

*Out of buttermilk? Make your own sour milk. For the amount needed for this recipe, place 2 tsp. lemon juice or vinegar in a glass measuring cup. Add enough milk to make ¾ cup liquid total; stir. Let stand 5 minutes before using.*

**1.** Preheat oven to 375°F. Line twelve 2½-inch muffin cups with paper bake cups; set aside.

**2.** In a medium bowl stir together the first four ingredients (through salt). Make a well in center of flour mixture; set aside.

**3.** In a medium bowl combine eggs, buttermilk, and 6 Tbsp. melted butter. Add egg mixture all at once to flour mixture. Stir just until moistened (batter should be lumpy). Fold in blueberries. Set aside 1 cup of batter.

**4.** Spoon remaining batter into prepared muffin cups, filling each half full. Spoon about 1 tsp. blueberry preserves into center of batter on each muffin. Spoon remaining batter over preserves to cover (muffin cups will be about two-thirds full). Bake 20 minutes or until golden brown.

**5.** Meanwhile, for citrus-sugar topping, stir together the 2 Tbsp. sugar, the orange zest, and lemon zest. Remove muffins from oven; brush with the 2 Tbsp. melted butter. Top muffins with citrus-sugar. Cool in muffin cups on a wire rack 15 minutes. Remove from muffin cups; serve warm.

PER SERVING *245 cal., 9 g fat (5 g sat. fat), 52 mg chol., 248 mg sodium, 38 g carb., 1 g fiber, 20 g sugars, 4 g pro.*

**DOUBLE-RASPBERRY MUFFINS**
Prepare Double-Blueberry Muffins as directed, except substitute fresh or frozen raspberries for the blueberries and raspberry preserves for the blueberry preserves.

**ORANGE-CHOCOLATE MUFFINS**
Prepare Double-Blueberry Muffins as directed, except substitute ¾ cup miniature semisweet chocolate pieces for the blueberries and orange marmalade for the blueberry preserves.

**WHITE CHOCOLATE-CHERRY MUFFINS** Prepare Double-Blueberry Muffins as directed, except substitute ¾ cup coarsely chopped white chocolate (4 oz.) for the blueberries and cherry preserves for the blueberry preserves. Omit citrus-sugar topping.

**LUMPY OR SMOOTH?** *The batter for the muffin on the right was overbeaten, resulting in a puffier muffin with a smooth top. Don't be fooled: The inside crumb is tougher and has little tunnels of air pockets throughout. The batter for the muffin on the left was mixed just until everything was combined—but still lumpy! While it may have a textured, golden-brown top, the inside is soft and tender.*

## TESTING NOTES

↑
1. Making a well (a deep indentation) in the flour mixture holds the liquid in one place and makes it easy to combine the flour and liquid mixtures—which, in turn, prevents overmixing. Add the liquid all at once, then get out the mixing spoon!

↑
2. Stir the liquid and flour mixtures together just until combined, then stop. There will be lumps and some spots of flour showing—that's OK. Mixing the batter until it's smooth is bad news for the texture and appearance of the baked muffin.

↑
3. Use two spoons to divide the thick batter among the muffin cups, filling each about halfway. Add a bit of the blueberry preserves for the filling, then top with the remaining batter, covering the preserves completely.

↑
4. While the muffins are still warm from the oven, use a pastry brush to spread the tops with melted butter and sprinkle with the citrus-sugar topping.

# 022   POTATO CINNAMON ROLLS

**TASTING COMMENTS:**  *We tweaked a prizewinning cinnamon roll recipe that contained potato flakes by adding real mashed potato to the dough—which adds moisture and structure without contributing to the development of gluten. They are so light and fluffy. Every time we photograph or test them, we think they can't be beat!—JH*

**PREP** 45 MINUTES   **RISE** 1 HOUR 15 MINUTES   **STAND** 10 MINUTES   **BAKE** 25 MINUTES AT 375°F   **COOL** 10 MINUTES

*The amount of liquid that flour will absorb varies—it depends on the type of flour, the amount of protein in the flour, and how much moisture is in the air. To avoid tough, heavy cinnamon rolls, use the lesser amount of flour in the given range, then gradually add only as much additional flour as needed to keep the dough from sticking as you knead.*

4¼ to 4¾ cups all-purpose flour
1 pkg. active dry yeast
1 cup milk
1 cup mashed cooked potato
⅓ cup butter, cut up
⅓ cup granulated sugar
1 tsp. salt
2 eggs
½ cup packed brown sugar
1 Tbsp. ground cinnamon
¼ cup butter, softened
1 recipe Powdered Sugar Icing (page 258), Cream Cheese Icing (page 72), or Browned Butter Frosting (page 72)

**1.** In a large bowl combine 1½ cups of the flour and the yeast; set aside. In a saucepan heat and stir the next five ingredients (through salt) just until warm (120°F to 130°F) and butter almost melts; add to flour mixture along with eggs. Beat with a mixer on low to medium 30 seconds, scraping sides of bowl. Beat on high 3 minutes. Stir in as much of the remaining flour as you can.

**2.** Turn dough out onto a lightly floured surface. Knead in enough remaining flour to make a moderately soft dough that is smooth and elastic (3 to 5 minutes total). Shape dough into a ball. Place in a lightly greased bowl; turn to grease surface of dough. Cover; let rise in a warm place until double in size (45 to 60 minutes).

**3.** Punch dough down. Turn out onto a lightly floured surface. Cover; let rest 10 minutes. Meanwhile, lightly grease a 13×9-inch baking pan; set aside. For filling, in a bowl stir together brown sugar and cinnamon; set aside.

**4.** Roll dough into an 18×12-inch rectangle. Spread the ¼ cup butter over dough; sprinkle with filling, leaving 1 inch unfilled along one long side. Roll up dough, starting from the filled long side. Pinch dough to seal seam.

**5.** Slice into 12 equal pieces. Arrange pieces, cut sides down, in prepared baking pan. Cover; let rise in a warm place until nearly double in size (about 30 minutes).

**6.** Preheat oven to 375°F. Bake 25 to 30 minutes or until golden brown. Cool in pan on a wire rack 10 minutes. Remove from pan. Drizzle or spread rolls with Icing.

**MAKE-AHEAD DIRECTIONS** Prepare rolls as directed through Step 5, except do not let rise after shaping. Cover loosely with oiled waxed paper and plastic wrap. Chill 2 to 24 hours. Before baking, let chilled rolls stand, covered, 30 minutes at room temperature. Uncover and bake as directed.

PER SERVING *396 cal., 11 g fat (6 g sat. fat), 61 mg chol., 283 mg sodium, 68 g carb., 2 g fiber, 31 g sugars, 7 g pro.*

**MASHED POTATO IN A HURRY** *Scrub a 10-oz. potato and leave the peel on. Prick it all over with a fork. Microwave 5 to 7 minutes or until tender. Halve potato and scoop pulp out of skin into a small bowl; discard skin. Mash pulp with a potato masher or mixer on low. Measure 1 cup of mashed potato.*

## YEAST

**ACTIVE DRY YEAST**
*This is the most common yeast for home baking. Active dry yeast comes in packets and larger jars. It's mixed with flour or dissolved in warm liquid before using in a recipe. Check the date on your package to make sure it has not expired.*

**QUICK-RISING YEAST**
*Also called fast-rising or instant yeast, this more active strain of yeast cuts the rise time by about a third. It can be substituted for active dry yeast except in recipes requiring the dough to rise in the refrigerator and in dough using sourdough starter.*

**CARAMEL-PECAN ROLLS** Prepare Potato Cinnamon Rolls as directed through Step 3. In a medium bowl stir together ½ cup melted butter, ¾ cup packed brown sugar, and ¼ cup light-color corn syrup. Stir in ¾ cup chopped pecans. Spread mixture in prepared pan. Continue as with Step 4, placing rolls on top of mixture in pan. After baking, immediately invert rolls onto a serving platter (spoon any nut mixture remaining in pan onto rolls). Omit the icing.

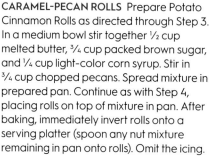

**APPLE-RAISIN ROLLS** Prepare rolls as directed, except for filling, in a small bowl stir together ⅓ cup granulated sugar, ⅓ cup chopped dried apples, ¼ cup raisins, 2 tsp. apple pie spice, and 1 tsp. orange zest (optional).

**CREAM CHEESE ICING** In a medium bowl combine one 3-oz. pkg. cream cheese, softened; 2 Tbsp. butter, softened; and 1 tsp. vanilla with a mixer on medium until combined. Gradually beat in 2½ cups powdered sugar until smooth. Beat in milk, 1 tsp. at a time, to reach spreading consistency.

**BROWNED BUTTER FROSTING** In a small saucepan heat ¾ cup butter over low heat until melted. Continue heating until butter turns a delicate light brown, stirring occasionally. Remove from heat. In a large bowl combine 3 cups powdered sugar, 2 Tbsp. milk, and 1 tsp. vanilla. Add browned butter. Beat with a mixer on low until combined. Beat on medium to high, adding additional milk, 1 tsp. at a time, to reach spreading consistency.

# TESTING NOTES

↑
1. Be gentle with your heat. If you heat the milk mixture beyond 130°F, you may kill the yeast, and nothing you do from this point will matter. Use a candy or instant-read thermometer to check your temp in the pan. If you need a visual clue, try this: When the butter is almost melted, you're ready to remove the mixture from the heat.

↑
2. Kneading develops the texture of your rolls. As you knead, the gluten in the flour develops. Set a timer for 3 minutes. On a lightly floured surface begin by folding your dough in half, then push down and away from you with the heels of your hands. Turn the dough, then repeat. Continue folding, pushing, then turning the dough, adding small amounts of flour to keep the dough from sticking to the surface (do not use more than the maximum amount of flour called for in the recipe). After kneading 3 to 5 minutes, your dough should be smooth, slightly sticky, and elastic. If you press into the dough, it will spring back.

3. To create a perfect warm place for raising dough, boil some water and pour it into a 2-cup measure. Cover dough with a kitchen towel and place it in a cold oven or the microwave with the steaming water in the 2-cup measure. Shut the door and let the dough rise for the amount of time specified in the recipe.
↓

↑
4. After letting the dough rise 45 minutes, look to see if it has nearly doubled in size. If so, gently press two fingers into the surface of the dough. If the indentations remain, the dough has risen adequately. If not, let it go another 15 minutes, then recheck.

5. Punch your fist into the center of the dough to deflate it. This is important so your dough does not have big pockets of air as you roll it out. Let the dough stand 10 minutes to relax the gluten, making the dough easier to roll out.

↑
6. Creating an 18×12-inch rectangle is important to making evenly shaped rolls. The hardest part of rolling is to make four good corners. Alternate rolling dough from the center to the edges with rolling dough from the center to the corners, diagonally.

7. To create square corners, gently lift and pull the corners, being careful not to stretch and tear the dough.
↓

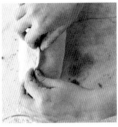

↑
8. Gently roll the dough into a spiral, starting with a long side. You may have to guide the roll along, moving your hands from one end of the dough to the other to get an even roll.

9. Gently pull the corners to make them square and even. This makes it easier to use the entire roll of dough without trimming.
↓

↑
10. Using your pointer finger and thumb, pinch the seam to seal the edges.

↑
11. Use a ruler to make sure you find the exact midpoint of the dough log. Cut the log in half using a serrated knife or kitchen string (these items won't squish the spiral). Place a loop of string around the log, then pull the ends of the string in opposite directions to cut through the dough.

# PIZZA, SANDWICHES & TACOS

# 023  HOMEMADE PIZZA

TASTING COMMENTS:  *A baking stone crisps the bottom of the crust because the dough cooks the instant it hits the intensely hot stone. The porousness of the fired-clay material also pulls moisture from the dough and gives it that crackly crust.—CW*

**PREP** 20 MINUTES  **RISE** 2 HOURS  **STAND** 10 MINUTES  **BAKE** 7 MINUTES AT 500°F

→ 5 **cups bread flour**
1 **Tbsp. sugar**
1½ **tsp. salt**
1 **tsp. active dry yeast**
1¾ **cups warm water (105°F to 115°F)**
2 **Tbsp. olive oil**
**Cornmeal**
½ **cup pizza sauce**
3 **cups shredded mozzarella, Fontina, and/or Asiago cheese (12 oz.)**

*Because bread flour has a higher protein content than all-purpose flour, it will give your crust a better texture. If you don't have it in your pantry, all-purpose will work.*

**1.** In an extra-large bowl stir together flour, sugar, salt, and yeast. Stir in water and oil until combined and all the flour is moistened.

**2.** Turn dough out onto a lightly floured surface. Knead dough until smooth and elastic (about 3 minutes). Place in a lightly greased bowl, turning once to grease surface of dough. Cover; let rise at room temperature until double in size (2 hours). If not using right away, cover with plastic wrap coated with nonstick cooking spray and chill up to 24 hours.

**3.** If chilled, let dough stand at room temperature 30 minutes. Remove dough from bowl (do not punch down). Divide dough into four portions. Gently shape each portion into a ball. Cover; let rest 10 minutes.

**4.** Preheat oven to 500°F. Place a pizza stone, if using, in the oven while it preheats. On a lightly floured surface roll or stretch each dough portion into a 10- to 11-inch circle. Transfer dough circles to a baking sheet sprinkled generously with cornmeal. Spread 2 Tbsp. pizza sauce on each dough circle. Top with cheese.

**5.** Gently slide one pizza at a time to the heated pizza stone or place baking sheet in the preheated oven. Bake 7 minutes for the pizza stone or 10 minutes for the baking sheet or until crust is golden.

**\*NOTE** This is a great basic cheese pizza recipe, but you can add your favorite additional toppings—such as 1 lb. cooked and drained bulk Italian sausage, 1 3.5-oz. package of pepperoni, or about 1½ cups chopped veggies. See pages 78-79 for more ideas.

PER SERVING *492 cal., 14 g fat (5 g sat. fat), 23 mg chol., 746 mg sodium, 69 g carb., 3 g fiber, 2 g sugars, 22 g pro.*

**VEGGIE PIZZA** Prepare as directed, except omit sausage and add 1½ cups assorted vegetables, such as chopped onion, sliced fresh mushrooms, sliced olives, chopped sweet peppers, and/or chopped tomatoes per pizza. Bake as directed.

**HAWAIIAN PIZZA** Prepare as directed, except substitute 6 slices Canadian-style bacon per pizza for the sausage. Add one 20-oz. can pineapple tidbits, drained. Bake as directed.

**PHILLY CHEESESTEAK PIZZA** Prepare as directed, except substitute 8 oz. cream cheese and, if desired, 3 Tbsp. prepared horseradish for the pizza sauce and 8 oz. deli roast beef, sliced into bite-size pieces, for the sausage. Add ¼ cup chopped sweet pepper and ¼ cup chopped onion per pizza. Substitute shredded Moneterey Jack cheese for the mozzarella cheese. Bake as directed.

**TACO PIZZA** Prepare as directed, except substitute salsa for the pizza sauce, 1 lb. ground beef for the sausage, and shredded cheddar cheese for the mozzarella. Stir ½ cup salsa into the cooked and drained ground beef. Bake as directed. Top each pizza with ¾ cup shredded lettuce, ½ cup chopped tomatoes, and ½ cup coarsely crushed tortilla chips.

**BARBECUE CHICKEN PIZZA** Prepare as directed, except substitute barbecue sauce for the pizza sauce and 8 oz. chicken, cooked and chopped, for the sausage. If desired, add sliced red onion, crumbled crisp-cooked bacon, and chopped tomato. Use a blend of cheddar and mozzarella cheeses. Bake as directed.

**HONEY-WHEAT PIZZA CRUST** Prepare dough as directed, except substitute 1 cup whole wheat flour for 1 cup of the bread flour and substitute 1 Tbsp. honey for the sugar.

## TESTING NOTES

↑
1. Yeast may seem fragile for some cooks, but if you watch the water temperature carefully, you won't kill the yeast. The best crusts rely on it.

↑
2. Once most of the dough has come together while mixing, use your hands to get it to come together completely into a ball before kneading.

3. Generously dust a baking sheet with cornmeal. Gently transfer a dough circle to the sheet. If you have enough cornmeal on the sheet, the dough will transfer onto the hot stone easily.
↓

4. Because the stone will be very hot, use the baking sheet to shimmy and shake the topped pizza dough onto the stone, gently pulling the baking sheet back toward you as the pizza settles on the stone.
↓

**BAKING STONES** *Baking stones get hot—really hot! That heat makes your pizza crust crispy on the bottom yet chewy in the middle. Place the stone in the oven while it preheats and be careful when transferring your pizza to the hot stone. Manufacturers vary with care recommendations, so follow the instructions specific to your stone.*

**MAKE-AHEAD DIRECTIONS** After dividing dough into four portions, wrap each portion in plastic wrap and place in airtight containers. Chill up to 24 hours or freeze up to 3 months. Thaw dough in refrigerator. Let it stand at room temperature for 30 minutes before rolling.

Barbecue
Chicken
Pizza

Basic
Homemade
Pizza

Veggie Pizza

Taco Pizza

Hawaiian
Pizza

Philly
Cheesesteak
Pizza

MAKES: *6 servings* TESTED BY: *Kelsey B.*

# 024 MAKE-IT-MINE DEEP-DISH PIZZA

TASTING COMMENTS: *Pizza can be a very personal thing! I love this recipe that allows you to customize your deep-dish experience to the tastes of your family or friends. —KB*

**PREP** 30 MINUTES **STAND** 10 MINUTES **RISE** 1 HOUR 20 MINUTES **BAKE** 55 MINUTES AT 400°F **COOL** 10 MINUTES

Cornmeal

1 cup warm water (105°F to 115°F)

1 pkg. active dry yeast

2¾ to 3¼ cups flour

⅓ cup vegetable or olive oil

½ tsp. salt

Protein

1 14.5-oz. can diced tomatoes, drained, or 2 medium tomatoes, seeded and chopped

Seasoning

Cheese

Fresh basil leaves (optional)

1. Grease a 10-inch springform pan, 10×2-inch heavy round cake pan, or a 13×9-inch baking pan. Sprinkle bottom and sides of pan with cornmeal.

2. In a large bowl combine the warm water and the yeast, stirring to dissolve yeast. Let stand 5 minutes. Stir in 2½ cups of the Flour, the ⅓ cup oil, and salt.

3. Turn dough out onto a lightly floured surface. Knead in enough of the remaining flour to make a moderately stiff dough that is smooth and elastic (about 5 minutes total). Shape dough into a ball. Place in a lightly greased bowl, turning once to grease surface. Cover and let rise in a warm place until double in size (50 to 60 minutes). Punch dough down. Cover and let rest 5 minutes.

4. Place dough in the prepared pan. Press and spread dough over

bottom and 1½ inches up the sides. Cover and let rise in a warm place until nearly double in size (30 to 35 minutes).

5. Preheat oven to 400°F. For filling, in a medium skillet combine cooked Protein, the tomatoes, and Seasoning. Cook and stir until heated through.

6. To assemble, arrange half of the Cheese over dough (all of the fresh mozzarella cheese). Spoon filling over cheese; sprinkle with remaining cheese.

7. Bake 55 to 60 minutes for 10-inch pans or 25 to 30 minutes for 13×9-inch baking pan or until edges of crust are golden and filling is heated through. If necessary, cover loosely with foil the last 10 minutes to prevent overbrowning. Cool on a wire rack 10 minutes. If desired, top with basil leaves.

**ANATOMY OF A DEEP-DISH PIZZA** *Traditional Chicago-style deep-dish calls for the dough to undergo two rises—one in the bowl and one in the pan. We figured out in tests of this personalized pizza that fresh mozzarella took on a different texture when it was placed on top—it became chewy and overly brown. If you use fresh mozzarella, put all of it on the bottom.*

**FLOUR (PICK ONE)**

Whole wheat flour

Half whole wheat and
half all-purpose

All-purpose

**PROTEIN (PICK ONE)**

1½ cups black beans,
lightly mashed

2 cups chopped
cooked chicken

1 lb. ground beef,
browned and drained

6 oz. sliced pepperoni

1 lb. mild bulk Italian
sausage, browned and
drained

**SEASONING (PICK ONE)**

1 tsp. dried Italian
seasoning, crushed

1 tsp. dried basil, crushed

1 tsp. dried oregano,
crushed

1 Tbsp. snipped fresh basil

1 Tbsp. snipped fresh
oregano

**CHEESE (PICK ONE)**

3 cups shredded Colby
Jack cheese (12 oz.)

3 cups shredded
cheddar cheese (12 oz.)

3 cups shredded
Mozzarella cheese
(12 oz.)

12 oz. sliced provolone
cheese

12 oz. sliced fresh
Mozzarella cheese

**THE PAN THAT CAN** *While a round pan will give
you the traditional "pizza pie" shape, if you don't
have one—or if you like your pizza pieces
square—you can use a 13×9 pan. We tested the
timings for a 13×9 pan because we thought,*
Everyone has one of those!

If you don't have a 10-inch springform pan or a heavy 10-inch cake pan, you can use a 13x9-inch baking pan to make this luscious deep-dish pie.

# 025 SKILLET BURGERS WITH SHALLOT-HERB BUTTER

TASTING COMMENTS: *Smoky, flame-kissed burgers may be a staple of grilling season, but there's something we love about the crisp, slightly charred crust on a pan-fried burger—and these are square! Serve them on toasted English muffin bread or ciabatta rolls.—CW*

**START TO FINISH** 30 MINUTES

*We used shallot in this herbed butter instead of onion because it is used raw. Raw shallot has lots of sweet onion flavor, but it doesn't have the harshness and bite of raw onion.*

- 1 large shallot, finely chopped (3 Tbsp.)
- 3 Tbsp. butter, softened
- 2 Tbsp. chopped Italian parsley
- ½ tsp. snipped fresh thyme
- ½ tsp. lemon zest
- 1½ lb. 80% to 85% lean ground beef
- ½ tsp. salt
- ¼ tsp. black pepper
- 8 oz. shiitake mushrooms, stemmed and sliced
- 1 Tbsp. olive oil
- 4 slices Swiss cheese
- 8 slices small firm square bread (such as English muffin toasting bread), toasted

**1.** In a small bowl stir together shallot, butter, parsley, thyme, and lemon zest until well combined. Set aside. Shape beef into four square patties about ½ inch larger than the bread. Season with salt and pepper.

**2.** Heat an extra-large heavy skillet over medium-high heat. Add 1 Tbsp. of the butter mixture to pan. When melted, add mushrooms. Cook and stir 3 minutes or just until tender. Transfer mushrooms to a medium bowl.

**3.** Add oil to skillet. When hot but not smoking, add patties to skillet. Cook 3 minutes or until browned and slightly charred. Turn and cook 3 minutes more or until done (160°F). Top patties with mushrooms, then cheese. Cover and cook 1 minute or until cheese is melted.

**4.** Meanwhile, spread remaining seasoned butter on four slices of toasted bread. Top with burgers and remaining bread.

PER SERVING *777 cal., 52 g fat (21 g sat. fat), 160 mg chol., 818 mg sodium, 36 g carb., 3 g fiber, 4 g sugars, 41 g pro.*

**HERB GARDEN** Whisk ½ cup softened butter until fluffy. Add 1 Tbsp. herbed pepper seasoning, 1 Tbsp. fresh lemon juice, and desired snipped fresh herbs. Shape into a 6-inch log in waxed paper. Twist ends to secure. Chill at least 30 minutes.

**GARLICKY TOMATO** Whisk ½ cup softened butter until fluffy. Add 1 Tbsp. tomato paste, 1 tsp. finely chopped green onion, and 1 tsp. minced roasted garlic. Shape and chill as directed at left.

**CITRUS SCALLION** Whisk ½ cup softened butter until fluffy. Add 1 Tbsp. lemon zest, 1 Tbsp. fresh lemon juice, and 1 Tbsp. finely chopped green onion. Shape and chill as directed at left.

*Try one of these fun butters the next time you make these tasty burgers!*

**MEET THESE MUSHROOMS** *Meaty mushrooms are a classic combination with beef— and more exotic varieties are increasingly available in supermarkets. Flavorful shiitakes are called for in this recipe, but branch out a bit with these beauties if you like. The pictured varieties are, from left: Trumpet Royale, shiitake, Brown Clamshell, Maitake Frondosa, Alba Clamshell, and oyster.*

# 026 MAKE-IT-MINE SLOPPY JOES

TASTING COMMENTS: *Make it yours! We tested the following combos: ground pork, zucchini, barbeque sauce, chipotles, and bolillo rolls; ground beef, carrot, sweet-and-sour sauce, and five-spice on ciabatta rolls; and a vegetarian version with onion, green pepper, and barbeque sauce—and we loved them all!—CC*

**START TO FINISH** 25 MINUTES

1½ lb. **Meat**

**Vegetable**

**Sauce**

**Seasoning**

**Bread, split and toasted**

**1.** In a large skillet cook Meat and Vegetable until meat is browned and vegetable is tender; drain off fat. Stir in Sauce and Seasoning. Bring to boiling; reduce heat. Simmer, uncovered, 5 minutes. Serve on toasted Bread.

## MEAT (PICK ONE)

Ground beef, pork, turkey, or chicken

2 cups cooked brown rice plus one 15-oz. can kidney beans, rinsed and drained

## SAUCE (PICK ONE)

1 cup bottled salsa plus ½ cup process cheese dip

½ cup sweet-and-sour sauce plus ½ cup tomato sauce

½ cup bottled barbecue sauce plus ⅓ cup orange marmalade

14-oz. jar pizza sauce

8-oz. can tomato sauce plus 2 Tbsp. water

## BREAD (PICK ONE)

6 kaiser rolls

6 ciabatta buns

6 pretzel buns

6 whole wheat or white hamburger buns

1 focaccia bread round, cut into 6 wedges

6 bolillo rolls

## VEGETABLE (PICK ONE)

1 cup chopped carrots

1 cup chopped zucchini

1 cup fresh or frozen corn kernels

½ cup chopped onion and ½ cup chopped green sweet pepper

## SEASONING (PICK ONE)

2 tsp. barbecue spice

2 tsp. chili powder

2 tsp. Worcestershire sauce and ½ tsp. garlic salt

1 tsp. finely chopped chipotle chile pepper in adobo sauce (tip, page 18)

1 tsp. five-spice powder

# 027 DELUXE GRILLED CHEESE SANDWICHES

**TASTING COMMENTS:** *This may not seem like something that needs testing, but we did—to be sure it was as good as it could be! We were even curious to see how the bread toasts when brushed with olive oil, mayo, or butter. Each was good in its own way!—JH*

**START TO FINISH** 20 MINUTES

1 1-lb. loaf unsliced bakery white bread

6 slices cheddar cheese

6 slices Swiss cheese

2 Tbsp. mayonnaise (optional)

1 Tbsp. mustard (optional)

3 Tbsp. olive oil

3 Tbsp. butter (optional)

*White cheddar or American is the classic cheese choice in this sandwich, we love other types, too—especially if we're jazzing it up with additional ingredients. Try Swiss, provolone, Gouda, Havarti, Monterey Jack (with or without peppers), or Colby.*

**1.** Slice bread into twelve ½-inch-thick slices. Top six slices with cheese slices. If desired, spread one side of remaining bread with mayonnaise and/or mustard; place on cheese, spread sides down. Brush both sides sandwiches with olive oil.

**2.** Heat a large skillet or griddle over medium heat. If desired, add 1 Tbsp. of the butter; heat until butter melts. Add two sandwiches to skillet. Cook 2 minutes or until bottoms are golden. Turn sandwiches over; cook 2 to 3 minutes more or until bottoms are golden and cheese is melted.

(Adjust heat as necessary to prevent overbrowning.) Repeat with remaining sandwiches.

PER SERVING *483 cal., 27 g fat (12 g sat. fat), 56 mg chol., 745 mg sodium, 40 g carb., 2 g fiber, 4 g sugars, 20 g pro.*

**OLIVE OIL** This turned out the crispest toast. And it was the lightest option—not quite as greasy as with butter or mayo.

**MAYO** The bread browned nicely with this option—and it added a pleasantly tangy flavor to the sandwich.

**BUTTER** This resulted in the most browning—and the most even browning. And then, of course, there was the great flavor of the butter.

This simple sandwich goes gourmet with the addition of just a few ingredients and by mixing up the bread choices. From the top: classic (just cheese), bacon and jam, tomato and basil, and tart apple and ham. Yum!

# 028 SHREDDED PORK ROAST SANDWICHES

TASTING COMMENTS: *Love the flavor of this roast! After shredding the meat, I used about ½ cup of the cooking liquid to keep the meat juicy and to add more of the flavor from the rub.—LB*

**PREP** 15 MINUTES   **ROAST** 2 HOURS 30 MINUTES AT 325°F

*This cut of meat is perfect for braising. The tough collagen fibers that run through the muscle completely break down if you cook the roast long enough—whether in the oven or the slow cooker.*

- 1 3-lb. boneless pork shoulder blade roast
- 8 cloves garlic, minced
- 2 tsp. ground coriander
- 2 tsp. ground cumin
- 2 tsp. dried oregano, crushed
- 1 tsp. onion powder
- ½ tsp. salt
- ½ tsp. black pepper
- ½ tsp. cayenne pepper
- 2 Tbsp. vegetable oil
- 1 cup beef broth
- 12 hamburger buns or kaiser rolls, split and toasted*
- Barbecue sauce (optional)
- Shredded cabbage (optional)

**1.** Preheat oven to 325°F. Trim excess fat from meat. In a small bowl combine the next eight ingredients (through cayenne). Sprinkle garlic mixture evenly over all sides of roast; rub in with your fingers. In a Dutch oven heat oil. Add roast; cook until browned on all sides, turning to brown evenly.

**2.** Pour beef broth over roast. Cover and roast 2½ to 3 hours or until very tender.

**3.** Using a slotted spoon, remove meat from Dutch oven. Shred meat; transfer to a large bowl. Skim fat from cooking liquid. Stir enough cooking liquid into shredded meat to moisten. Serve on toasted buns. If desired, add barbecue sauce and/or cabbage.

**\*TIP** To toast the buns, preheat broiler. Place split buns, cut sides up, on a broiler pan. Broil 4 to 5 inches from the heat about 1 minute or just until browned. Be sure to check the buns frequently to avoid burning.

**SLOW COOKER DIRECTIONS**
Prepare Shredded Pork Roast Sandwiches as directed in Step 1. Place roast in a 3½- to 5-qt. slow cooker; add beef broth. Cover and cook on low 8 to 10 hours or on high 4 to 5 hours. Continue as directed in Step 3.

PER SERVING *295 cal., 10 g fat (3 g sat. fat), 68 mg chol., 461 mg sodium, 23 g carb., 1 g fiber, 3 g sugars, 26 g pro.*

*Don't skip searing! Your roast will look AND taste better!*

## TESTING NOTES

1. Rub the spice mixture onto all sides of the roast. The spices may become clumpy due to the moisture on the surface of the roast.

2. Quickly sear the meat in hot oil at a high temperature to create a richly flavored, caramelized "crust."

*we liked the amount of heat in the rub. If you prefer things spicier, increase the cayenne.*

3. Skim excess fat from the cooking liquid by pouring the liquid into a glass measuring cup and letting the fat float to the top. Tip the cup slightly so you can skim a spoon just under the surface of the fat layer.

4. Roast until you can easily pull the meat apart and see the softened collagen fibers. Pull in opposite directions to shred the pork into long, thin pieces with the grain —the direction the bundles of muscle fibers are aligned on a piece of meat.

# 029 PORK TENDERLOIN SANDWICHES

**TASTING COMMENTS:** *The first rule of a great pork tenderloin sandwich is that the meat has to exceed the size of the bun. The other is a tender, juicy piece of pork in a perfectly crisp coating. This is it!—SM*

**PREP** 20 MINUTES **COOK** 6 MINUTES

1 lb. pork tenderloin

¼ cup all-purpose flour

¼ tsp. garlic salt

¼ tsp. black pepper

1 egg

1 Tbsp. milk

½ cup seasoned fine dry bread crumbs

2 Tbsp. vegetable oil

4 large hamburger buns or kaiser rolls, split and toasted

Ketchup, mustard, onion slices, and/or dill pickle slices

1. Trim fat from meat. Cut meat crosswise into four pieces. Place each piece between two pieces of plastic wrap. Use the flat side of a meat mallet to pound the pork lightly to ¼-inch thickness. Discard plastic wrap.

2. In a shallow bowl combine flour, garlic salt, and pepper. In another shallow bowl whisk together egg and milk. In a third bowl place bread crumbs. Dip pork into flour mixture to coat. Dip into egg mixture; coat with bread crumbs.

3. In a large heavy skillet cook pork, half at a time, in hot oil over medium heat 3 to 4 minutes or until meat is slightly pink in center, turning once (add more oil during cooking if necessary).

4. Serve tenderloin slices on warm buns with ketchup, mustard, onion slices, and/or dill pickle slices.

PER SERVING *424 cal., 13 g fat (3 g sat. fat), 127 mg chol., 776 mg sodium, 42 g carb., 2 g fiber, 7 g sugars, 33 g pro.*

*Get creative with your breading options. From the top: crushed whole grain thin wheat crackers, crushed multigrain tortilla chips, crushed cornflakes, and the classic: sesasoned fine dry bread crumbs.*

*Breading is a three-step process. The flour gives the egg something to stick to so the bread crumbs stick to the egg. The result: crispy perfection!*

## TESTING NOTES

1. Cut tenderloin crosswise into four equal pieces.

2. Working from center to edges, pound pork pieces to an even ¼-inch thickness.

3. To make pieces rounder, fold any long edges toward the center and pound again until even.

4. Cook until coating is browned and pork is a little pink in the middle. Cut into a slice to check doneness.

MAKES: *10 servings*  TESTED BY: *Colleen W.*

## 030 OAXACAN BEEF TACOS

TASTING COMMENTS: *The flavor of this roast is outstanding. It cooks for 2 hours in a smoky, spicy, rich sauce that is absorbed by the meat as it simmers. After shredding the meat, add some of the sauce to moisten it and pass the rest at the table.—CW*

**PREP** 20 MINUTES  **COOK** 2 HOURS

*Chuck is very flavorful but on the tough side since it comes from the shoulder—one of the most well-worked parts of the animal. Long cooking in liquid turns it fork-tender—perfect for shredding and rolling up in tacos.*

- 2 Tbsp. olive oil
- 3 lb. beef chuck, trimmed and cut into 2- to 3-inch pieces
- 2 dried ancho chile peppers, stemmed, seeded, and cut into 1-inch pieces
- 1 medium white onion, coarsely chopped
- 4 cloves garlic, halved lengthwise
- 1½ tsp. dried Mexican oregano or dried oregano, crushed
- 1 tsp. ground cumin
- ½ tsp. salt
- 1 14.5-oz. can reduced-sodium chicken broth
- 1 14.5-oz. can diced fire-roasted tomatoes (undrained)
- 3 Tbsp. cider vinegar
- 1 to 2 chipotle peppers in adobo sauce, chopped, plus 2 tsp. adobo sauce (tip, page 18)

- 2 sprigs fresh epazote* or 1 cup coarsely chopped fresh cilantro, tender stems and leaves
- Corn or flour tortillas, warmed
- Assorted toppings, such as chopped or sliced radishes, shredded red and/or green cabbage, crumbled queso fresco, chopped avocado, cilantro, sliced jalapeño peppers (tip, page 18), Mexican crema, sour cream, green onions, quartered cherry tomatoes, and/or lime wedges

**1.** Heat oil in a wide heavy pot or large deep skillet over medium-high heat. Add beef and cook 8 minutes, turning to brown all sides.

**2.** Add the next six ingredients (through salt). Cook 5 minutes, stirring occasionally. Add the next four ingredients (through adobo chile peppers). Bring to boiling; add epazote. Reduce heat to low. Cover; cook 1¾ to 2 hours or until beef is very tender, stirring occasionally.

**3.** Remove from heat and transfer beef to a large dish. Let sauce cool slightly; spoon into a blender. Blend until smooth (or blend in pan with an immersion blender). Using two forks, coarsely shred beef and return to pan. Add desired amount of sauce to moisten.** Return to low heat and keep warm until ready to serve.

**4.** Serve with tortillas and desired toppings.

**\*TIP** Found in Mexican markets.

**\*\*TIP** This recipe can be made to this point and refrigerated up to 3 days.

PER SERVING *451 cal., 25 g fat (8 g sat. fat), 119 mg chol., 621 mg sodium, 26 g carb., 4 g fiber, 4 g sugars, 30 g pro.*

*To warm corn tortillas, wrap a stack in foil and heat in a 350°F oven 15 minutes.*

Ancho chiles are dried poblano peppers.

Mexican oregano has a stronger flavor than Mediterranean oregano.

Epazote is a pungent wild herb.

MAKES: *8 servings*   TESTED BY: *Sarah B.*

# 031   BAJA-STYLE FISH TACOS

TASTING COMMENTS: *For the lightest, crispiest fish, there better be bubbles! Adding an ice-cold beer to batter adds flavor, but more important, the beer becomes frothy as the batter is stirred and creates air bubbles that make the coating light and crunchy.—SB*

*Use whatever beer you have on hand (nonalcoholic brews work well, too). The key to a perfect batter is ice-cold beer. The cold temperature helps maintain the carbonation, which ultimately gives you a light, crispy batter.*

**START TO FINISH** 35 MINUTES

½ cup mayonnaise

½ cup plain yogurt

1 Tbsp. lime juice

1 canned chipotle chile pepper in adobo sauce, finely chopped (tip, page 18)

½ tsp. dried oregano, crushed

¼ tsp. ground cumin

⅛ tsp. salt

⅛ tsp. black pepper

1½ lb. fresh or frozen tilapia, cod, grouper, or halibut fillets

1½ cups all-purpose flour

½ tsp. salt

¼ tsp. black pepper

1½ cups beer or nonalcoholic beer

Vegetable oil for deep-fat frying

8 6-inch corn tortillas or 7-inch flour tortillas, warmed

1½ cups shredded red and/or green cabbage or packaged shredded cabbage with carrot (coleslaw mix)

Lime wedges

**1.** For sauce, in a small bowl stir together the first eight ingredients (through ⅛ tsp. black pepper). Cover and chill.

**2.** Thaw fish, if frozen. Rinse fish; pat dry with paper towels. Cut fish lengthwise into 1-inch-wide strips; cut strips into bite-size pieces.

**3.** For the batter, in a medium bowl combine flour, the ½ tsp. salt, and the ¼ tsp. black pepper. Slowly add beer, stirring until batter is thick and slightly bubbly.

**4.** Preheat oven to 200°F. In an extra-large skillet heat 1 inch of oil to 365°F. Working with about one-third of the fish at a time, dip each piece in batter, turning to coat. Fry fish in the hot oil 3 to 5 minutes or until coating is golden brown and fish flakes easily, turning once. Transfer fish to a paper towel-lined baking sheet; keep warm in oven while frying remaining fish.

**5.** Divide fish among tortillas; top with cabbage and serve with sauce and lime wedges.

PER SERVING *474 cal., 27 g fat (4 g sat. fat), 48 mg chol., 371 mg sodium, 35 g carb., 2 g fiber, 2 g sugars, 22 g pro.*

If you'd like more heat in your sauce, stir in a little bit of the adobo sauce from the chipotle chile.

**FISH PICKS** *Most any mild whitefish works well in these tacos. Favorite everyday choices include tilapia (B) and cod (D). Your pocketbook will take a bigger hit with grouper (A) and halibut (C), but they can be worth a splurge. No matter which fish you use, choose firm, evenly sized fillets that are free from blemishes, bruises, or red spots. Plan to cook fresh fish the same day you buy it. If that's not possible, wrap fish loosely in plastic wrap and store in the coldest part of the refrigerator; use within 2 days.*

## TESTING NOTES

1. After rinsing fish pieces with cool water, dry them thoroughly by patting gently with paper towels on all sides. A dry surface helps the batter evenly coat and stick to the fish.
↓

↑
2. Add cold beer to the dry ingredients slowly, stirring gently with a rubber spatula or whisk. You don't want to lose all of the carbonation by overstirring. Expect the batter to be fairly thick and even a little lumpy. Batter that is too thin will not adhere well to the fish and may fall off during frying. Dip fish into the batter, one piece at a time, and allow the excess batter to drip back into the bowl; too much batter may turn gummy when cooked. For the best consistency, always prepare beer batter just before you use it.

↑
3. Don't crowd fish in the pan when frying. Adding too many pieces at once causes the temperature of the oil to drop quickly and the fish to cook unevenly. Plan to fry about one-third of the fish at a time. When the batter turns a light golden brown, use long-handle tongs to carefully remove fish from the hot oil and place on a paper towel–lined baking sheet. Between batches, use a deep-frying thermometer to be sure the oil temperature is back up to 365°F before adding more fish to the pan.

↑
4. Properly cooked fish is opaque with a flaky texture. To test for doneness, insert a fork into the fish and gently twist. The fish is done as soon as it begins to flake easily. Always test fish for doneness at the minimum cooking time. For maximum crispiness, serve fish (and all fried foods) within 15 minutes of frying.

MAKES: *8 servings*   TESTED BY: *Sarah B.*

# HEALTHIER FISH TACOS

TASTING COMMENTS:   *Skillet-cooking seasoned fish instead of battering and frying it—and making a few ingredient swaps—cuts the calorie count for these lightened-up tacos by half and the fat by more than 75 percent.—SB*

**PREP:** 50 MINUTES   **STAND:** 20 MINUTES

1½  tsp. chili powder
¼  tsp. salt
¼  tsp. black pepper
1½  lb. fresh or frozen tilapia, cod, grouper, or halibut fillets
2  Tbsp. vegetable oil
8  6-inch corn tortillas or 7-inch flour tortillas, warmed
1½  cups broccoli slaw mix
1  recipe Fruit Salsa
  Plain Greek yogurt

**1.** In a small bowl stir together chili powder, salt, and pepper. Sprinkle both sides of each fish fillet with the chili powder mixture.

**2.** In a large skillet heat oil over medium heat. Add half of the fish fillets to the hot oil. Fry fish 4 to 6 minutes or until fish flakes easily when tested with a fork, turning once. Remove from skillet; keep warm.

**3.** Cook the remaining fish fillets, adding a little more oil if necessary. Use a fork to break fish into small pieces.

**4.** Divide fish among tortillas. Top with broccoli slaw mix, Fruit Salsa, and yogurt.

**FRUIT SALSA**  In a medium bowl stir together 1½ cups finely chopped fresh pineapple or mango; ½ to 1 canned chipotle chile pepper in adobo sauce, finely chopped (tip, page 18); 2 Tbsp. snipped fresh cilantro; 1 Tbsp. honey; 1 tsp. lime zest or lemon zest; and 1 Tbsp. lime juice or lemon juice.

PER SERVING: *212 cal., 6 g fat (1 g sat. fat), 43 mg chol., 169 mg sodium, 20 g carb., 2 g fiber, 6 g sugars, 20 g pro.*

# MEAT
# MAINS

# 032  MEAT LOAF

TASTING COMMENTS: *We knew the ideal meat loaf is a tender and juicy loaf that holds together and isn't compact or dry. We also knew that to accomplish this you have to use two different types of ground meat—a higher protein for structure and a higher fat for flavor and tenderness. We played around with lots of combinations—including ground turkey—to get the ideal. —CW*

**PREP** 25 MINUTES  **BAKE** 1 HOUR AT 350°F  **STAND** 10 MINUTES

*Bread crumbs soak up some of the fat from the meat and lighten the mixture so it doesn't get too dense. To make soft bread crumbs, cut one slice of bread into cubes and place the cubes in a food processor or blender. Process or blend with on/off turns until crumbs are desired consistency. One bread slice makes about ¾ cup bread crumbs.*

- 1 Tbsp. vegetable oil
- ½ cup finely chopped fresh mushrooms
- ½ cup shredded carrot
- ⅓ cup finely chopped onion
- 2 cloves garlic, minced
- 2 eggs, lightly beaten
- ¼ cup milk
- 3 Tbsp. ketchup
- 1 Tbsp. Dijon-style mustard
- 1 Tbsp. Worcestershire sauce
- ½ tsp. kosher salt
- 1 cup soft bread crumbs
- 1 lb. ground beef chuck*
- 1 lb. ground beef sirloin*
- ½ cup ketchup
- ¼ cup packed brown sugar
- 2 tsp. Dijon-style mustard

**1.** Preheat oven to 350°F. In a large skillet heat oil over medium-high heat. Add mushrooms, carrot, onion, and garlic; cook and stir 4 to 5 minutes or until tender.

**2.** In a large bowl combine the next six ingredients (through salt). Stir in bread crumbs and vegetable mixture until thoroughly combined. Add ground beef; mix well. Line a 3-qt. rectangular baking dish with foil. Shape mixture into a 9×5-inch loaf and place in the prepared dish.

**3.** For glaze, in a small bowl combine the ½ cup ketchup, the brown sugar, and the 2 tsp. mustard; set aside.

**4.** Bake 1 hour or until done (160°F), spooning glaze over meat loaf the last 25 minutes. Let stand 10 minutes before serving.

***TIP** sIf desired, substitute 8 oz. bulk sweet Italian sausage, uncooked ground turkey, or ground pork for 8 oz. of ground beef.

PER SERVING *369 cal., 18 g fat (6 g sat. fat), 123 mg chol., 649 mg sodium, 24 g carb., 1 g fiber, 13 g sugars, 26 g pro.*

**NEXT-DAY MEAT LOAF SANDWICHES!** *Cut leftover meat loaf into ¾-inch slices and warm through on a lightly greased, preheated grill pan, carefully turning once. If you like, top each piece with a cheese slice and cook until melted. Serve between bread slices with mustard, ketchup, mayonnaise, arugula, and/or roasted red sweet pepper strips.*

# TESTING NOTES

↑
1. Mushrooms, carrots, onions, and garlic add nutrients, flavor, and moisture, but they also extend the meat loaf mixture. Cut or shred the veggies in small, uniform pieces so they cook evenly and the mixture will hold together when shaped. Briefly sautéing the veggies first ensures they will lose their crunch when baked.

↑
2. It's important to mix the wet and dry ingredients well before adding the meat. This ultimately reduces the amount of mixing necessary once you do add the meat. Be sure to use a bowl large enough to hold the entire mixture.

↑
3. Use your fingers or a wooden spoon to thoroughly but gently mix the ground meat into the egg-bread crumb mixture until just combined. Use a light touch: Overmixing can make the meat loaf dense and tough.

↑
4. To prevent the meat mixture from sticking to your hands, moisten your hands with cold water before shaping the loaf. Gently pat and shape the meat mixture into an oblong loaf that is slightly smaller than the rectangular dish. This improves browning and lets some of the fat drain from the loaf into the dish.

**MEAT COMBOS** *The best combination for meat loaf is a mixture of ground chuck (80% lean, 20% fat) and sirloin (90% lean, 10% fat). Because of its higher fat content, ground chuck adds flavor and moisture to the loaf; lean sirloin adds good structure. To change up your meat mixture, try the combos below. If your meat mix is on the lean side, cover the meat loaf with foil for the first 35 minutes of baking to keep it from drying out.*

### GROUND BEEF + BULK SWEET ITALIAN SAUSAGE

### GROUND TURKEY BREAST + GROUND PORK

### GROUND BEEF CHUCK + GROUND VEAL

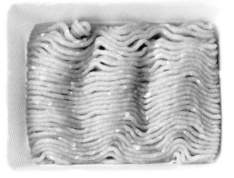

# MAKE-IT-MINE GLAZES

TASTING COMMENTS: *Ketchup may be the classic meat loaf topper, but we thought we'd branch out a bit with these special glazes. —CW*

**APRICOT-MUSTARD GLAZE** Stir together ½ cup apricot preserves and 2 Tbsp. Dijon-style mustard.

**CRANBERRY GLAZE** Stir together ½ cup ketchup and ¼ cup whole cranberry sauce.

**PEACH-CHILE GLAZE** Stir together ½ cup peach preserves, 2 tsp. Asian chili sauce with garlic, and 2 tsp. grated fresh ginger.

**STRAWBERRY GLAZE** In a blender combine 1 cup strawberries, ½ cup plum jam, 3 cloves garlic, 1 tsp. soy sauce, ¼ tsp. ground ancho chile pepper, ¼ tsp. ground ginger, and ⅛ tsp. salt. Cover and blend until smooth. In a small saucepan heat strawberry mixture until boiling; boil gently 10 minutes. Cool slightly before spooning over meat loaf.

Strawberry Glaze

Apricot-Mustard Glaze

Cranberry Glaze

Peach-Chile Glaze

# 033  STEAK WITH PAN SAUCE

TASTING COMMENTS: *Grilled steak is great, but a pan-cooked steak can be just as delicious. We seared the steaks before roasting to create a crisp, caramelized exterior and develop flavorful browned bits that became the foundation for the pan sauce. —LB*

**PREP** 20 MINUTES  **STAND** 30 MINUTES  **ROAST** 10 MINUTES AT 400°F

*Always use unsalted butter when preparing pan sauce. It lets you control the flavor while adding richness and body to the sauce.*

- 2 beef top loin or ribeye steaks, cut 1 to 1½ inches thick, or 4 beef tenderloin steaks, cut 1 to 1½ inches thick (1½ to 2 lb. total)
- ½ tsp. kosher salt
- ½ tsp. freshly ground black pepper
- 6 Tbsp. cold unsalted butter
- ½ cup dry red wine or apple juice
- ⅓ cup reduced-sodium beef broth
- 3 Tbsp. finely chopped shallot or 2 cloves garlic, minced
- 2 Tbsp. heavy cream

1. Allow steaks to stand at room temperature 30 minutes. Preheat oven to 400°F. Trim fat from steaks; pat dry with paper towels. Sprinkle salt and pepper over steaks. Heat a large oven-going skillet over medium-high heat. Add 2 Tbsp. of the butter to hot skillet; reduce heat to medium. Add steaks; cook 4 minutes or until browned, turning once. Transfer skillet to oven. Roast, uncovered, 10 to 13 minutes or until medium rare (an instant-read thermometer registers 145°F when inserted in centers of steaks). Transfer steaks to a serving platter. Cover with foil; let stand while preparing sauce.

2. For pan sauce, drain fat from skillet. Add wine, broth, and shallot to skillet. Bring to boiling, whisking constantly to scrape up any crusty browned bits from bottom of skillet. Boil gently, uncovered, over medium heat 6 minutes or until liquid is reduced to about ¼ cup.

3. Whisk in cream. Boil gently 1 to 2 minutes more or until slightly thickened. Whisk in remaining 4 Tbsp. butter, 1 Tbsp. at a time, until butter is melted and sauce is thickened.

PER SERVING *529 cal., 39 g fat (19 g sat. fat), 173 mg chol., 437 mg sodium, 3 g carb., 0 g fiber, 1 g sugars, 37 g pro.*

RIBEYE  TOP LOIN  TENDERLOIN

**STEAK OUT!** *Whether you choose ribeye, top loin, or tenderloin steaks, look for well-marbled meat with vibrant color and a moist (but not wet) surface. For more-even cooking, let steaks stand at room temperature about 30 minutes before searing.*

*For best results, don't use a nonstick skillet because it won't caramelize the steaks properly and may not be safe for use in the oven. Stainless-steel and cast-iron skillets tolerate high heat levels and retain heat well, making either one ideal for this recipe.*

↑
1. Make sure the pan is really hot before you add the steaks. If it's hot enough, the steak will brown instantly; if not, it will turn pale gray. Use tongs, and be cautious not to pierce the meat, which will release flavorful juices.

↑
2. Deglaze the pan by adding wine and broth, then scrape the bottom of the skillet to pick up the flavorful browned bits left behind by the steaks.

↑
3. To determine doneness, insert an instant-read thermometer into the thickest part of a steak at an angle; be sure it is not touching the surface of the pan or any large areas of fat. Cook steaks to 145°F for medium rare or 160°F for medium. Always let steaks rest before serving to allow the juices to redistribute within the steak.

## SAUCY FLAVOR BOOSTS

*Vary the flavor of the sauce with one of these simple stir-ins.*

**HERBS** 1 tsp. snipped fresh thyme, tarragon, or oregano added with the shallot

**MUSTARD** 1 tsp. Dijon-style mustard or balsamic vinegar added with the shallot

**CAPERS** 1 tsp. rinsed and drained capers stirred into the finished sauce

MAKES: 6 servings    TESTED BY: Kelsey B.

# 034    ASIAN SHORT RIBS

**TASTING COMMENTS:** Browning the ribs first adds extra flavor and deepens the color of the rich sauce. Just don't brown them all at once—you'll miss the benefits of searing and go straight to stewing!—KB

**PREP** 30 MINUTES    **BAKE** 2 HOURS 45 MINUTES AT 350°F

- 2½ cups reduced-sodium beef broth
- ¾ cup hoisin sauce
- 3 Tbsp. reduced-sodium soy sauce
- 2 tsp. toasted sesame oil
- 1½ tsp. five-spice powder
- ⅛ tsp. cayenne pepper (optional)
- 3½ to 4 lb. beef short ribs, cut into serving-size pieces
- ¼ tsp. black pepper
- 1 Tbsp. vegetable oil
- ½ cup chopped onion
- 3 to 4 cloves garlic, minced
- 1 tsp. grated fresh ginger
- 1½ cups sliced fresh shiitake mushrooms (stems removed) or button mushrooms
- Hot cooked rice (optional)
- Green onions, bias-sliced into 1-inch pieces (optional)

**1.** Preheat oven to 350°F. In a medium bowl stir together the first six ingredients (through cayenne pepper if using). Trim fat from ribs; sprinkle with black pepper. In a 4- to 5-qt. Dutch oven heat oil over medium-high heat. Add ribs, half at a time; cook until browned on all sides. Remove ribs to a large bowl. Add onion, garlic, and ginger to Dutch oven. Cook and stir 1 to 2 minutes or until onion is lightly browned.

**2.** Return ribs to Dutch oven; add broth mixture. Bring to boiling. Cover Dutch oven; transfer to oven. Bake 2 hours, stirring once or twice. Add mushrooms; stir. Bake, covered, 45 minutes more or until ribs are tender.

**3.** Transfer ribs to a deep platter; keep warm. Transfer cooking liquid to a large glass measure. Skim fat from cooking liquid. For sauce, return cooking liquid to Dutch oven; bring to boiling. Cook, uncovered, 2 to 3 minutes or until thickened. Pour some of the sauce over ribs. Pass remaining sauce. If desired, serve with rice and sprinkle with green onions.

PER SERVING 316 cal., 16 g fat (5 g sat. fat), 65 mg chol., 1,044 mg sodium, 18 g carb., 1 g fiber, 10 g sugars, 24 g pro.

well-marbled

one bone

**PICK THE RIGHT RIBS!** *For this recipe, choose English-style short ribs, which are 2 to 4 inches long with one rib-bone section. Look for meaty, well-marbled ribs and use a knife to remove any large areas of visible fat.*

## TESTING NOTES

1. Although it takes a little more time to brown the ribs half at a time, it's worth it in the end to do this step in two batches. If you brown all of the ribs at once, too much liquid is released from the meat. Instead of searing and taking on a dark caramelized crust, the meat stews and gets soft on the outside.

↓

↑

3. To test the doneness of short ribs, insert a fork into the thickest part. They are done when the fork twists easily and the meat pulls apart with no resistance.

4. Don't skip the last step! Simmering the skimmed sauce 2 to 3 minutes over medium-high heat concentrates the flavor and gives you a slightly thickened sauce that coats a spoon.

↓

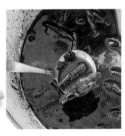

↑

2. Shiitake stems are very tough! Remove the stems before adding the mushrooms to this dish. If you like to make your own vegetable stock, save the stems. They add a meaty note to homemade stock—perfect for a veggie risotto.

**GREAT GRATING** *To mince fresh ginger, first remove the tough, woody skin using a spoon or table knife. Then grate using a Microplane or the smallest holes on a box grater. Grate only what you need for each use. Wrap unpeeled ginger in a paper towel and refrigerate up to 3 weeks. For longer storage, place unpeeled ginger in a freezer bag; freeze up to 1 year.*

# 035 OVEN-ROASTED BEEF TENDERLOIN

TASTING COMMENTS: *We've learned over the years that the less you mess with a very special cut of meat such as a tenderloin, the better the results. That's why the rub for this roast is just oil, salt, and pepper. The three different sauces accent but don't interfere with the buttery texture and delicate flavor of the meat.—JH*

**PREP** 30 MINUTES   **ROAST** 35 MINUTES AT 425°F   **STAND** 15 MINUTES

*As its name implies, the tenderloin is most tender (and most expensive) cut of beef. It's an oblong cut that comes from just under the ribs and next to the backbone of the animal, a muscle that doesn't do much work. Don't overcook it!*

- 1 Tbsp. olive oil
- 1 3-lb. beef tenderloin roast, trimmed
- 1½ tsp. kosher salt
- 1 tsp. black pepper
- 1 recipe Mediterranean Dipping Sauce, Peppercorn-Horseradish Sauce, and/or Soy-Ginger Dipping Sauce
- **Fresh parsley sprigs (optional)**

1. Preheat oven to 425°F. Brush olive oil over meat. For rub, in a small bowl stir together salt and pepper. Sprinkle rub over meat; rub in with your fingers.

2. Place roast on a rack set in a shallow roasting pan. Insert an oven-going meat thermometer into center of roast. Roast, uncovered, 35 to 40 minutes or until 135°F for medium rare. (For medium, roast 45 to 50 minutes or until 150°F.)

3. Transfer roast to a cutting board. Cover roast with foil; let stand 15 minutes. Slice meat across the grain. Serve with sauce(s). If desired, top with fresh parsley sprigs.

PER SERVING *261 cal., 19 g fat (7 g sat. fat), 91 mg chol., 293 mg sodium, 0 g carb., 0 g fiber, 0 g sugars, 22 g pro.*

**MEDITERRANEAN DIPPING SAUCE** In a small bowl whisk together ¼ cup champagne vinegar, ¼ cup finely snipped fresh tarragon, 2 Tbsp. finely chopped shallot, 2 Tbsp. chopped capers, 2 tsp. Dijon-style mustard, and ½ tsp. salt. Gradually whisk in ¼ cup olive oil.

**PEPPERCORN-HORSERADISH SAUCE** In a small bowl stir together one 8-oz. carton sour cream, 3 Tbsp. prepared horseradish, 1 Tbsp. snipped fresh chives, 2 tsp. white wine vinegar, and 1 tsp. coarsely ground black peppercorns. Cover and chill at least 1 hour before serving.

**SOY-GINGER DIPPING SAUCE** In a small bowl whisk together ½ cup reduced-sodium soy sauce; ¼ cup lime juice; 2 Tbsp. thinly sliced green onion; 2 tsp. grated fresh ginger; 2 tsp. Asian sweet chili sauce; and 2 cloves garlic, minced. Gradually whisk in 2 Tbsp. sesame oil and 1 Tbsp. canola oil.

**A CHEAPER CHOICE** *Not feeling flush enough for a beef tenderloin? Try a 4-lb. beef top round roast. Roast it in a 350°F oven 1½ to 1¾ hours or until a meat thermometer registers 135°F for medium rare. Roasting past medium rare is not recommended for this cut because it is tougher and cooking it beyond this doneness causes it to lose its tenderness.*

## TESTING NOTES

1. Let the meat rest, lightly covered in foil, for 15 minutes after it comes out of the oven. If you slice it too soon, you will lose the juices and be left with dry, flavorless meat. Always cut across the grain—against the direction the muscle fibers run—for the tenderest slices.

2. If you cut with the grain—or in the same direction the muscle fibers run—the meat slices will be tough and may pull apart—not what you want in a slice of beef tenderloin.

# 036  MAKE-IT-MINE BEEF POT ROAST

TASTING COMMENTS: *we love the versatility of this one-pot recipe. It was designed and tested so that whichever ingredients you choose, it will be perfectly cooked and delicious. The key to the tender, tasty meat is a long braise in flavorful liquid. —SB*

**PREP** 30 MINUTES  **COOK** 1 HOUR 45 MINUTES

- 1 2½-to 3-lb. beef chuck arm pot roast, beef chuck shoulder pot roast, or beef chuck 7-bone pot roast
- Salt
- Black pepper
- 2 Tbsp. vegetable oil
- ¾ cup Liquid
- 1 Tbsp. Liquid Seasoning
- 1 tsp. Dried Herb, crushed
- ½ tsp. salt
- 1 lb. Potatoes
- 1 lb. Vegetables, cut into 1- to 2-inch pieces
- ½ cup cold water
- ¼ cup all-purpose flour
- Pepper Seasoning (optional)

**1.** Trim fat from meat. Sprinkle meat with salt and pepper. In a 4- to 6-qt. Dutch oven brown roast on all sides in hot oil. Drain off fat. Combine desired Liquid, Liquid Seasoning, Dried Herb, and ½ tsp. salt. Pour over roast. Bring to boiling; reduce heat. Simmer, covered, 1 hour.

**2.** Meanwhile, if using new potatoes, peel a strip of skin from the center of each potato. If using medium potatoes or sweet potatoes, peel and quarter. Add Potatoes and Vegetables to Dutch oven with meat. Return to boiling; reduce heat. Simmer, covered, 45 to 60 minutes or until meat and vegetables are tender. Using a slotted spoon, transfer meat and vegetables to a platter, reserving juices in Dutch oven. Keep warm.

**3.** For gravy, measure cooking juices; skim off fat. If necessary, add enough water to juices to equal 1½ cups. Return to Dutch oven. In a bowl stir together the cold water and flour until smooth. Stir into juices in pan. Cook and stir over medium heat until thickened and bubbly. Cook and stir 1 minute more. If desired, season with Pepper Seasoning.

**OVEN DIRECTIONS**
Preheat oven to 325°F. Prepare as directed through Step 1. Bake, covered, 1 hour. Prepare Potatoes as directed. Add Potatoes and Vegetables to Dutch oven with meat. Cover and bake 45 to 60 minutes more or until meat and vegetables are tender. Prepare gravy in a saucepan as directed in Step 3.

**SLOW COOKER DIRECTIONS**  Trim fat from meat. Sprinkle meat with salt and pepper. Brown roast as directed in Step 1. Place Vegetables and Potatoes in a 4½- or 5-qt. slow cooker. Place roast on top of vegetables. Combine the Liquid, Liquid Seasoning, Dried Herb, and ½ tsp. salt. Pour over roast in cooker. Cover and cook on low 9 to 11 hours or on high 4½ to 5½ hours. Prepare gravy in a saucepan as directed in Step 3.

*The amount of zip you add to this pot roast depends on which Pepper Seasoning you pick (see opposite).*

**BEEF ROAST (PICK ONE)**

Beef chuck

7-bone pot roast

Beef chuck arm pot roast

**DRIED HERB (PICK ONE)**

Basil

Italian seasoning

Herbes de Provence

Oregano

Rosemary

Thyme

**PEPPER SEASONING (PICK ONE)**

Black pepper

Crushed red pepper

Cayenne pepper

Steak seasoning

**LIQUID SEASONING (PICK ONE)**

Barbecue sauce

Dijon-style mustard

Worcestershire sauce

Steak sauce

Soy sauce

**LIQUID (PICK ONE)**

Apple juice

½ cup beef broth plus ¼ cup dry red wine

Tomato juice

Beef broth

**POTATOES (PICK ONE)**

Fingerling

Tiny new

Yellow

Sweet

Russet

**VEGETABLES (PICK ONE OR MORE)**

Trimmed fennel bulbs

Mushrooms

Peeled carrots or parsnips

Celery

Peeled butternut squash

Sliced leeks or shallots

Onion wedges or peeled pearl onions

Peeled turnips or rutabaga

You can make your mother's pot roast (or not!) with this highly customizable recipe. whatever the other elements may be, the meat always comes out fork-tender and juicy.

MAKES: *12 servings*   TESTED BY: *Linda B.*

# 037   CLASSIC LASAGNA

**TASTING COMMENTS:** *Simpler versions of this dish call for just tomato sauce, but the addition of béchamel—a classic, creamy white sauce—really took it up a notch. The richness of the white sauce balances the acidity and sweetness of the tomato sauce to create a truly special dish.—LB*

**PREP** 30 MINUTES   **COOK** 15 MINUTES   **BAKE** 30 MINUTES AT 375°F   **STAND** 15 MINUTES

- 12 dried lasagna noodles
- 8 oz. ground beef
- 8 oz. bulk Italian sausage or bulk pork sausage*
- 1 cup chopped onion
- 2 cloves garlic, minced
- 1 14.5-oz. can diced tomatoes, undrained
- 1 8-oz. can tomato sauce
- 1 Tbsp. dried Italian seasoning, crushed
- 1 tsp. fennel seeds, crushed
- ¼ tsp. black pepper
- 1 egg, lightly beaten
- 1 15-oz. carton ricotta cheese or 2 cups cottage cheese, drained
- ¼ cup grated Parmesan cheese
- 1 recipe Béchamel Sauce
- 2 cups shredded mozzarella cheese (8 oz.)
- Grated Parmesan cheese (optional)
- Snipped fresh basil (optional)

*Fennel seeds have a licoricelike flavor similar to anise. They provide the distinctive flavor to Italian sausage. Crushing the seeds intensifies their flavor. Use a mortar and pestle or rolling pin to crush the seeds.*

1. Preheat oven to 375°F. Cook lasagna noodles according to package directions; drain. Rinse with cold water; drain well. Set aside.

2. For meat sauce, in a large skillet cook beef, sausage, onion, and garlic over medium-high heat until meat is browned. Drain off fat. Stir in the next five ingredients (through pepper). Bring to boiling; reduce heat. Cover and simmer 15 minutes, stirring occasionally.

3. For filling, in a medium bowl combine egg, ricotta cheese, and the ¼ cup Parmesan cheese; set aside.

4. Spread about ¼ cup of the meat sauce in a 3-qt. rectangular baking dish. Place three of the noodles on sauce. On the sauce layer one-fourth of the filling, one-fourth of the Béchamel Sauce, one-fourth of the remaining meat sauce, and one-fourth of the mozzarella cheese. Repeat layers three times. If desired, sprinkle with additional Parmesan cheese.

5. Bake, uncovered, 30 to 35 minutes or until heated through and bubbly. Let stand 15 minutes. If desired, top with basil.

**MAKE-AHEAD DIRECTIONS**
Prepare Classic Lasagna as directed through Step 4. Cover lasagna with plastic wrap and chill in the refrigerator 4 to 24 hours. Preheat oven to 375°F. Uncover lasagna. Bake 45 to 50 minutes or until hot in the center (160°F).

*\*TIP* If you prefer, substitute 8 oz. lean ground beef for the sausage.

**BÉCHAMEL SAUCE** In a medium saucepan heat 2 Tbsp. butter over medium heat until melted. Add 3 cloves garlic, minced; cook and stir 1 minute (this infuses the butter with garlic flavor). Stir in 3 Tbsp. all-purpose flour, ¼ tsp. salt, and ¼ tsp. black pepper until combined. Stir in 2 cups milk all at once. Cook and stir until thickened and bubbly. Cook and stir 1 minute more. Remove from heat. Stir in ¼ cup grated Parmesan cheese.

PER SERVING *380 cal., 21 g fat (11 g sat. fat), 86 mg chol., 567 mg sodium, 25 g carb., 2 g fiber, 5 g sugars, 21 g pro.*

**\*\*TIP** For mess-free assembly, spoon the filling into a resealable plastic bag. Snip off one corner of the bag; squeeze the bag to pipe the filling over the noodles in the baking dish, then spread evenly.

**VEGETABLE LASAGNA** *Prepare Classic Lasagna as directed in Steps 1 and 2, except omit beef and sausage. Add 2 Tbsp. olive oil to the skillet; heat over medium-high heat. Add 1 lb. fresh cremini mushrooms, quartered, and 1 yellow or red sweet pepper, cut into strips, with the onion and garlic; cook 5 minutes. Stir in 1½ cups coarsely chopped zucchini and/or yellow summer squash; cook 3 to 5 minutes more or until vegetables are tender. Continue as directed in Step 3.*

## TESTING NOTES

↑
1. If you worry about working with sticky noodles after cooking them, try this: Place the noodles on sheets of plastic wrap or parchment paper on a sheet pan. Place three noodles in each layer, add plastic wrap, and repeat until you've used all the noodles. This might take a little time, but it will keep your noodles separated.

2. The basis of your béchamel begins with cooking garlic in melted butter. Cooking the garlic for a quick minute mellows its raw bite without allowing it to burn and become acrid. Watch it carefully!
↓

↑
3. Classic béchamel is made with equal parts flour and butter. This recipe uses more flour, so it's a slightly thicker sauce for layering in lasagna.

↑
4. Once the milk is added, whisk constantly until béchamel is thick and bubbly. Cook the last minute to ensure the starch grains in flour swell for maximum thickening power.

5. Remove the pan from heat and add ¼ cup grated Parmesan cheese. The sauce should be thick enough to coat the back of a spoon.
↓

1. Spread ¼ cup meat sauce on the bottom of the baking dish to prevent the noodles from sticking when baked.

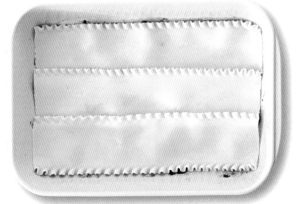

2. Add three of the cooked noodles to the dish lengthwise. They will overlap slightly.

3. Spread one-fourth of the filling onto the noodles** (tip, page 118)

4. Spoon about one-fourth of the Béchamel Sauce over the filling.

5. Spoon about one-fourth of the remaining meat sauce over the béchamel.

6. Cover the meat sauce with about one-fourth of the shredded mozzarella cheese. Repeat all layers three times, finishing with meat sauce and cheese.

MAKES: *4 servings* TESTED BY: *Carla C.*

# 038 SKILLET PORK CHOPS WITH APPLES AND ONIONS

TASTING COMMENTS: *we left the peel on the apples because we thought the color was pretty. You could use Granny Smith apples, but you might want to peel them. Their green skin turns gray when cooked. —CC*

**START TO FINISH** 35 MINUTES

- 4 **bone-in pork chops, cut ½ inch thick (about 2 lb.)**
- ½ tsp. **salt**
- ¼ tsp. **cracked black pepper**
- 1 Tbsp. **olive oil**
- 1 Tbsp. **butter**
- 1 **large yellow onion, cut into ½-inch-thick wedges**
- 2 **red cooking apples, such as Braeburn, cored and cut into ½-inch-thick wedges**
- ½ cup **chicken broth**
- ¼ cup **heavy cream**
- 3 Tbsp. **coarse ground mustard**
- 5 sprigs **fresh thyme**
- 1 Tbsp. **snipped fresh sage**

**1.** Season pork chops with salt and pepper. In an extra-large skillet heat oil and butter over medium-high heat until butter is melted. Add chops and cook 5 minutes, turning once. Transfer to a plate.

**2.** Add onion to skillet. Cook and stir 3 minutes, stirring occasionally. Add apples, broth, and cream, stirring to scrape up any browned bits from bottom of skillet. Stir in mustard and thyme. Reduce heat. Cover; simmer 8 minutes.

**3.** Return chops and accumulated juices to skillet. Simmer, uncovered, 4 to 5 minutes or until pork is done (145°F) and sauce is slightly thickened. Remove from heat. Discard thyme and sprinkle with fresh sage. Let stand 3 minutes.

PER SERVING *442 cal., 27 g fat (9 g sat. fat), 111 mg chol., 642 mg sodium, 17 g carb., 3 g fiber, 12 g sugars, 32 g pro.*

*we tested this recipe with bone-in chops, but you could use boneless chops as well. As long as they're about ½ inch thick, the cook time won't change and you will still get juicy results!*

*To wedge an onion, cut it in half from the root end to the top and remove the papery skin. Place each half cut side down on a cutting board and cut into even slices.*

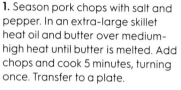

# 039   ROASTED BALSAMIC PORK TENDERLOIN

TASTING COMMENTS:   *Basting the roast with cooking liquid three times during cooking—once before it goes in the oven and twice during roasting—creates a tasty, caramelized crust.—KB*

**PREP** 25 MINUTES   **ROAST** 25 MINUTES AT 375°F

- 1 1½-lb. pork tenderloin
- ¼ tsp. kosher salt
- ¼ tsp. black pepper
- 1 Tbsp. olive oil
- 1 sprig fresh rosemary
- ¼ cup chopped red onion
- 1 clove garlic, minced
- ½ to ¾ cup reduced-sodium chicken broth
- 2 Tbsp. balsamic vinegar
- 2 Tbsp. snipped fresh Italian parsley
- 1 Tbsp. butter, softened
- 2 tsp. Dijon-style mustard

**1.** Preheat oven to 375°F. Using a small sharp knife, remove fat and silverskin from tenderloin. Fold thin end under; secure with a toothpick. Season with salt and pepper.

**2.** Heat oil in a large heavy oven-going skillet over medium-high heat. Add tenderloin and cook 6 minutes, turning to brown on both sides. Remove tenderloin from skillet.

**3.** Add rosemary, onion, and garlic to skillet. Cook and stir 2 minutes or until onion begins to soften. Add ½ cup broth and the vinegar to skillet; bring to boiling. Return tenderloin to skillet and spoon mixture over tenderloin.

**4.** Transfer skillet to oven and roast 25 minutes or until done (145°F), spooning cooking liquid over tenderloin twice.

**5.** Transfer pork to a cutting board. Cover with foil; let stand while preparing sauce.

**6.** For pan sauce, carefully place hot skillet over medium-high heat; bring cooking liquid to boiling. Add remaining ¼ cup broth, if needed, and stir constantly to scrape up any browned bits from the bottom of skillet. Remove from heat. Remove rosemary. Whisk in parsley, butter, and mustard until butter is melted.

**7.** Slice tenderloin crosswise into ¼-inch-thick slices. Serve with pan sauce.

PER SERVING *256 cal., 10 g fat (3 g sat. fat), 118 mg chol., 366 mg sodium, 3 g carb., 0 g fiber, 2 g sugars, 36 g pro.*

*When we tested this recipe, the ½ cup chicken broth had evaporated after roasting, so we needed the additional ½ cup broth for the pan sauce. You may or may not need it.*

*Serve slices of this juicy roast on homemade herbed biscuits. (See page 161 for a recipe.)*

## TESTING NOTES

Folding the thin end of a pork tenderloin under and securing it with a toothpick ensures the roast will cook evenly.

# POULTRY

# 040 BUTTERMILK-BRINED FRIED CHICKEN WITH CREAMY GRAVY

TASTING COMMENTS: *Every time we make this recipe, we're amazed by how much flavor is created with such simple ingredients! Process is key: First, brining tenderizes and adds moisture to the chicken. And then frying the coated chicken, just a few pieces at a time maintains the temperature of the oil so the breading fries up crunchy, not soggy!—SM*

**PREP** 30 MINUTES  **CHILL** 2 HOURS  **COOK** 12 MINUTES PER BATCH

*Choose a vegetable oil that has a smoking point above 400°F. You can use any of these oils for fried chicken: peanut, canola, corn, safflower, and sunflower.*

- 3 cups buttermilk
- ⅓ cup kosher salt
- 2 Tbsp. sugar
- 2½ to 3 lb. meaty chicken pieces (breast halves, thighs, and drumsticks)
- 2 cups all-purpose flour
- ¼ tsp. salt
- ¼ tsp. black pepper
- ¾ cup buttermilk
- Vegetable oil
- 1 recipe Creamy Gravy (page 128)

**1.** For brine, set an extra-large resealable plastic bag in a large glass measuring cup or large bowl. Add the 3 cups buttermilk, the kosher salt, and sugar to bag; stir. Using a chef's knife, cut chicken breast halves in half crosswise. Add all of the chicken to the brine; seal bag. Turn bag to coat chicken. Chill 2 to 4 hours. Remove chicken from brine. Drain chicken; pat dry with paper towels. Discard brine.

**2.** In a large bowl combine flour, the ¼ tsp. salt, and the pepper. Place the ¾ cup buttermilk in a shallow dish. Coat chicken with flour mixture; dip in buttermilk and coat again with flour mixture.

**3.** Meanwhile, in a deep, heavy pot or deep-fat fryer heat 1½ inches oil to 350°F. Using tongs, carefully add a few pieces of chicken to hot oil.

(Oil temperature will drop; adjust the heat to maintain temperature at 350°F.) Fry chicken 12 to 15 minutes or until chicken is done (170°F for breasts; 175°F for thighs and drumsticks) and coating is golden, turning once. Drain on a wire rack or paper towels. If desired, keep fried chicken warm in a preheated 300°F oven while frying remaining chicken pieces and making gravy.

PER SERVING *618 cal., 36 g fat (7 g sat. fat), 110 mg chol., 1,701 mg sodium, 37 g carb., 1 g fiber, 5 g sugars, 36 g pro.*

**SPICY BUTTERMILK-BRINED FRIED CHICKEN** Prepare as directed, except add 1½ tsp. cayenne pepper to the flour mixture.

**ON THE SIDE** *Pick the perfect potato to accompany this crunchy fried chicken. When it's hot out of the fryer, try Mashed Potatoes (recipe, page 194). For hot chicken or cold leftover chicken (so good on a picnic!), try Classic Potato Salad (recipe, page 206).*

## TESTING NOTES

1. When frying chicken, the pieces should be similar in size so they cook evenly in the same amount of time. You'll need to cut breast pieces in half using a sturdy, sharp chef's knife.

↓

2. The salt- and buttermilk-based brine actually breaks down the muscle fibers and allows the meat to absorb more moisture and flavor. Soak chicken in the brine at least 2 hours but no more than 4.

↑

3. A double dip in the seasoned flour mixture with a buttermilk bath in between ensures the chicken pieces are thoroughly coated with flavorful breading that won't fall off during frying. To keep the flour mixture from becoming overly messy and gummy during dipping, start by dividing it evenly between two shallow bowls. Use one bowl for the first coating and the other only after the chicken has been dipped into the buttermilk.

4. To ensure chicken fries evenly without burning or becoming greasy, it is important to maintain the oil temperature as close to 350°F as possible at all times during the frying process. Use a deep-frying thermometer to monitor the temperature and adjust the heat as necessary

5. For the best results, fry chicken in smaller batches and don't crowd in the pan. As you finish each batch, drain on paper towels and place the fried pieces on a wire rack that has been set on a baking sheet; keep warm in a 300°F oven until ready to serve.

↓

↑

6. You can't be sure your chicken is done inside just by looking at the outside. To be 100% certain, check the internal temperature with an instant-read thermometer (it is done when breasts are 170°F and thighs and drumsticks are 175°F). Insert the thermometer into the thickest part of the chicken without touching bone. Bone conducts heat faster than meat, so if a thermometer is touching bone, the reading will be high and inaccurate.

**MAKES:** *13/4 cups*  **TESTED BY:** *Sammy M.*

# CREAMY GRAVY

**TASTING COMMENTS:**  *The type of drippings you use influences the flavor of your gravy. Bacon makes it it smoky; butter makes it rich and nutty.—SM*

**PREP** 50 MINUTES  **STAND** 20 MINUTES

3 Tbsp. fried chicken drippings, butter, or bacon drippings

3 Tbsp. all-purpose flour

1¾ cups milk

¼ tsp. salt

⅛ tsp. black pepper

Milk (optional)

1. In a large skillet heat fried chicken drippings, butter, or bacon drippings over medium heat. Stir in flour until mixture is smooth, bubbly, and starting to brown. Whisk in milk, salt, and pepper. Cook over medium heat, whisking constantly, until thickened and bubbly. Cook and whisk 1 minute more. Reduce heat if gravy bubbles too hard. If desired, thin with additional milk.

**BISCUITS + GRAVY** *Prepare the Creamy Gravy as directed, except stir in 8 oz. cooked and drained bulk pork sausage. Serve over Flaky Biscuits, page 66.*

## TESTING NOTES

1. Fat adds flavor to gravy, and it's important to use the amount called for in a recipe. Adding too much fat makes gravy greasy and adding too little yields bland, lackluster results. If you don't have fried chicken drippings, you can substitute butter or bacon drippings.

↑
2. After heating drippings in the skillet, add flour and stir constantly with a wooden spoon until the mixture is bubbly and starts to turn a light golden brown. This step is important to prevent lumps. You're coating the flour particles with fat, which keeps them separated and prevents them from clumping together.

↑
3. When you add milk to the cooked flour mixture in the skillet, be sure to whisk constantly throughout the remaining cook time. The nonstop motion helps keep lumps from forming, and the heat ensures that the flour gets fully cooked—important for thickening and eliminating any raw flour taste. Don't skip that last 1 minute of cook time—it's the final step to ensure the starch grains in the flour swell and cause the gravy to thicken properly. The gravy is done when it starts to thicken and coats the back of a spoon.

↑
4. Gravy can be made ahead and reheated. To reheat, in a medium saucepan cook and stir the gravy over medium-low heat 2 to 3 minutes. You might have to add a little more milk to make it smooth and creamy.

# 041  **OVEN-BARBECUED CHICKEN**

TASTING COMMENTS:   *we did not miss the skin on this oven-baked chicken. It has fewer calories than skin-on chicken, and because the sauce can penetrate the meat more easily, it has more flavor, too!—JH*

**PREP** 25 MINUTES   **BAKE** 45 MINUTES AT 375°F

*use a variety of meaty chicken pieces (breast halves, thighs, and/or drumsticks) or choose only your favorite. You can save money by cutting up a whole chicken yourself.*

- 4 lb. meaty chicken pieces
- 2 Tbsp. vegetable oil
- 1 cup finely chopped onion
- 2 Tbsp. kosher salt
- 1 Tbsp. minced garlic
- ¼ cup butter
- 1 Tbsp. paprika
- 1 Tbsp. chili powder
- 1½ tsp. crushed red pepper
- ½ tsp. freshly ground black pepper
- 1½ cups water
- 1 cup cider vinegar
- 1 cup packed dark brown sugar
- 2 Tbsp. Worcestershire sauce
- 1 cup tomato paste
- ¼ cup molasses

*we like the rich, molasses-y flavor that dark brown sugar gives this sauce!*

1. Preheat oven to 375°F. Line a 15×10-inch baking pan with parchment paper or foil; set aside. Skin chicken. In an extra-large skillet heat oil over medium heat. Add chicken; cook until browned on all sides. If necessary, brown chicken in batches, adding more oil if needed. Arrange chicken pieces, bone sides up, in the prepared baking pan. Bake 35 minutes.

2. Meanwhile, for sauce, in a large saucepan cook onion, salt, and garlic in hot butter over medium-low heat 10 to 15 minutes or until onion is tender, stirring occasionally. Add paprika, chili powder, crushed red pepper, and black pepper; cook and stir 1 minute more. Add the water, cider vinegar, brown sugar, and Worcestershire sauce; bring to boiling. Whisk in tomato paste and molasses until smooth. Boil gently, uncovered, 15 to 20 minutes or until sauce is thickened and reduced to about 4 cups, stirring occasionally.

3. Turn chicken pieces bone sides down. Brush about 1 cup sauce on chicken. Bake 10 to 20 minutes more or until chicken is no longer pink (170°F for breasts; 175°F for thighs and drumsticks). Reheat the remaining sauce; pass with chicken. Refrigerate any leftover sauce in an airtight container up to 1 week.

PER SERVING  *420 cal., 10 g fat (4 g sat. fat), 142 mg chol., 1,724 mg sodium, 40 g carb., 2 g fiber, 23 g sugars, 41 g pro.*

*A basting brush makes easy work of coating chicken with sauce. Look for one made of silicone, which is heat-resistant and easy to clean.*

## TESTING NOTES

1. The most difficult part of removing the skin is hanging on! Here's a trick: Use a paper towel to grip the skin and pull it away from the meat. If the skin doesn't pull off easily, use kitchen shears to cut away the skin.

2. Browning the chicken in a little oil before baking helps develop a golden brown color on the outside while keeping it moist and tender on the inside.

3. To get the best consistency for brushing, boil the sauce gently—you should see small bubbles across the surface of the sauce in the pan. Stir occasionally because the sauce around the edges may begin to thicken before the sauce in the center.

4. While all chicken is safe at 165°F, aesthetically we liked the dark meat at 175°F and breast meat at 170°F. You can also check doneness by piercing the thickest part of the thigh with a fork. The meat should be tender and no longer pink and juices should run clear.

**PLAY IT SAFE** *Set the sauce to be used as a brush-on aside from the sauce to be passed at the table. Place the basting brush, spoons, and any other utensils used on uncooked or partially cooked poultry only in this portion. Cook the chicken at least 5 minutes after brushing with sauce.*

# 042 CHICKEN PARMIGIANA

TASTING COMMENTS: *Our Test Kitchen is equipped with every kind of tool you can imagine, but if you don't have a meat mallet, pound the chicken with the bottom of a heavy skillet or a rolling pin. —CW*

**START TO FINISH** 45 MINUTES

1 Tbsp. butter

⅓ cup chopped onion

1 clove garlic, minced

1 14.5-oz. can diced tomatoes, undrained

½ tsp. sugar

⅛ tsp. salt

Dash black pepper

¼ cup snipped fresh basil

4 6-to 8-oz. skinless, boneless chicken breast halves

1 egg, lightly beaten

2 Tbsp. milk

⅓ cup seasoned fine dry bread crumbs

¼ cup grated Parmesan cheese

½ tsp. dried oregano, crushed

3 Tbsp. olive oil or vegetable oil

¼ cup shredded mozzarella cheese (1 oz.)

**1.** For sauce, in a medium saucepan melt butter over medium heat. Add onion and garlic; cook until tender, stirring occasionally. Stir in tomatoes, sugar, salt, and pepper. Bring to boiling; reduce heat. Simmer, uncovered, 10 minutes or until desired consistency, stirring occasionally. Stir in basil. Keep sauce warm.

**2.** Meanwhile, place each chicken breast half between two pieces of plastic wrap. Using the flat side of a meat mallet, pound chicken lightly until about ¼ inch thick. Remove and discard plastic wrap.

**3.** In a shallow dish combine egg and milk. In another shallow dish stir together bread crumbs, 3 Tbsp. of the Parmesan cheese, and the oregano. Dip chicken into egg mixture, then into crumb mixture, turning to coat.

**4.** In an extra-large skillet heat oil over medium heat. Add chicken; cook 4 to 6 minutes or until golden, turning once. Transfer chicken to a platter.

**5.** Spoon sauce over chicken. Top with mozzarella cheese and the remaining 1 Tbsp. Parmesan cheese. Let stand 2 minutes or until mozzarella cheese is melted.

PER SERVING *439 cal., 22 g fat (6 g sat. fat), 173 mg chol., 750 mg sodium, 14 g carb., 2 g fiber, 5 g sugars, 44 g pro.*

**VEAL PARMIGIANA** Prepare as directed, except substitute 1 lb. boneless veal sirloin or round steak, cut ½ inch thick, for the chicken breast halves. Cut meat into four serving-size pieces and pound until ¼ inch thick.

**CREAMY TOMATO CHICKEN PARMIGIANA** Prepare as directed, except after simmering the sauce until desired consistency, slowly add 3 Tbsp. heavy cream or half-and-half, stirring constantly. Cook and stir 3 minutes more; stir in basil.

*Don't have fresh basil on hand? The rule of thumb for substituting dried herbs for fresh is to use one-third of the amount of dried herbs. So in this recipe, use 4 tsp. dried basil and add it with the salt and pepper.*

**TENDERIZING TIPS** *Pounding meat breaks up connective tissues, making the meat more tender. It also flattens the chicken to an even thickness, allowing it to cook quickly and evenly. To avoid splatters, place the chicken breast between two pieces of plastic wrap. Starting from the thickest part of the chicken breast, lightly pound the chicken using the flat side of a meat mallet.*

## TESTING NOTES

1. Place the egg mixture and bread crumb mixture in shallow dishes, such as pie plates, for easy dipping.

2. Working with one piece at a time, dip the chicken into the egg mixture. Hold the chicken over the dish, allowing the excess egg mixture to drip off.

3. Dredge both sides of the chicken in the bread crumb mixture, using your fingers to lightly press the crumbs onto the chicken for an even coating.

4. Place the chicken on a piece of waxed paper. Repeat with remaining chicken pieces.

# 043  CHICKEN WITH PAN SAUCE 8 WAYS

**TASTING COMMENTS:** *Boneless, skinless chicken breasts are a blank canvas that take to a variety of flavors. Making a pan sauce is a fast, easy way to jazz them up.—LB*

**START TO FINISH** 35 MINUTES

- **2** skinless, boneless chicken breast halves (6 to 8 oz. each)
- **¼** tsp. salt
- **¼** tsp. freshly ground black pepper
- **1** Tbsp. olive oil
- **½** cup dry white wine or chicken broth
- **½** cup chicken broth
- **¼** cup finely chopped shallot or onion
- **2** Tbsp. heavy cream
- **¼** cup cold butter

*Chicken breasts halves have gotten very large—some range upward of 12 ounces to a pound! Whenever we can, we prefer to cook with breast halves in the 6- to 8-oz. range.*

**1.** Halve each chicken breast horizontally. Place each chicken breast piece between two pieces of plastic wrap. Using the flat side of a meat mallet, pound chicken lightly to about ¼ inch thick. Discard plastic wrap. Sprinkle chicken with salt and pepper.

**2.** In a very large skillet heat the oil over medium-high heat. Add chicken to skillet. Cook chicken 5 to 6 minutes or until no longer pink, turning once. Transfer chicken to a platter; cover with foil to keep warm. Remove skillet from heat.

**3.** Add wine, broth, and shallot to the hot skillet. Return skillet to heat. Cook and stir to scrape up the browned bits from the bottom of the pan. Bring to boiling. Boil gently, uncovered, 10 minutes or until liquid is reduced to ¼ cup. Reduce heat to medium-low.

**4.** Stir in cream. Add butter, 1 Tbsp. at a time, stirring until butter melts after each addition. Sauce should be slightly thickened. Season to taste with additional salt and pepper. Serve sauce over chicken.

PER SERVING *287 cal., 20 g fat (10 g sat. fat), 96 mg chol., 458 mg sodium, 3 g carb., 0 g fiber, 1 g sugars, 19 g pro.*

**SKINLESS, BONELESS CHICKEN BREAST HALVES**
*Horizontally halve thicker pieces of chicken, such as oversize chicken breasts, into more manageable and portion-appropriate, uniform sizes. Press down lightly on the top of the piece of chicken as you cut all the way through. Use a kitchen scale to weigh chicken pieces. (Most of our recipes call for 4- to 6-ounce skinless, boneless chicken breast halves.)*

**MUSHROOM** Add 1 cup sliced assorted fresh mushrooms with shallot; do not add wine and broth. Cook until tender and golden. Add wine and broth; continue as directed.

**TOMATO-PARMESAN** Add ½ cup quartered grape tomatoes to skillet with shallot. Stir 2 Tbsp. grated Parmesan into the finished sauce.

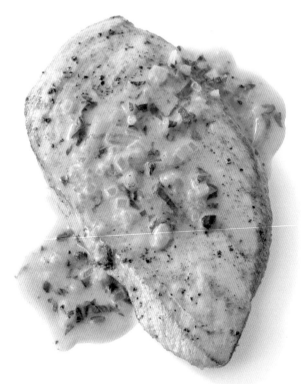

**HERB** Stir 2 to 3 tsp. snipped fresh basil, chervil, parsley, oregano, and/or dill weed into the finished sauce.

**BACON-LEEK** Add ½ cup sliced leek to skillet with shallot. Top with 3 slices crumbled, crisp-cooked bacon.

**CILANTRO-CHIPOTLE** Stir 1 Tbsp. snipped fresh cilantro and ½ tsp. finely chopped chipotle chile pepper in adobo sauce into the finished sauce.

**LEMON-THYME** Stir 2 tsp. lemon juice and 2 tsp. snipped fresh thyme into the finished sauce. Serve with lemon slices.

**MUSTARD** Stir 1 Tbsp. snipped fresh italian parsley and 2 tsp. Dijon-style mustard into finished sauce.

**BALSAMIC-CAPER** Stir 2 tsp. balsamic vinegar and 2 tsp. drained capers into finished sauce.

# 044   HERB-ROASTED CHICKEN

TASTING COMMENTS:   *Keeping the surface of the chicken dry ensures the crispest skin. Be sure to thoroughly pat it dry after rinsing—residual water creates steam during roasting, which keeps the proteins from browning. The other key to perfect roasted chicken is a dry rub. It boosts flavor without adding surface moisture.—SB*

**PREP** 20 MINUTES   **ROAST** 1 HOUR 15 MINUTES AT 375°F   **STAND** 10 MINUTES

1   3½-to 4-lb. whole broiler-fryer chicken

2   Tbsp. butter, melted

2   cloves garlic, minced

1   tsp. dried basil, crushed

1   tsp. dried sage, crushed

½   tsp. dried thyme, crushed

¼   tsp. salt

¼   tsp. black pepper

*Allow your chicken to sit at room temperature for 20 to 30 minutes before roasting. Taking the refrigerator chill off the chicken will allow it to roast evenly throughout.*

**1.** Preheat oven to 375°F. Rinse chicken body cavity; pat dry with paper towels. Skewer neck skin to back; tie legs to tail. Twist wing tips under back. Place chicken, breast side up, on a rack in a shallow roasting pan. Brush with melted butter; rub with garlic.

**2.** In a small bowl stir together the remaining ingredients; rub onto chicken. If desired, insert a meat thermometer into center of an inside thigh muscle. (Thermometer should not touch bone.)

**3.** Roast, uncovered, 75 to 90 minutes or until chicken is done (at least 170°F in the thigh) and drumsticks move easily in sockets. Remove chicken from oven. Cover and let stand 10 minutes before carving.

PER SERVING *590 cal., 39 g fat (14 g sat. fat), 201 mg chol., 568 mg sodium, 27 g carb., 4 g fiber, 5 g sugars, 35 g pro.*

**HERB-ROASTED CHICKEN AND VEGETABLES** Prepare as directed, except in a large bowl combine 1 lb. red-skin potatoes, cut into 1-inch pieces; 3 carrots, halved lengthwise and cut into 1-inch pieces; 1 medium turnip, peeled and cut into 1½-inch pieces; and 1 medium onion, cut into 1-inch pieces. Add 2 Tbsp. melted butter, 1 Tbsp. vegetable oil, ¼ tsp. salt, and ¼ tsp. black pepper; toss gently to coat. Arrange vegetables around chicken in pan the last 45 to 50 minutes of roasting, stirring vegetables once or twice.

**KEEP IT SHALLOW** *A shallow roasting pan with a rack allows air to circulate around the chicken as it roasts, resulting in even cooking and ultimate browning. We recommend using a sturdy roasting pan with heavy-duty handles for the easiest maneuvering. However, the price can be a detractor. In a pinch, purchase a large, sturdy foil roasting pan and place it on a baking sheet while roasting.*

## TESTING NOTES

1. Use kitchen string to secure the legs to the tail. Wrap the string around the legs and tail, pull it tight, and tie a knot. After 50 minutes to an hour (when chicken is two-thirds through its roasting time), cut the strings on the drumsticks.
↓

2. Tuck the wing tips behind the back. Tucking the wings and tying the legs keeps them tight and secure against the body of the chicken, creating a uniform shape. This also helps the chicken roast at an even rate and prevents burning.
↓

↑
3. Chicken is safe to eat when cooked to 165°F. After testing this recipe, however, we thought the bird looked and tasted better when it registered at least 170°F. Insert an oven-going thermometer into the deepest part of the thigh, making sure the probe does not touch bone.

# 045   CLASSIC CHICKEN POT PIE

TASTING COMMENTS: *This homey comfort-food dish went through many tests and tweaks to get it just right. The biggest issue was the sauce. We wound up almost doubling the amount of liquid to create a creamy, saucy pie that was luscious and didn't eat dry. —CW*

**PREP** 30 MINUTES   **BAKE** 40 MINUTES AT 400°F   **STAND** 10 MINUTES

- ½ cup butter
- ½ cup all-purpose flour
- 1 14.5-oz. can chicken broth
- 1½ cups milk
- 3 cups chopped cooked chicken (about 1 lb.)
- 1 16-oz. pkg. frozen mixed vegetables
- ½ of a 14.4-oz. pkg. frozen pearl onions (1½ cups)
- 1 tsp. poultry seasoning
- ½ tsp. salt
- ⅛ tsp. black pepper
- 1 recipe Pastry Topper for Pot Pie
- 1 Tbsp. milk
- ¼ cup grated Parmesan cheese (1 oz.)
- Freshly snipped Italian parsley (optional)

*The meat from a deli-roasted chicken works perfectly. A rotisserie chicken will yield 2½ to 3 cups of meat.*

**1.** Preheat oven to 400°F. In a large saucepan melt butter over medium heat; stir in flour. Cook and stir 1 minute. Stir in broth and the 1½ cups milk. Cook and stir until slightly thickened and bubbly. Stir in chicken, vegetables, onions, poultry seasoning, salt, and pepper. Cook and stir until heated through. Keep warm.

**2.** Prepare Pastry Topper for Pot Pie. On a lightly floured surface roll pastry from center to edges into an oval or rectangle 1 inch larger than a 3-qt. oval or rectangular baking dish (about 14×10 inches). Transfer hot chicken mixture to baking dish. Cut pastry into 1½-inch-wide strips. Weave strips over hot filling in a wide lattice pattern. Trim pastry ½ inch beyond edge of dish. Brush top with the 1 Tbsp. milk. Sprinkle with Parmesan cheese.

**3.** Bake 40 minutes or until lightly browned and edges are bubbly. Let stand 10 minutes before serving. If desired, sprinkle with parsley.

PER SERVING *618 cal., 37 g fat (16 g sat. fat), 100 mg chol., 913 mg sodium, 48 g carb., 4 g fiber, 4 g sugars, 25 g pro.*

**PASTRY TOPPER FOR POT PIE** In a large bowl stir together 2½ cups all-purpose flour and 1 tsp. salt. Using a pastry blender, cut in ½ cup shortening and ¼ cup butter, cut up, until pieces are pea size. Sprinkle 1 Tbsp. cold water over part of the flour mixture; toss with a fork. Push moistened pastry to side of bowl. Repeat moistening flour mixture, using 1 Tbsp. cold water at a time (½ to ⅔ cup total), until flour mixture is moistened. Gather into a ball, kneading gently until it holds together.

*Our cream sauce starts with a thickened mixture of chicken broth and milk, which gives it the perfect balance of rich and savory.*

## TESTING NOTES

1. Whisk flour into melted butter in a saucepan, stirring constantly. The butter will coat the flour molecules, preventing them from sticking together and forming lumps when milk is added.

2. Once the flour and butter are combined, gradually add the broth and milk to the flour mixture, whisking constantly to incorporate the flour mixture into the liquid.

3. Keep whisking slowly until you have a thickened and bubbly sauce.

# 046   CHICKEN PAD THAI

**TASTING COMMENTS:** *Noodles are the central ingredient in this classic Thai dish, so we fiddled around with them on multiple tests—we tried different types and soaked them in hot water for varying lengths of time—to achieve a perfect just-chewy texture.—JH*

There are many brands of Asian chili sauce with garlic available. Look for an ingredients list that includes a bright combination of chile peppers, garlic, and vinegar.

Fresh sprouts can be vulnerable to salmonella contamination. Rinse and drain them well before cooking thoroughly—stir-frying for 2 minutes should eliminate any potential risk.

**START TO FINISH** 45 MINUTES

- 8 oz. dried linguine-style rice noodles*
- 1 lime
- ¼ cup salted peanuts, finely chopped
- ¼ cup fish sauce
- 2 Tbsp. packed brown sugar
- 2 Tbsp. rice vinegar
- 1 Tbsp. water
- 1 Tbsp. Asian chili sauce with garlic
- 3 Tbsp. vegetable oil
- 1 lb. boneless, skinless chicken breast halves, cut into bite-size strips
- 1 Tbsp. minced garlic
- 1 egg, lightly beaten
- 1 cup fresh bean sprouts, rinsed and drained
- ⅓ cup sliced green onions
- 2 Tbsp. snipped fresh cilantro
- Lime wedges (optional)

**1.** Place rice noodles in a large bowl. Add enough boiling water to cover; let stand 10 to 15 minutes or until softened but still slightly chewy (al dente), stirring occasionally. Drain well in a colander.

**2.** Meanwhile, remove ½ tsp. zest and squeeze 2 Tbsp. juice from lime. For peanut topping, in a bowl combine peanuts and lime zest. In another bowl whisk together lime juice and the next five ingredients (through chili sauce) until smooth.

**3.** In an extra-large nonstick skillet heat 1 Tbsp. of the oil over medium-high heat. Add chicken and garlic to skillet; cook and stir 6 minutes or until chicken is tender and no pink remains. Transfer chicken to a bowl.

**4.** Add egg to the hot skillet, tilting skillet to spread egg in an even layer (egg may not fill bottom of skillet); cook without stirring 30 seconds. Using a wide spatula, carefully turn egg over; cook 30 to 60 seconds more or just until set. Transfer egg to a plate. Using a sharp knife, cut into bite-size strips.

**5.** In same skillet heat the remaining 2 Tbsp. oil over medium-high heat 30 seconds. Add sprouts; stir-fry 2 minutes. Add chicken and drained noodles (noodles may clump together but will separate when the sauce is added). Stir in fish sauce mixture; cook 1 to 2 minutes more or until heated through. Transfer chicken mixture to a serving plate. Top with egg strips and peanut topping. Sprinkle with green onions and cilantro. If desired, serve with lime wedges.

***TIP** Look for rice noodles in the Asian section of large supermarkets or at a store specializing in Asian foods.

PER SERVING *549 cal., 19 g fat (3 g sat. fat), 119 mg chol., 1,816 mg sodium, 60 g carb., 2 g fiber, 10 g sugars, 32 g pro.*

**SHRIMP PAD THAI** Prepare as directed, except substitute 1 lb. medium shrimp in shells for the chicken. Thaw shrimp, if frozen. Peel and devein shrimp. Rinse shrimp; pat dry with paper towels. In Step 3, cook shrimp 2 to 3 minutes or until opaque.

**TOFU PAD THAI** Prepare as directed, except substitute one 16-oz. pkg. extra-firm tub-style tofu for the chicken. Drain tofu; cut into strips. Pat dry with paper towels. In Step 3, cook tofu 2 to 3 minutes or until browned.

## TESTING NOTES

**1.** If you oversoak your noodles, they'll be mushy and fall apart. If undersoaked, they may drink up too much sauce, making your final dish less saucy. Test one of the noodles after soaking for 10 minutes to check the texture—you might have to taste it. Let the noodles soak just until soft and translucent, stirring occasionally. They should be pliable without being too gummy.
↓

↑
**2.** For a restaurantworthy pad Thai, here's an easy technique to make beautiful thin strips of cooked egg: Cook the egg over medium-high heat, tilting the pan to spread the egg in an even layer. Cook, without stirring, 30 seconds until the egg begins to set up.

↑
**3.** Use a spatula to turn the egg and cook just until set. When done, the eggs won't look wet but will look dry and slightly shiny. Slight browning is OK; just be careful not to overcook the egg. Turn the egg out onto a plate and cut into pieces with a knife or spatula

**4.** Combine the sprouts, chicken, and drained noodles in your skillet. The noodles have a tendency to stick together a bit at this point. Don't worry! They will separate as you stir in the sauce. After stirring in the sauce, cook 1 to 2 minutes more.
↓

### RICE NOODLES
Pad Thai is typically made with linguine-style rice noodles (pictured here). We thought they were best in this recipe, but you could substitute thin rice stick noodles (vermicelli-style) or wider straight-cut noodles. They may behave differently in your finished recipe.

# 047 CRUNCHY CHOPPED CHICKEN SALAD

TASTING COMMENTS: *Everyone loves options! This salad really lends itself to variation. We tested it with this combination, but any crunchy vegetables would be a good fit.—SM*

**PREP** 45 MINUTES   **BAKE** 8 MINUTES AT 400°   **COOK** 8 MINUTES

- 6 thin slices prosciutto (about 4 oz.)
- ½ cup olive oil
- 4 skinless, boneless chicken breast halves
- Salt
- Black pepper
- Paprika
- 2 lemons
- 2 Tbsp. finely chopped shallot
- ⅔ cup thinly sliced, peeled small carrots
- 2½ cups chopped zucchini
- ¾ cup chopped red sweet pepper
- ¾ cup chopped yellow sweet pepper
- ¼ cup chopped red onion
- 5 oz. blue cheese, crumbled
- Romaine lettuce leaves

*Prosciutto is intended to be eaten in its raw and cured state, but we love it cooked, too. It's very thin, so it gets super crispy and delicately textured—a really nice addition to this salad.*

1. Preheat oven to 400°F. Place prosciutto in a single layer on a large baking sheet. Bake 8 to 10 minutes or until crisp; set aside.

2. In a large nonstick skillet heat 1 Tbsp. of the olive oil over medium heat. Sprinkle chicken with salt, black pepper, and paprika; add to skillet. Cook 8 to 10 minutes or until chicken is no longer pink (170°F), turning once. Cool slightly; slice.

3. For dressing, remove zest from one lemon and juice both lemons to equal ⅓ cup juice. In a small bowl whisk together remaining olive oil, lemon juice, lemon zest, and shallot. Season to taste with salt and black pepper; set aside.

4. In a large bowl combine sliced chicken, carrots, zucchini, sweet peppers, and onion. Toss with dressing. Add blue cheese. Line salad bowls with romaine. Spoon chicken salad on romaine. Top with prosciutto.

PER SERVING *434 cal., 28 g fat (8 g sat. fat), 86 mg chol., 923 mg sodium, 14 g carb., 5 g fiber, 5 g sugars, 35 g pro.*

*We love the lemon dressing in the main recipe for this salad, but a red wine vinaigrette is good, too.*

**RED WINE VINAIGRETTE**
In a jar combine ⅓ cup red wine vinegar, ⅓ cup olive oil, 2 Tbsp. shallot, 2 tsp. snipped fresh rosemary, and salt to taste. Shake well.

**CHOPPED OPTIONS** *Add or swap out some of the ingredients in this crunchy salad to customize it to your taste. Make it vegetarian with garbanzo beans instead of chicken. Or use chopped kale, green or Kalamata olives, sliced celery, chopped fennel, or crumbled feta cheese.*

MAKES: *24 servings*   TESTED BY: *Colleen W.*

# 048   GRILLED CHICKEN WINGS

TASTING COMMENTS: *We love this recipe for entertaining because the rubs, sauces, and dips can be combined in so many different ways to satisfy so many different tastes. It also doesn't require a lot of hands-on (we call it "active") time—the wings simply soak in a brine and then a rub for hours at a time.—CW*

**PREP** 20 MINUTES   **MARINATE** 2 HOURS   **GRILL** 20 MINUTES PER BATCH

24 whole chicken wings (5 to 6 lb. total)

3 cups buttermilk

2 Tbsp. bottled hot pepper sauce

Wings Rub (see pages 148–149)

Wings Sauce (see pages 148–149)

Wings Dip (see pages 148–149)

Carrot and celery sticks

1. Place chicken wings in a large resealable plastic bag set in a shallow dish. Add buttermilk and hot sauce. Seal bag; turn to coat chicken. Marinate in the refrigerator 2 to 8 hours, turning bag occasionally. Drain wings; discard bag and buttermilk mixture. Pat wings dry with paper towels; place in a clean large resealable plastic bag.

2. Sprinkle Wings Rub over chicken wings; seal bag. Shake bag to coat wings with seasonings. If desired, chill 6 to 24 hours.

3. Prepare grill for indirect heat using a drip pan. Grill half the wings, covered, over drip pan 20 to 25 minutes or until chicken is no longer pink, turning once. Place wings in a shallow baking pan. Keep warm in a 300°F oven while grilling the remaining wings.

4. If necessary, transfer wings to an extra-large bowl. Drizzle with Wings Sauce; toss gently to coat. Serve with your choice of Wings Dip and carrot and celery sticks.

*We added carrots to the celery traditionally served with hot wings. Even if your particular wings aren't spicy, the veggie sticks provide a crunchy, cooling counterpoint to the chicken.*

*Choose one of the rub recipes on page 148 and apply it to the wings as directed after this step. At this point, you can go ahead and fire up the grill. Or refrigerate the spiced wings up to 24 hours.*

## TESTING NOTES

1. Buttermilk's acidity helps tenderize the meat; adding a little hot sauce to the mix gives it some kick.

2. After draining the marinade, be sure to remove as much moisture from the wings as possible by patting them dry with paper towels. This will help the spice rub stay right where you want it.

## WINGS RUB (CHOOSE 1)

**SAVORY** Stir together 1 Tbsp. dried oregano, crushed; 1 Tbsp. cayenne pepper; 1 Tbsp. black pepper; and 1 tsp. garlic powder.

**CAJUN** Stir together 1 Tbsp. black pepper; 1 tsp. dried thyme, crushed; 1 tsp. onion powder; 1 tsp. garlic powder; 1 tsp. cayenne pepper; and ½ tsp. salt.

**CHILI** Stir together 1 Tbsp. paprika, 1 tsp. ground cumin, 1 tsp. chili powder, ½ tsp. salt, ½ tsp. ground coriander, ½ tsp. black pepper, and ¼ tsp. cayenne pepper.

**BBQ** Stir together 1 Tbsp. packed brown sugar, 1 Tbsp. chili powder, 2 tsp. onion powder, 2 tsp. garlic salt, 2 tsp. paprika, 1 tsp. dry mustard, and 1 tsp. cayenne pepper.

## WINGS SAUCE (CHOOSE 1)

**BLUE BUFFALO** In a small saucepan combine 1 cup bottled cayenne pepper sauce (Frank's RedHot), ½ cup butter, ¼ cup white wine vinegar, 1 tsp. Worcestershire sauce, and ½ tsp. garlic powder. Cook over medium heat until butter is melted; cool. Stir in ¼ cup finely crumbled blue cheese.

**CHIMICHURRI** In a blender or food processor combine 2 cups fresh Italian parsley leaves, ¾ cup fresh cilantro leaves, ½ cup red wine vinegar, ½ cup olive oil, and 4 cloves garlic. Cover and blend or process until nearly smooth. Transfer to a serving bowl; stir in ½ tsp. salt and ½ tsp. crushed red pepper.

## WINGS DIP

**FRESH CHIVE RANCH** In a small bowl whisk together ½ cup sour cream, ⅓ cup buttermilk, 2 Tbsp. snipped fresh chives, 2 tsp. lemon juice, ½ tsp. garlic powder, ¼ tsp. salt, and ⅛ tsp. black pepper.

**BLUE CHEESE** In a small bowl whisk together 1 cup mayonnaise, 1 cup crumbled blue cheese (4 oz.), 1 Tbsp. red wine vinegar, 1 Tbsp. lemon juice, ¼ tsp. garlic salt, and ¼ tsp. celery seeds.

**CREAMY PARMESAN** In a small bowl stir together ¾ cup mayonnaise; ¼ cup sour cream; 3 Tbsp. grated Parmesan cheese; 2 Tbsp. white wine vinegar; 2 cloves garlic, minced; ½ tsp. dried Italian seasoning, crushed; and ¼ tsp. black pepper.

**WASABI-AVOCADO** In a small bowl whisk together ¾ cup mayonnaise, ½ cup mashed avocado, ¼ cup sour cream, ¼ cup snipped fresh cilantro, 1 Tbsp. wasabi paste, 1 Tbsp. rice wine vinegar, and 2 tsp. sriracha sauce.

**TZATZIKI** In a small bowl stir together 1 cup plain Greek yogurt; 1 cup seeded and chopped cucumber; ½ cup sour cream; 3 Tbsp. olive oil; 1 Tbsp. lemon juice; 1 Tbsp. snipped fresh mint or dill; 4 cloves garlic, minced; and ½ tsp. salt. If desired, stir in additional lemon juice to taste.

**KOREAN HEAT** In a small saucepan combine ½ cup sriracha sauce or Asian chili paste (sambal oelek), ⅓ cup packed brown sugar, 3 Tbsp. soy sauce, and 3 Tbsp. rice vinegar. Cook and stir over medium heat 5 minutes. Remove from heat. Stir in 1 tsp. toasted sesame oil.

**LOUISIANA BEER** In a small saucepan cook ¼ cup chopped onion and ¼ cup chopped red sweet pepper in 1 Tbsp. hot vegetable oil over medium heat 4 minutes or until tender. In a bowl stir together ½ cup beer, ½ cup cold water, 1 Tbsp. cornstarch, 1 Tbsp. Cajun seasoning, and ¼ tsp. salt; add to onion mixture. Cook and stir until thickened and bubbly. Cook and stir 2 minutes more.

# FISH & SEAFOOD

MAKES: *8 servings*   TESTED BY: *Juli H.*

# 049  PLANK-SMOKED SALMON WITH GRILLED-PEPPER RELISH

TASTING COMMENTS: *we like the subtle touch of smoke provided by cooking the salmon on a plank— just enough to enhance but not overwhelm the flavor of the fish.—JH*

**PREP** 25 MINUTES   **SOAK** 1 HOUR   **MARINATE** 1 HOUR   **GRILL** 18 MINUTES

- 1 **2-lb. fresh or frozen salmon fillet with skin**
- 1 **cedar or alder grilling plank (15×6½×³⁄₈ inches)**
- ¼ cup **reduced-sodium soy sauce**
- ¼ cup **balsamic vinegar**
- 3 Tbsp. **honey**
- 1 Tbsp. **grated fresh ginger**
- ½ tsp. **crushed red pepper**
- 3 **red, yellow, and/or orange sweet peppers**
- 3 Tbsp. **thinly sliced fresh basil**
- 2 Tbsp. **chopped pitted Kalamata olives**
- 2 tsp. **olive oil**
- 2 tsp. **balsamic vinegar**
- ¼ tsp. **salt**
- ¼ tsp. **black pepper**
- ¼ cup **thinly bias-sliced green onions**

*Salmon is a meaty fish with a distinct flavor, making it a natural for smoking on the grill. Look for wild-caught salmon from the East Coast, like coho or sockeye, or the West Coast, like chinook. Atlantic salmon is most often farm-raised and may have less flavor.*

**1.** Thaw salmon, if frozen. Rinse salmon; pat dry with paper towels. Soak plank in enough water to cover for 1 hour.

**2.** For marinade, in a bowl combine the next five ingredients (through crushed red pepper). Place salmon in a large resealable plastic bag set in a shallow dish. Pour marinade over salmon. Seal bag; turn to coat salmon. Marinate in the refrigerator 1 hour, turning bag occasionally. (Do not marinate longer.) Drain salmon, discarding marinade.

**3.** Grill sweet peppers directly over medium heat 10 to 12 minutes or until blistered and charred, turning occasionally. Enclose peppers in foil; let stand 15 minutes. Using a sharp knife, loosen edges of skins; gently pull off in strips and discard. Chop peppers into ½-inch pieces, discarding stems, seeds, and membranes.

**4.** Place plank on the rack of the uncovered grill directly over medium heat 3 to 5 minutes or until plank begins to crackle and smoke. Place salmon, skin side down, on grilling plank. Cover and grill 18 to 22 minutes or until fish flakes easily.

**5.** For relish, in a medium bowl stir together the chopped sweet peppers and the next six ingredients (through black pepper).

**6.** Sprinkle salmon with green onions and serve with the relish.

PER SERVING *196 cal., 9 g fat (1 g sat. fat), 62 mg chol., 197 mg sodium, 5 g carb., 1 g fiber, 3 g sugars, 23 g pro.*

## TESTING NOTES

↑

1. Soaking the wood plank in water is essential to smoking! To let the wood fully absorb water, put the plank in water for 1 hour. Weight down the wood to prevent it from floating: Fill another bowl of water and place it on top so the plank is submerged. Soaking makes the wood smoke and char slowly without catching fire.

↑

2. Marinating a higher-fat fish like salmon works well because the flesh readily absorbs the flavors. The sweet and tangy soy-flavor marinade pairs well with salmon. Turn the salmon occasionally to make sure the marinade is coating all sides equally. Remove the salmon from the marinade after 1 hour and discard the extra liquid. If you let the fish marinate too long, the acid (from the balsamic vinegar and brown sugar) will begin to "cook" the fish by coagulating the protein.

↑

3. You'll know the salmon is done when it starts to flake when tested with a fork. Salmon naturally turns opaque, losing some of its pink translucent appearance when done. Start checking at the minimum timing to avoid overcooking.

↑

4. Don't skip the relish for this salmon. The two complement each other incredibly well. Peeling the peppers is the trickiest part of the relish. Make it easy on yourself: After blistering and charring the peppers on the grill, wrap them in foil. This traps the natural steam coming off the peppers from grilling. The steam loosens the skin, making it easier for you to peel.

**SALMON CAKES** *Don't let the leftovers get lost in the back of your fridge. Use them up in this incredible salmon cake recipe you'll keep forever.*

Chill half of the smoked salmon (about 15 oz. cooked salmon). In a large bowl beat 1 egg with a fork; stir in ¾ cup soft bread crumbs, ¼ cup thinly sliced green onions, and 1 Tbsp. snipped fresh basil or cilantro. Using two forks, flake the chilled smoked salmon into small pieces. Add salmon to bread crumb mixture; stir to combine. Shape mixture into four ¾-inch-thick cakes. In an extra-large skillet heat 1 Tbsp. butter and 1 Tbsp. olive oil over medium heat.

Arrange salmon cakes in a single layer in the skillet. Cook about 8 minutes or until done (an instant-read thermometer inserted in the center of each cake registers 160°F) and lightly browned, turning once halfway through cooking time. For topping, in a small bowl stir together ¼ cup mayonnaise, ¼ cup sour cream, 1 Tbsp. snipped fresh cilantro, 1 tsp. finely shredded lime peel, and 1 Tbsp. lime juice. Serve over salmon cakes. Makes 4 servings.

*Grilling planks can be found in the grilling section of hardware and home supply stores. Cedar and alder are the woods selected most often for smoking salmon.*

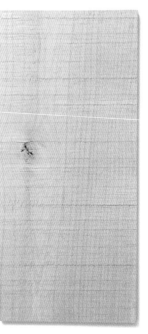

# 050   SALMON IN PARCHMENT

TASTING COMMENTS: *Cooking fish "en papillote," or in a paper package, keeps it very moist and infuses it with great flavor. I made sure my pieces of fish were of similar thickness and size so they all cooked evenly.—SB*

**PREP** 30 MINUTES   **BAKE** 30 MINUTES AT 350°F

*Select a 1-lb. fresh skinless salmon or halibut fillet that is at least ¾ inch thick but no more than 1 inch thick. Use a sharp knife to cut fillets into four equal-size pieces.*

- 1 lb. fresh or frozen skinless salmon, halibut, cod, or arctic char fillets, ¾ to 1 inch thick
- 4 cups fresh vegetables (such as sliced carrots,* trimmed fresh green beans,* sliced zucchini or yellow summer squash, and/or sliced red, yellow, and/or green sweet peppers)
- ½ cup sliced green onions
- 1 Tbsp. snipped fresh oregano or 1 tsp. dried oregano, crushed
- 2 tsp. orange zest
- ¼ tsp. salt
- ¼ tsp. black pepper
- 4 cloves garlic, halved
- 4 tsp. olive oil
  Salt
  Black pepper
- 1 medium orange, halved and thinly sliced
- 4 sprigs fresh oregano (optional)

1. Preheat oven to 350°F. Thaw fish, if frozen. Rinse fish; pat dry with paper towels. Cut into four serving-size pieces if necessary. Tear off four 14-inch squares of parchment paper. (Or tear off four 24-inch pieces of 18-inch-wide heavy foil. Fold each in half to make four 18×12-inch pieces.)

2. In a large bowl combine the next seven ingredients (through garlic).

3. Divide vegetable mixture among the four pieces of parchment or foil, placing vegetables to one side of parchment or in center of each piece. Place one fish piece on top of each vegetable portion. Drizzle 1 tsp. of the oil over each fish piece. Sprinkle lightly with additional salt and black pepper; top with orange slices. Fold parchment over fish and vegetables; fold in the open sides several times to secure, curving the edge into a circular pattern. (For foil, bring together two opposite foil edges and seal with a double fold. Fold the remaining edges together to completely enclose the food, allowing space for steam to build.) Place the packets in a single layer in a 15×10-inch baking pan.

4. Bake 30 minutes or until carrots are tender and fish flakes easily (cut an "X" in the top of the parchment packet to check for doneness or open a foil packet). If desired, top with fresh oregano sprigs.

*NOTE If using carrots and/or green beans, precook them. In a covered medium saucepan cook the carrots and/or green beans in a small amount of boiling water 2 minutes; drain.

PER SERVING *262 cal., 12 g fat (2 g sat. fat), 62 mg chol., 388 mg sodium, 14 g carb., 4 g fiber, 7 g sugars, 25 g pro.*

**OREGANO** *For a quick snip, remove oregano leaves from the stem, toss them into a measuring cup, then snip with kitchen shears.*

**ROSEMARY** *Although the recipe calls for oregano, rosemary is another strong-flavor herb that works well. Reduce the amount to 2 tsp. fresh rosemary.*

1. Fold your parchment in half to mark the center. Arrange your veggies in the middle of one side of the parchment.

2. Top vegetable mixture with a piece of fish, drizzle with olive oil, and sprinkle with salt and black pepper.

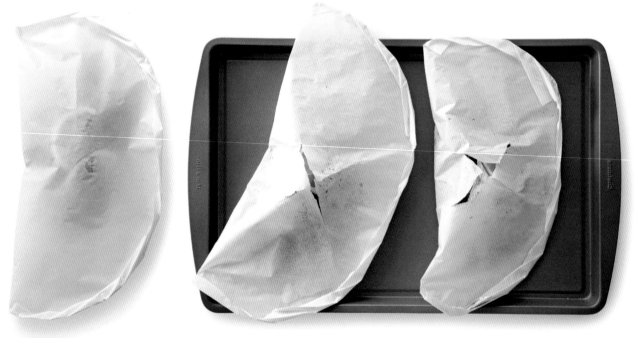

5. When sealed, the finished parchment package is perfect for cooking fish and chicken. A gentle, moist heat evenly cooks the fish without drying. Parchment is oven-safe up to 425°F.

6. You'll have to cut packets open to check for doneness. Check after 25 minutes if your fish is ¾ inch thick. If your fish is closer to 1 inch thick, check at 30 minutes.

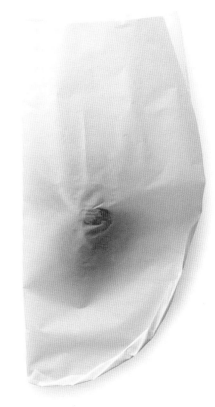

**3.** Before enclosing packets, top each fish piece with thinly sliced orange. A combination of orange and lemon slices works, too.

**4.** Fold parchment over fish. Begin at the bottom, folding and pleating the parchment toward the fish. Continue to fold and pleat, moving toward the top and making a half-moon shape.

**YOU CAN USE FOIL, TOO** *To make foil packets, tear off four 24×18-inch pieces of heavy-duty foil; fold each piece in half. Place veggies and fish in center of foil. Bring together two opposite sides and seal with a double fold. Fold remaining edges together to enclose completely.*

# 051   FISH AND CHIPS

TASTING COMMENTS:  *we tested this recipe with cod—it's the classic fish-and-chips fish, and we like its meaty texture and buttery flavor—but you could use haddock, pollock, or halibut as well.—LB*

*Red wine vinegar is made from from red wine that is fermented until it turns sour. In the same way, nutty, toasty-tasting malt vinegar is made from ale or beer. A shake or two is a great counterpoint to the richness of the crisp, batter-fried fish.*

**START TO FINISH** 1 HOUR

1 lb. fresh or frozen skinless fish fillets, about ½ inch thick

1¼ lb. medium potatoes (about 4)

Vegetable oil or shortening for deep-fat frying

1 cup all-purpose flour

½ cup beer

1 egg

¼ tsp. baking powder

¼ tsp. salt

¼ tsp. black pepper

Coarse salt

1 recipe Tartar Sauce (optional)

Malt vinegar or cider vinegar (optional)

Lemon wedges (optional)

**1.** Thaw fish, if frozen. Preheat oven to 300°F. Cut fish into 3×2-inch pieces. Rinse fish; pat dry with paper towels. Cover and chill until needed.

**2.** For chips, cut the potatoes lengthwise into ½-inch-wide wedges. Pat dry with paper towels. In a 3-qt. saucepan or deep-fat fryer heat 2 inches of vegetable oil to 325°F over medium heat. Fry potatoes, one-fourth at a time, 2 minutes. Using a slotted spoon, transfer potatoes to paper towels to drain. Heat oil to 375°F over medium-high heat. Add potatoes, one-fourth at a time, and cook 2 to 3 minutes or until crisp and golden. Remove potatoes; drain on paper towels. Transfer chips to a wire rack set on a baking sheet. Keep warm in oven.

**3.** Meanwhile, place ½ cup of the flour in a shallow dish. For batter, in a medium bowl combine remaining ½ cup flour and the next five ingredients (through pepper). Whisk until smooth. Dip fish into the flour dish, turning to coat all sides; shake off excess flour. Dip fish into batter, turning to coat all sides.

**4.** Fry fish, two or three pieces at a time, in the hot (375°F) oil 4 to 6 minutes or until coating is golden brown and fish flakes easily, turning once. Remove fish and drain on paper towels. Transfer fish to a second baking sheet; keep warm in the oven while frying remaining fish. Sprinkle fish and chips with coarse salt. If desired, serve with Tartar Sauce, vinegar, or lemon wedges.

PER SERVING *552 cal., 29 g fat (4 g sat. fat), 101 mg chol., 449 mg sodium, 43 g carb., 4 g fiber, 1 g sugars, 27 g pro.*

**TARTAR SAUCE**  In a small bowl stir together ¾ cup mayonnaise, ¼ cup sweet or dill pickle relish, 2 Tbsp. finely chopped onion, 1 Tbsp. snipped fresh dill weed or 1 tsp. dried dill weed, 1 tsp. lemon juice, and 2 tsp. capers (optional). Cover and chill at least 2 hours before serving. Store any leftovers in an airtight container in the refrigerator up to 1 week.

**LOW-FAT TARTAR SAUCE**  Prepare as directed, except substitute ½ cup light mayonnaise and ¼ cup plain low-fat yogurt for the ¾ cup mayonnaise.

**SWEET OR TART AND TANGY?** *A good tartar sauce is a rich and creamy concoction with bursts of salty, pungent, herbal flavors and crisp bits of pickle. Whether you use dill or sweet pickle relish is really up to your personal taste—both work equally well.*

## TESTING NOTES

↑
1. After scrubbing the potatoes thoroughly with a vegetable brush, cut them in half lengthwise, then cut each half into ½-inch-wide wedges.

↑
2. Pat the wedges dry with a paper towel. The dryer the potatoes are when they go in the hot oil, the less the oil will spatter.

↑
3. There are two tricks to achieving fried-potato perfection. One is to fry the potatoes in small batches. The temperature of the oil plunges when the food is added. If the oil isn't hot enough, the food comes out greasy and soggy. Adding too many potatoes at once lowers the oil temperature too quickly. The other trick is to fry twice—once at 325°F to cook the interior so it's light and fluffy and a second time at 375°F so the exterior gets crisp and golden.

↑
4. After the second fry, drain the potatoes on paper towels, then transfer to a wire rack set on a baking sheet and keep warm in the oven. Because the rack allows hot air to circulate under the potatoes, they'll stay crisp while you fry the fish.

# 052   SHRIMP SCAMPI

TASTING COMMENTS: *This classic recipe has been around our archives for a long time. We've made it with other types of pasta, but we like how the delicate strands of angel hair allow the shrimp to be the star.—CW*

**START TO FINISH** 20 MINUTES

1½ lb. fresh or frozen large shrimp

8 oz. dried angel hair pasta

¼ cup butter, melted

¼ cup olive oil

6 cloves garlic, minced

¼ tsp. salt

⅛ tsp. crushed red pepper

2 Tbsp. snipped fresh Italian parsley

1 tsp. lemon zest

Lemon wedges (optional)

**1.** Thaw shrimp, if frozen. Peel and devein shrimp, leaving tails intact if desired. Rinse shrimp; pat dry with paper towels.

**2.** In a large pot cook pasta according to package directions; drain. Return pasta to pot.

**3.** Meanwhile, in a large skillet heat butter, olive oil, and garlic over medium-high heat. Add shrimp, salt, and crushed red pepper. Cook and stir 3 minutes or until shrimp are opaque. Stir in parsley and lemon zest. Add shrimp mixture to pasta; toss to combine. If desired, serve with lemon wedges.

PER SERVING *565 cal., 27 g fat (9 g sat. fat), 269 mg chol., 428 mg sodium, 44 g carb., 2 g fiber, 2 g sugars, 38 g pro.*

**IS IT DONE YET (OR OVERDONE)?** *Shrimp cooks very quickly—and unfortunately, it is easy to overcook to a rubbery state. Perfectly cooked shrimp is opaque, glossy, and loosely curled, like the shrimp at left above. Shrimp that is overcooked begins to curl up more tightly and looks dry on the surface because it has lost too much moisture.*

*Italian or flat-leaf parsley has a slightly more intense flavor than curly-leaf parsley, but you can use either one in this recipe.*

*Shrimp Scampi is an adaptation made by Italian immigrant cooks. Scampi are actually small, lobsterlike crustaceans (also called langoustines, pictured top right). Shrimp were more plentiful in this country, so they adapted the butter-garlic-olive oil preparation to shrimp but kept both names.*

## TESTING NOTES

↑
1. Open shell down the underside of the shrimp. Starting at the head, pull off the shell.

↑
2. Use a sharp knife to cut down the center of the back to reveal the black vein.

↑
3. Use the tip of the knife to remove the vein. Rinse under cold running water.

## 053 SEARED SCALLOPS WITH CITRUS BEURRE BLANC AND WARM SLAW

TASTING COMMENTS: *This recipe was inspired by a more complicated dish with difficult-to-find ingredients. We tweaked it to make it approachable but still delicious! —JH*

**PREP** 20 MINUTES   **COOK** 25 MINUTES

- 1 red grapefruit
- 1 navel orange
- 1 cup dry white wine
- 1 medium lemon, juiced
- 2 small shallots, thinly sliced
- 1½ lb. fresh or frozen sea scallops, thawed
- ½ tsp. salt
- ½ tsp. freshly ground black pepper
- 1½ Tbsp. olive oil
- 3 oz. thinly sliced prosciutto
- 6 Tbsp. butter, cubed, at room temperature
- 5 cups shredded napa cabbage
- 3 radishes, thinly sliced

*If you can't eat grapefruit (it interferes with some common medications) or just don't like it, substitute another orange.*

**1.** Using a small knife, cut a thin slice off top and bottom of grapefruit. Stand fruit upright. Slice skin and white pith away from flesh. Hold fruit over a bowl; cut next to the membranes to remove fruit segments. Squeeze membranes to collect juices. Repeat with orange.

**2.** In a small saucepan combine juices from bowl, the white wine, and lemon juice. Bring to boiling; reduce heat to medium. Boil gently, uncovered, 15 minutes or until reduced to about ⅓ cup. Stir in shallots; remove from heat.

**3.** Meanwhile, pat scallops dry with a paper towel. Season with salt and pepper. Heat olive oil in a large skillet over medium-high heat. Cook half of the prosciutto at a time 3 minutes or until browned and crisp, turning occasionally. Drain and cool prosciutto on paper towels. Coarsely crumble.

**4.** Add about 1 Tbsp. butter to skillet. When butter is very hot but not browned, sear scallops in batches 1 minute per side or until golden brown. Transfer to a plate and keep warm in a 200°F oven.

**5.** Add cabbage to skillet. Cook and stir until just beginning to soften. Add radishes. Cook and stir gently until just warmed through. Gently stir in citrus segments. Using a slotted spoon, divide slaw among four dinner plates. Add shallot mixture to any liquids left in the skillet and bring to a boil. Remove skillet from heat and stir in remaining 5 Tbsp. butter just until melted.

**6.** Place scallops on slaw; spoon sauce over scallops and top with prosciutto.

PER SERVING *515 cal., 26 fat (13 g sat. fat), 109 mg chol., 1,143 mg sodium, 22 g carb., 3 g fiber, 10 g sugars, 38 g pro.*

## TESTING NOTES

↑
1. To get perfect sections of citrus with no pith attached (called "supreming"), slice off the top and bottom of an orange or grapefruit.

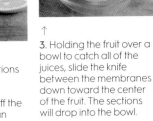

↑
3. Holding the fruit over a bowl to catch all of the juices, slide the knife between the membranes down toward the center of the fruit. The sections will drop into the bowl.

**FRESH OR FROZEN** *Buy fresh scallops if they are harvested locally or you have access to a reputable fish counter at your grocery store. Otherwise, high-quality, chemical-free frozen scallops are comparable and convenient. It's best to thaw them in the refrigerator overnight, but soaking frozen scallops in a bowl of cold water until thawed will work in a pinch. Pat dry before cooking.*

**DRY OR WET** *Fresh scallops come either dry- or wet-packed, but dry is always the way to go. Wet-packed scallops come bathed in a phosphate solution that keeps them plump longer but leaves a soapy aftertaste.*

**KNOW YOUR SCALLOPS** *Thimble-size bay scallops are sweet and perfect for paella but are too small to be seared. Sea scallops are larger and meatier than bay scallops. Diver scallops do not denote a type of scallop, but rather the fact that they were harvested by hand.*

↑
2. Slice off the skin and bitter pith in small sections, following the curve of the fruit.

*Sea scallops*

*Bay scallops*

**PULLING THE FOOT** *Scallops have a tough bit of muscle called an adductor or foot on the side that helps them open and shut their shells. It's easy to remove: Just gently give it a tug to pull it off.*

*Raw*

*Medium*

*Well Done*

### ARE THEY DONE YET?
*You can easily tell by the way scallops look and feel (compare these scallops that have been cut in half):*

**RAW**
The scallop is jiggly and appears slightly pink and translucent throughout.

**MEDIUM**
The scallop has started to firm up, with a little give when touched, and is opaque in places. For some, this is the perfect doneness.

**WELL DONE**
Now the scallop is fully white and completely firm when poked. Chefs may disagree, but many people prefer scallops this way.

This lovely dish is company-special but is easy enough to put together (and with just a few ingredients!) that you won't stress about making it.

# 054   CRAB CAKES

TASTING COMMENTS:   *The key to awesome crab cakes is to keep things simple. Our version is flavored only with green onion and a little seafood seasoning so the delicate flavor of the crab comes through.—CC*

**PREP** 40 MINUTES   **CHILL** 1 HOUR

2 Tbsp. chopped green onion

2 Tbsp. butter

1 Tbsp. all-purpose flour

¼ tsp. seafood seasoning

⅛ tsp. black pepper

½ cup milk

1 6- to 8-oz. pkg. frozen lump crabmeat, thawed; one 6-oz. can refrigerated lump crabmeat, drained and flaked; or 1 cup fresh crabmeat, flaked and cartilage removed

2 Tbsp. panko bread crumbs, fine dry bread crumbs, or cornmeal

¼ cup all-purpose flour

1 egg

1 tsp. water

¾ cup panko bread crumbs or fine dry bread crumbs

2 Tbsp. vegetable oil

¼ cup Rémoulade, Lemon-Dill Sour Cream, or Mustard Chutney

*The most familiar seafood seasoning comes in a yellow tin. It is a blend of dry mustard, paprika, celery salt, bay leaf, black pepper, crushed red pepper, mace, cloves, allspice, nutmeg, cardamom, and ginger.*

**1.** In a small saucepan cook onion in 1 Tbsp. hot butter until tender. Stir in the 1 Tbsp. flour, the seafood seasoning, and pepper. Add milk all at once. Cook and stir until thickened and bubbly. Transfer to a medium bowl. Cover and chill 1 hour or until cold.

**2.** Stir crabmeat and the 2 Tbsp. panko into chilled sauce. Place the ¼ cup flour in a shallow dish. In a second shallow dish beat together egg and the water. Place the ¾ cup panko in a third shallow dish.

**3.** For each crab cake, shape about 2 Tbsp. of the crab mixture into a small patty. Dip patty into flour; turn to coat. Dip in egg mixture, then in bread crumbs. Place on waxed paper.

**CHOOSE YOUR CRUMBS** *The crumbs (or cornmeal) in these crab cakes perform two functions. The crumbs that are stirred into the crab mixture act as a binder to keep the crab cakes together when cooked. The crumbs in which the uncooked cakes are dredged create the crispy coating. Panko, fine dry bread crumbs, and cornmeal work equally well—which you choose is a matter of personal taste.*

**4.** In a large skillet heat oil and remaining 1 Tbsp. butter over medium heat. Add half of the crab cakes; cook 3 minutes on each side or until golden brown. Repeat with remaining crab cakes. Serve with Rémoulade, Lemon-Dill Sour Cream, or Mustard Chutney.

PER SERVING *328 cal., 15 g fat (5 g sat. fat), 92 mg chol., 415 mg sodium, 39 g carb., 1 g fiber, 20 g sugars, 10 g pro.*

**RÉMOULADE** In a bowl combine ¾ cup mayonnaise; 1 Tbsp. each thinly sliced green onion, fresh snipped parsley, finely chopped red pepper, Creole or brown mustard, and lemon juice; 1 tsp. drained capers; and ½ tsp. each paprika and hot pepper sauce.

**LEMON-DILL SOUR CREAM** In a bowl combine ¾ cup sour cream and 1 Tbsp. each lemon zest, dill, and chives.

**MUSTARD CHUTNEY** In a bowl combine ½ cup purchased mango chutney (snip large pieces), 1½ tsp. Dijon-style mustard, and 1 tsp. lemon juice.

1. The base of these crab cakes is essentially a white sauce made with butter, flour, seafood seasoning, and milk. It's cooked to thicken it, then chilled until cold. Chilling the milk mixture thickens it further so the crab cakes will hold together when fried.
↓

2. Using a small ice cream scoop when forming the crab cakes keeps them evenly sized and gives them a nice shape.
↓

**CRAB OPTIONS** *Unless you live next to an ocean, fresh (never frozen) crabmeat may be hard to come by. There are other options, including canned, frozen, refrigerated pasteurized tubs, and refrigerated vacuum-sealed packs. Lump crabmeat refers to meat that comes from the crustacean's body. It's ideal for crab cakes. You can also use backfin meat, which is broken pieces of lump mixed with smaller pieces of white body meat. Crab cakes made with backfin have a finer texture than those made with lump crabmeat.*

MAKES: *4 servings*  TESTED BY: *Kelsey B.*

# 055  THAI GREEN SEAFOOD CURRY

TASTING COMMENTS: *we tested this recipe with each type of curry paste to be sure it worked with any of them. They were all very good, but each person at the taste panels had a favorite—that's why it's good to have multiple tasters!—KB*

**START TO FINISH** 35 MINUTES

1 lb. fresh or frozen medium shrimp in shells and/or sea scallops

1 Tbsp. canola oil

3 cloves garlic, minced

1 cup unsweetened coconut milk

⅓ cup reduced-sodium chicken broth

1 Tbsp. fish sauce

2 tsp. packed brown sugar

2 Tbsp. green or yellow curry paste or 3 Tbsp. red curry paste

1 medium red or yellow sweet pepper, cut into thin bite-size strips

½ of a small eggplant, peeled if desired and cut into bite-size pieces (2 cups)

¼ cup thinly sliced fresh basil leaves

1 tsp. lime zest

2 cups hot cooked jasmine rice*

Fresh basil leaves

Lime wedges

*unsweetened coconut milk typically comes in a can. Don't confuse it with the sweetened product or with any coconut-flavor waters or beverages on the market today. Be sure to stir the milk before measuring; the solids and liquid separate in the can over time.*

**1.** Thaw shrimp and/or scallops, if frozen. Peel and devein shrimp, leaving tails intact if desired. Rinse and pat dry with paper towels. In a wok or large nonstick skillet heat oil over medium-high heat. Add garlic; cook 30 seconds.

**2.** In a bowl combine coconut milk, broth, fish sauce, brown sugar, and curry paste. Add to wok; bring mixture to boiling. Boil gently, uncovered, 5 minutes, stirring occasionally. Stir in the shrimp and/or scallops, sweet pepper, and eggplant. Boil gently 5 minutes more or until seafood turns opaque, vegetables are just tender, and sauce has thickened slightly, stirring occasionally.

**3.** Remove from heat. Stir in the ¼ cup basil and the lime zest. Serve over hot cooked rice. Top with fresh basil leaves and serve with lime wedges.

**\*TIP** For 2 cups cooked rice, in a medium saucepan combine 2 cups water and 1 cup uncooked jasmine rice. If desired, add a little salt. Bring to boiling; reduce heat. Simmer, covered, 20 minutes or until water is absorbed and rice is tender.

PER SERVING *368 cal., 16 g fat, (11 g sat. fat), 137 mg chol., 887 mg sodium, 34 g carb., 4 g fiber, 5 g sugars, 22 g pro.*

**THAI CHICKEN CURRY** Prepare as directed, except substitute 12 oz. skinless, boneless chicken thighs, cut into 1-inch strips, for the seafood. Add after bringing liquid to boiling in Step 2 .

**CURRY PASTE COLORS** *Because each type of curry paste is made with different chiles, aromatic herbs, and spices, the flavor of your dish will be greatly influenced by which paste you use. Red curry paste—the most versatile—is made from red chiles and often includes chili powder to deepen the flavor. Green curry paste is made with green chiles and may include some coriander, basil, and/or kaffir lime leaves. It is thought to be the hottest, followed by yellow curry paste. Turmeric is added to yellow curry paste, along with a much smaller amount of red chiles, to get the yellow color.*

## TESTING NOTES

1. Instead of browning the shrimp and scallops in a stir-fry, it's common to poach them in the coconut milk mixture. This moist-heat method allows the shrimp and scallops to take on the flavors of the curry paste and coconut milk.

↓

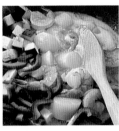

↑

2. This is where a wok pays off. You can cook and stir a lot of ingredients without losing them to your stove-top burner! Stir in the chopped eggplant and sweet pepper. Continue to cook about 5 minutes or until shrimp or scallops turn opaque or chicken is done. Vegetables should be just tender, and the sauce will have thickened.

↑

3. Thinly sliced basil is easy to achieve in just a few steps. After you've picked the basil leaves, stack them on top of one another and roll the stack into a small tubelike shape. Use a knife to cut thin slices from the basil roll, making sure to cut all the way through so strips detach from the roll.

## INGREDIENTS YOU NEED TO KNOW

**FISH SAUCE** Be prepared! The odor of fish sauce might deter you, but the flavor becomes incredible when combined with the rest of the ingredients. Fish sauce is made from the liquid of salted, fermented fish.

**LIME PEEL** Traditional curries call for kaffir lime leaves. They're thick, dark green, and aromatic but hard to find. We used shredded lime peel here. Look for kaffir lime leaves in an Asian market.

**EGGPLANT** Typically, Japanese or Thai eggplant is used in curry recipes. If you can't find these varieties, a regular eggplant will do. When cooked, the skin may become tough and bitter, so peel it if you like.

# VEGETARIAN

# 056 FOUR-CHEESE MACARONI & CHEESE

TASTING COMMENTS: *This can be served straight from the saucepan or with a brown crusty topper. Quick-broiling the buttered bread crumbs rather than baking the whole dish for an extended period of time kept the texture creamy. —SB*

*we love panko crumbs as a topping! They have a larger surface area and flakier texture than fine dry bread crumbs, so when they're tossed with butter and baked, they eat super light and crispy!*

**PREP** 30 MINUTES   **BROIL** 2 MINUTES

Nonstick cooking spray

1 16-oz. pkg. dried cavatappi or corkscrew-shape pasta

3 Tbsp. unsalted butter

⅓ cup finely chopped onion

3 Tbsp. all-purpose flour

½ tsp. kosher salt

¼ tsp. freshly ground black pepper

2½ cups milk

8 oz. Gouda cheese, shredded (2 cups)

4 oz. sharp cheddar cheese, shredded (1 cup)

4 oz. Swiss cheese, shredded (1 cup)

½ cup grated Parmesan cheese

1 tsp. unsalted butter

⅔ cup panko bread crumbs

Snipped fresh Italian parsley (optional)

1. Preheat broiler. Coat a 2½- or 3-qt. broiler-safe gratin or baking dish with cooking spray; set aside. Bring a large pot of lightly salted water to boiling. Add pasta and cook according to package directions. Drain and return to the warm pot.

2. Meanwhile, in a large saucepan melt the 3 Tbsp. butter over medium heat. Add onion; cook and stir 3 minutes. Stir in flour, kosher salt, and pepper. Add milk all at once. Cook, whisking constantly, until thickened and bubbly. Cook and whisk 2 minutes more; remove from heat.

3. Add Gouda, cheddar, and Swiss cheeses and ¼ cup of the Parmesan cheese, whisking until cheeses are melted and sauce is smooth. Add the cheese sauce to cooked pasta; stir to combine. Transfer to the prepared dish.

4. In a small microwave-safe bowl melt the 1 tsp. butter. Stir in panko and the remaining ¼ cup Parmesan cheese; sprinkle over pasta mixture. Broil 5 to 6 inches from the heat 2 minutes or until top is browned. If desired, top with parsley.

PER SERVING *739 cal., 34 g fat (20 g sat. fat), 111 mg chol., 858 mg sodium, 72 g carb., 3 g fiber, 9 g sugars, 36 g pro.*

*Shred your cheeses by hand! Packaged shredded cheeses may contain added starches that affect the sauce's texture.*

## TESTING NOTES

Process cheese is often the key to the creamiest mac and cheese, but the four aged cheeses in this recipe provide lots of great flavor with no loss of creaminess.

1. Whisk flour into the melted butter mixture in the saucepan, stirring constantly. The butter will coat the flour molecules, which prevents them from sticking together and forming lumps when milk is added. Stir constantly to keep the mixture from sticking to the pan.

2. Once the flour and butter are combined, gradually add the milk to the flour mixture, whisking constantly. Keep whisking slowly until you have a thickened and bubbly sauce. Continue cooking for 2 minutes to finish cooking the flour. Remove the pan from heat before you add the cheeses. Residual heat and continual whisking will melt the cheese slowly and evenly.

# 057 EGGPLANT PARMIGIANA

TASTING COMMENTS: *Eggplant is a spongy and absorbent vegetable. When frying slices for this dish, we had to add extra oil to the pan so they wouldn't stick and burn. —LB*

**PREP** 20 MINUTES **COOK** 9 MINUTES

- 1 small eggplant (12 oz.)
- 1 egg, lightly beaten
- 1 Tbsp. water
- ¼ cup all-purpose flour
- 2 Tbsp. vegetable oil
- ⅓ cup grated Parmesan cheese
- 1 cup meatless spaghetti sauce
- ¾ cup shredded mozzarella cheese (3 oz.)
- Shredded fresh basil (optional)

*Choose eggplants that are firm and feel heavy for their size. If the skin gives slightly when you press your fingernail against it, the eggplant is ripe. Small eggplants tend to be sweeter and more tender than large ones.*

**1.** Wash and peel eggplant; cut crosswise into ½-inch-thick slices. Combine egg and the water; dip eggplant slices into egg mixture, then into flour, turning to coat both sides.

**2.** In a large skillet cook eggplant, half at a time, in hot oil over medium-high heat 4 to 6 minutes or until golden, turning once. (If necessary, add additional oil and reduce heat to medium if eggplant browns too quickly.) Drain on paper towels.

**3.** Wipe the skillet with paper towels. Arrange the eggplant slices in the skillet; sprinkle with the Parmesan cheese. Top with spaghetti sauce and mozzarella cheese. Cook, covered, over medium-low heat 5 to 7 minutes or until heated through. If desired, top with basil.

**BAKED EGGPLANT PARMIGIANA**
Preheat oven to 400°F. Prepare as directed, except in Step 2, place the eggplant slices in a single layer in an ungreased 2-qt. rectangular baking dish. (If necessary, cut slices to fit.) Sprinkle with Parmesan cheese. Top with spaghetti sauce and mozzarella cheese. Bake, uncovered, 12 to 15 minutes or until heated through. If desired, top with basil.

PER SERVING *250 cal., 15 g fat (5 g sat. fat), 70 mg chol., 563 mg sodium, 20 g carb., 5 g fiber, 8 g sugars, 12 g pro.*

*The baked option takes a few minutes longer to cook than the skillet version, but the coating on the eggplant stays crisper—which is nice!*

## TESTING NOTES

1. The skin on eggplant can be tough and a little bitter when cooked. Peel it using a sharp, sturdy vegetable peeler.

2. Cook the eggplant slices only half at a time. If you crowd the pan with more than that, the slices will steam rather than fry and your coating will be soggy instead of crisp.

# 058   BAKED ZITI WITH THREE CHEESES

TASTING COMMENTS:   *This indulgent dish is one of our most popular recipes—and it can be enjoyed by everyone. Not only is it vegetarian, but it is easily made gluten-free just by using gluten-free pasta. Just don't freeze it—it's best enjoyed the day it's made.—CW*

**PREP** 30 MINUTES   **BAKE** 30 MINUTES AT 425°F

- 4 cups dried ziti or penne pasta (12 oz.)
- 1 14.5-oz. can fire-roasted diced tomatoes, undrained
- 1 cup chopped onion
- 12 cloves garlic, minced
- 2 Tbsp. olive oil
- ½ cup dry white wine
- 2 cups heavy cream
- 1 cup finely shredded Parmesan cheese
- ¾ cup Gorgonzola or other blue cheese, crumbled (3 oz.)
- ½ cup Fontina cheese, shredded (2 oz.)
- ½ tsp. salt
- ¼ tsp. black pepper
- Snipped fresh Italian parsley (optional)

*Fire-roasted tomatoes are kind of a magical ingredient. They add smoky flavor and pretty charred flecks to all kinds of dishes. If you can find fire-roasted crushed tomatoes, you could substitute those for the diced tomatoes. Your casserole will just be less chunky.*

1. Preheat oven to 425°F. In a large saucepan cook pasta according to package directions; drain. Place in an ungreased 3-qt. rectangular baking dish; stir in undrained tomatoes.

2. Meanwhile, in a large saucepan cook onion and garlic in hot oil over medium heat just until tender. Carefully stir in wine; cook 3 minutes or until liquid reduces by half. Add cream; heat to boiling. Boil gently, uncovered, 5 minutes or until mixture thickens slightly, stirring frequently. Remove from heat. Stir in cheeses, salt, and pepper.

3. Pour cheese sauce over pasta. Bake, covered, 30 to 35 minutes or until sauce is bubbly. Stir. If desired, sprinkle with parsley.

PER SERVING *717 cal., 46 g fat (26 g sat. fat), 141 mg chol., 883 mg sodium, 54 g carb., 3 g fiber, 5 g sugars, 21 g pro.*

**TOTALLY TUBULAR** *Tube pastas such as (from left) ziti, penne, and rigatoni are perfect for use in casseroles. The bigger the pasta, the better it is at catching chunky bits of sauce. If the word "rigate" is part of the name, it means the pasta has ridges, which helps sauce cling as well. Any of these work in this dish.*

**CHEESY TRIO** *Each of the cheeses in this rich casserole offers something that makes the sum of its parts so good. The blue cheese provides bites of pleasingly sharp, tangy flavor. The Parmesan infuses the dish with its distinctive nuttiness. And the Fontina— which adds a fruity, herbaceous flavor—also contributes creaminess and meltability.*

MAKES: *4 servings*   TESTED BY: *Sammy M.*

# 059 MAKE-IT-MINE VEGETABLE STIR-FRY

TASTING COMMENTS:   *we tested this recipe five times—not because it wasn't good, but because we wanted to try all different combinations of veggies and sauces! Each test yielded valuable tweaks.—SM*

**START TO FINISH** 30 MINUTES

1 Tbsp. vegetable oil

3 cups **Group 1 Vegetables**

2 cloves **garlic,** minced

3 cups **Group 2 Vegetables**

**Sauce**

**Toppers**

**Splash-Ons**

**1.** In an extra-large skillet or wok heat oil over medium-high heat. Add Group 1 Vegetables and garlic. Cook and stir 3 minutes. Add Group 2 Vegetables. Cook and stir 3 to 5 minutes more or until vegetables are crisp-tender. Push vegetables to side of skillet. Add Sauce to center of skillet; bring to boiling. Cook and stir until slightly thickened. Toss to coat the vegetables; heat through.

**2.** Transfer stir-fry to a dish. Add Toppers and Splash-Ons.

**TIP** To make this a heartier main dish, stir-fry 12 oz. lean beef, pork, or chicken before cooking vegetables. Remove meat from the skillet or wok before cooking vegetables, then stir back in after adding Sauce to heat through.

## GROUP 1 VEGETABLES
### (PICK A COMBINATION)

Butternut squash, cubed

Carrots, thinly bias-sliced

Cauliflower florets

Celery, thinly bias-sliced

Green beans, cut into
1-inch pieces

Sweet potatoes, cubed

Mushrooms, quartered

Onion wedges, thin

## GROUP 2 VEGETABLES
### (PICK A COMBINATION)

Broccoli florets

Sweet peppers, cut into
bite-size strips

Snow pea pods

Zucchini or yellow
summer squash, sliced

Asparagus, cut into
1-inch pieces

## SAUCE (PICK ONE)

Stir together ¼ cup reduced-
sodium soy sauce, 1 Tbsp. rice
vinegar, 1 Tbsp. packed brown
sugar, 1 tsp. ground ginger,
and ¼ tsp. crushed red
pepper.

Stir together ⅓ cup orange
juice, 2 Tbsp. orange
marmalade, 1 Tbsp. reduced-
sodium soy sauce, and 1 tsp.
grated fresh ginger.

Add ⅓ cup bottled sweet-and-
sour sauce, stir-fry sauce,
peanut sauce, or reduced-
sodium teriyaki sauce.

## TOPPERS (PICK ONE)

Chopped peanuts, toasted
almonds or hazelnuts, or
roasted cashews

Chow mein noodles

Sesame seeds

Snipped fresh cilantro

## SPLASH-ONS
### (PICK ONE)

Sriracha sauce

Chili garlic paste

Fish sauce

Reduced-sodium
soy sauce

Toasted sesame oil

Given the options for vegetables, sauces, toppers, and splash-ons—plus your choice of adding optional meat, poultry, or shrimp—the variations of this veggie stir-fry are nearly limitless.

# 060   **RATATOUILLE**

TASTING COMMENTS:   *We looked at both versions—the skillet version and the baked version—side by side at Taste Panel. We really like that there are two ways to serve it—as a fast weeknight side or prettily arranged in a baking dish so it was more company-special but still rustic. We added more garlic to both! —JH*

**START TO FINISH** 40 MINUTES

- ½ **cup chopped onion**
- 1 **clove garlic, minced**
- 1 **Tbsp. olive oil or vegetable oil**
- 3 **cups cubed, peeled eggplant**
- 1 **medium zucchini or yellow summer squash, halved lengthwise and cut into ¼-inch slices (1½ cups)**
- 1 **cup chopped, peeled tomatoes or one 14.5-oz. can diced tomatoes, drained**
- ¾ **cup chopped green sweet pepper**
- 3 **Tbsp. dry white wine, chicken broth, or vegetable broth**
- ¼ **tsp. salt**
- ⅛ **tsp. black pepper**
- 1 **Tbsp. snipped fresh basil or oregano**

*Peeling your tomatoes and eggplant is suggested, but it's not a necessity—especially if you are making the baked version. We like the look of the eggplant skin in the casserole.*

1. In a large skillet cook onion and garlic in hot oil over medium heat until onion is tender. Stir in the next seven ingredients (through black pepper). Bring to boiling; reduce heat. Simmer, covered, 10 minutes or until vegetables are tender. Uncover and cook 5 minutes more or until most of the liquid evaporates, stirring occasionally. Season to taste with additional salt and black pepper. Stir in basil just before serving.

PER SERVING *85 cal., 4 g fat (1 g sat. fat), 0 mg chol., 156 mg sodium, 11 g carb., 4 g fiber, 5 g sugars, 2 g pro.*

**RATATOUILLE CASSEROLE** *Prepare as directed, except in a medium bowl stir together one 10.75-oz. can tomato puree; 2 Tbsp. balsamic vinegar; 2 Tbsp. dry white wine; 1 Tbsp. chopped fresh basil; 2 cloves garlic, minced; ½ tsp. salt; and ¼ tsp. black pepper. Spoon into the bottom of a 2-qt. rectangular baking dish. Arrange the sliced vegetables in the dish, alternating vegetables and standing the slices up with cut sides touching. Brush vegetables with 1 Tbsp. olive oil. Bake at 350°F 1 hour or until tender and bubbly. Let stand 10 minutes before serving. Garnish with additional fresh basil.*

MAKES: *4 servings*   TESTED BY: *Sarah B.*

# 061   CUBAN RED BEANS AND RICE

TASTING COMMENTS: *If you want to cook your own beans, soak ½ lb. (2 to 2½ cups) dried beans overnight and cook 60 to 90 minutes. You will get the 3½ cups you need for this recipe.—SB*

**START TO FINISH** 35 MINUTES

*Using vegetable broth in this recipe makes it vegetarian and suitable for vegans as well!*

- 1 large sweet onion, cut into thin wedges
- 1 cup chopped green or red sweet pepper
- 4 cloves garlic, minced
- 1 Tbsp. canola oil
- ½ cup snipped fresh cilantro
- ½ tsp. dried oregano, crushed
- ½ tsp. ground cumin
- ¼ tsp. black pepper
- 2 15- to 16-oz. cans pinto beans and/or red kidney beans, rinsed and drained
- 1 cup vegetable broth
- ¼ cup lime juice
- 2 cups hot cooked brown rice
- Lime wedges and/or small hot chile peppers (tip, page 18) (optional)

**1.** In a large saucepan cook onion, sweet pepper, and garlic in hot oil over medium heat 5 to 7 minutes or until tender, stirring occasionally. Add ¼ cup of the cilantro, the oregano, cumin, and black pepper. Cook and stir 1 minute.

**2.** Add beans and broth. Bring to boiling; reduce heat. Simmer, uncovered, 15 to 20 minutes or until liquid is thickened to desired consistency.

**3.** Stir in lime juice. Serve beans over rice and sprinkle with remaining cilantro. If desired, serve with lime wedges and/or hot chile peppers.

PER SERVING *369 cal., 6 g fat (1 g sat. fat), 0 mg chol., 933 mg sodium, 67 g carb., 13 g fiber, 0 g sugars, 17 g pro.*

## COOKING RICE
Cooking rice can be time-consuming. If you don't have the time or inclination to cook whole grain rice for your meal, try one of the easy alternatives.

| TYPE | BENEFITS | COOK TIME | CHARACTERISTICS |
|---|---|---|---|
| WHOLE GRAIN BROWN RICE | Whole grain rice is the most nutritious. It contains all portions of the grain. | 45 minutes | Cooking whole grain rice gives you the most control over nutrition and texture. |
| INSTANT BROWN RICE | Instant rice is whole grain rice that has been precooked and dehydrated. Some texture and nutrients are lost in the process, but cooking time is minimal. | 10 minutes | Texture is slightly less firm than whole grain rice. Many nutrients lost in the manufacturing process are added back. |
| READY-TO-EAT BROWN RICE | Ready-to-eat rice is fully cooked and packaged and can be heated in seconds. Check labels to determine which products have the best nutritional values. | 90 seconds | Nutritional values can be equal to whole grain rice. |

**SPICE IS NICE** *Beans and rice have been embraced by cultures all over the world—and for good reason. They're cheap, tasty, nutritious, and versatile. These red beans are flavored with oregano, cilantro, and cumin—a combination that makes the dish Cuban meets Cajun.*

## 062 TOFU-CELLOPHANE NOODLE STIR-FRY WITH YU CHOY

TASTING COMMENTS: *We don't always specify a nonstick skillet, but when it's necessary, we do. Tofu sticks pretty easily, so a nonstick skillet was the only way to go in this recipe. It has such interesting flavor from the hoisin, ginger, cinnamon, and cloves!—JH*

**START TO FINISH** 35 MINUTES

*There are several varieties of tofu out there, ranging in texture from silken—which as its name implies is very soft and custardy—to extra-firm. Extra-firm is the type that's best for stir fries because it holds its shape and doesn't break apart.*

- 1 12-oz. pkg. extra-firm tofu, drained and cut into ¾-inch pieces
- 4 oz. cellophane noodles (bean threads)
- 2 Tbsp. reduced-sodium soy sauce
- 2 Tbsp. rice vinegar
- 1 to 2 tsp. Asian chili paste (sambal oelek)
- 1 tsp. toasted sesame oil
- 2 Tbsp. canola oil
- 4 oz. shiitake mushrooms, stems removed and caps sliced ½ inch thick (1½ cups)
- 2 cloves garlic, thinly sliced
- 5 oz. yu choy, cut into 2-inch pieces (3 cups)
- 3 green onions, trimmed and cut into 1½-inch pieces
- ¼ cup water
- 3 Tbsp. hoisin sauce
- 2 tsp. grated fresh ginger
- ¼ tsp. ground cinnamon
  Dash ground cloves
- 6 lime wedges
- ¼ cup dry-roasted peanuts, chopped

**1.** Drain tofu on a plate lined with paper towels while preparing remaining ingredients.

**2.** Fill a large saucepan with water and bring to boiling. Add cellophane noodles and remove pan from heat; let stand 2 to 3 minutes or until softened. Drain; rinse with cool water and return to saucepan. Stir in soy sauce, vinegar, chili paste, and sesame oil.

**3.** In a large nonstick skillet heat 1 Tbsp. of the canola oil over medium heat. Add tofu; cook 5 to 7 minutes until lightly browned, tossing occasionally. Transfer tofu to pan with noodles and gently toss to combine.

**4.** Add remaining 1 Tbsp. canola oil to skillet. Add mushrooms. Cook and stir 3 minutes. Add garlic; cook and stir 1 minute. Add yu choy and green onions; cook and stir 2 minutes or just until wilted. Add the next five ingredients (through cloves); cook and stir 1 minute. Add noodle mixture and cook until heated through, stirring occasionally.

**5.** Transfer stir-fry to a dish. Squeeze 2 lime wedges over top and sprinkle with peanuts. Serve with the remaining lime wedges.

PER SERVING *361 cal., 18 g fat (2 g sat. fat), 0 mg chol., 548 mg sodium, 40 g carb., 4 g fiber, 7 g sugars, 13 g pro.*

**TO PRESS OR NOT TO PRESS?** *Some recipes recommend pressing tofu for up to an hour before cooking to extract moisture. We found that pressing the tofu had little effect on the texture of the finished food. Instead, make sure you thoroughly drain the tofu and gently pat it with paper towels to reduce surface moisture.*

**CELLOPHANE NOODLES** Also called glass noodles, these delicate threads are made from mung bean starch. When cooked, they have a delightfully chewy texture.

**SHIITAKE MUSHROOMS** A common ingredient in Asian dishes, they have a meaty texture and distinctive flavor. The stems are woody—always remove them.

**ASIAN CHILI PASTE** Sambal oelek, as it's also known, is made only of fiery red chiles, vinegar, and salt. It has a simpler flavor than sriracha sauce but is quite a bit hotter.

**YU CHOY** This leafy Asian vegetable (top right) is sometimes called choy sum. If you can't find it, substitute an equal amount of broccoli rabe (bottom left) or 2 baby bok choy (top left), coarsely chopped, plus 1½ cups small broccoli florets (bottom right).

MAKES: *6 servings*   TESTED BY: *Colleen W.*

# 063   **CLASSIC RISOTTO**

TASTING COMMENTS: *For the creamiest risotto, the rice must get toasty first! Toasting prepares the rice for absorbing the hot broth. It may seem like a minor step, but don't be tempted to skip it.—CW*

**START TO FINISH** 40 MINUTES

½ cup chopped onion

2 cloves garlic, minced

2 Tbsp. olive oil

1 cup uncooked Arborio rice

3 cups vegetable broth or chicken broth*

½ cup white wine or chicken broth

1 cup frozen baby or regular peas

¼ cup grated Parmesan cheese

Lemon zest (optional)

**1.** In a 3-qt. saucepan cook onion and garlic in hot oil over medium heat 5 minutes or until onion is tender, stirring occasionally. Add rice. Cook 5 minutes or until rice is golden, stirring frequently.

**2.** Meanwhile, in a 1½-qt. saucepan bring broth to boiling; reduce heat. Cover and keep broth simmering.

**3.** Carefully stir wine into rice mixture. Cook over medium heat until absorbed. Carefully stir ½ cup of the broth into the rice mixture. Cook over medium heat until broth is absorbed, stirring frequently. Continue adding broth, ½ cup at a time, stirring frequently until broth is absorbed, adding peas with the last ½ cup broth. Rice should be tender and creamy (should take about 25 minutes total).

**4.** Stir in cheese; heat through. If desired, sprinkle with lemon zest. Serve immediately.

**\*TIP** If desired, substitute ½ cup dry white wine for ½ cup of the broth, gently heating the wine separately and stirring it into the rice as the first ½ cup of liquid.

PER SERVING *188 cal., 6 g fat (1 g sat. fat), 3 mg chol., 544 mg sodium, 30 g carb., 2 g fiber, 3 g sugars, 5 g pro.*

**SHORTCUT RISOTTO** Prepare Classic Risotto as directed through Step 1. Carefully stir in all of the broth. Bring to boiling; reduce heat. Simmer, covered, 20 minutes (do not lift lid). Remove from heat. Stir in peas. Cover; let stand 5 minutes. Stir in cheese; heat through. If desired, sprinkle with lemon zest.

**CLASSIC RISOTTO WITH VEGETABLES** Prepare Classic Risotto as directed, except add ¼ cup coarsely shredded carrot with the peas. Add 2 cups fresh spinach, shredded, and 1 Tbsp. snipped fresh thyme with the cheese (or ½ tsp. dried thyme, crushed, with the carrot).

**TRY FARRO!** *Farro, an ancient grain with a nutty flavor similar to brown rice, comes in whole grain, semipearled, and pearled varieties. For risotto, choose the pearled variety, which cooks in a shorter time because the hull has been removed. Soak farro in water for 30 minutes before cooking, then follow the same process as with the Arborio rice, adding broth a bit at a time and cooking each addition until absorbed.*

1. Toasting the rice heats the grain exterior quickly so it can absorb liquid slowly.

2. Adding hot broth to the rice helps the rice release its starch slowly and cook evenly. Adding cold broth may result in a hard, uncooked kernel in the center of the rice grain. Gradually add each ½ cup of broth only after the majority of the liquid in the saucepan is absorbed. At the end of cooking, add a smaller amount of broth and taste the risotto before you add more broth.

3. If you are planning to make the caramelized onion version of this risotto recipe, use sweet onions—they tend to be juicy with a mild taste. Some popular sweet varieties include Maui, Vidalia, and Walla Walla onions.

4. Always use freshly grated Parmesan cheese for risotto. Purchased grated cheese may result in a gritty texture and a less-assertive cheese flavor.

### FARRO RISOTTO WITH VEGETABLES
Prepare Classic Risotto as directed, except substitute pearled farro for the Arborio rice and add ¼ cup coarsely shredded carrot with the peas. Add 2 cups fresh spinach, shredded, and 1 Tbsp. snipped fresh thyme with the cheese. (If you prefer to use dried thyme, add ½ tsp. dried thyme, crushed, with the carrot.)

### CLASSIC RISOTTO WITH SHRIMP
Prepare Classic Risotto with Vegetables as directed, except omit peas. Stir 1½ cups cooked, peeled medium shrimp into rice with the carrot.

### CLASSIC RISOTTO WITH CARAMELIZED ONIONS
Prepare Classic Risotto as directed, except omit peas. While risotto is cooking, in a large skillet heat 1 Tbsp. olive oil. Add 2 cups sliced, halved onions; cook, covered, over medium-low heat 15 minutes. Cook, uncovered, 10 to 15 minutes more or until onions are golden, stirring frequently. Stir caramelized onions and 1 cup bite-size pieces cooked asparagus into rice with the last ½ cup broth.

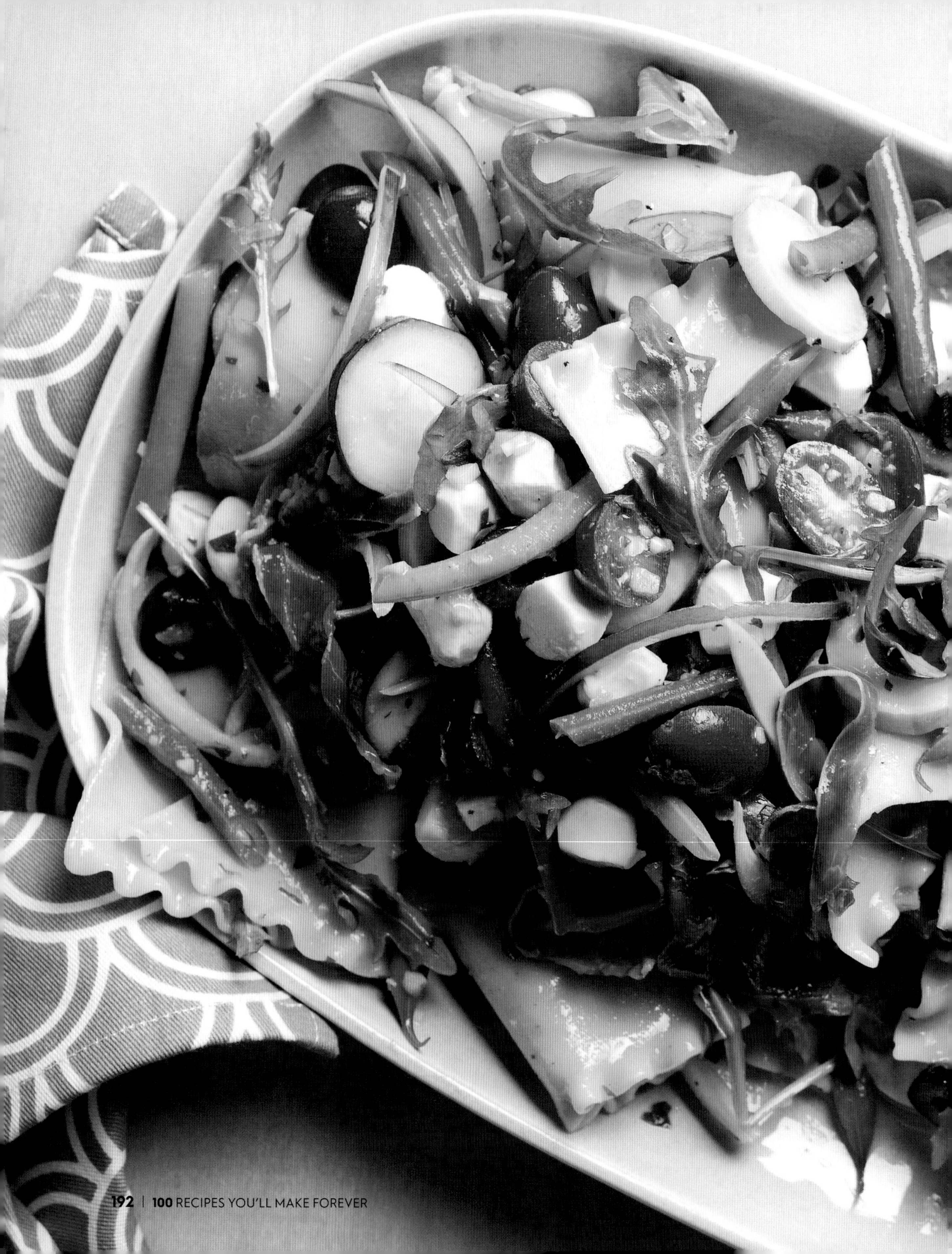

# SIDE DISHES
# & BREADS

# 064   MASHED POTATOES

TASTING COMMENTS: *To get the fluffiest mashed potatoes, we let the potatoes dry in the pan for 2 minutes before mashing to remove excess moisture. Be careful not to overmash or you might get sticky rather than fluffy potatoes.—CW*

**PREP** 30 MINUTES   **COOK** 20 MINUTES

- 3 lb. russet, Yukon gold, or red potatoes, peeled* and cut into 2-inch pieces
- ¼ cup butter
- ½ to ¾ cup milk, heavy cream, or half-and-half
- 1 tsp. salt
- ½ tsp. black pepper
- Butter, melted (optional)
- Snipped fresh chives (optional)

*Start the potatoes in cold water. They will cook more evenly. (If you dump them into boiling water, the outsides will cook faster than the insides.)*

**1.** In a 4- to 5-qt. Dutch oven cook potatoes, covered, in enough lightly salted boiling water to cover 20 to 25 minutes or until tender; drain. Return the hot, drained potatoes to the hot Dutch oven. Add the ¼ cup butter. Let stand, uncovered, 2 to 3 minutes. Meanwhile, in a small saucepan heat the milk over low heat until very warm.

**2.** Mash potatoes with a potato masher or beat on low just until light and fluffy.* (You can also use a ricer; see page 196.)** Stir in the warm milk, salt, and pepper. Gradually stir in additional milk to reach desired consistency. If desired, serve with additional butter and chives.

**\*NOTE** If you want to leave the peel on the potatoes, use a potato masher rather than a mixer to mash the potatoes.

**\*\*NOTE** If using a ricer, stir in melted butter after pressing through ricer.

**MAKE-AHEAD DIRECTIONS**
Prepare as directed. Transfer to a bowl; cool slightly. Cover tightly; chill up to 48 hours. Place mashed potatoes in a greased 4- to 5-qt. slow cooker. Cover and cook on low 3½ to 4 hours or until heated through. Stir before serving. Or place cooled mashed potatoes in a greased 2-qt. rectangular baking dish. Cover tightly and chill up to 48 hours. To serve, preheat oven to 350°F. Bake, covered, 45 minutes. Uncover and bake 10 to 15 minutes more or until heated through.

PER SERVING *118 cal., 5 g fat (3 g sat. fat), 13 mg chol., 296 mg sodium, 17 g carb., 2 g fiber, 2 g sugars, 2 g pro.*

**YUKON GOLD** *These waxy-texture potatoes with golden-yellow skin and flesh are great mashers. They have a rich, almost sweet flavor, and they mash to a creamy consistency. The skins are thin, so peeling is optional.*

**RUSSET** *These potatoes contain more starch than the other two, so they create fluffier potatoes. The skin is thick—peeling is recommended.*

**RED** *These fine-texture, white-flesh potatoes possess a mild flavor and creamy waxiness; peeling is optional.*

## TESTING NOTES

1. Make sure there is enough cold water covering the potatoes so they have room for good boiling. An inch or 2 inches above the potatoes is good. When the water boils, cover the pan and reduce the heat so the water continues to simmer without bubbling over.

↓

2. After draining the potatoes, it's important to return them to the hot pan and let stand a couple minutes so the residual heat dries them out. Reducing this extra moisture creates lighter, fluffier potatoes.

↑

3. Although it would be easy to pick up the jug and pour cold milk into the potatoes, it's worth the effort to heat it up. Hot milk keeps the potatoes hot until they get to the table. Some people like their potatoes fluffy and soft; others prefer them heavy and almost stiff. The amount of milk you add and how much you beat the potatoes determine the end product. Start by adding the least amount of milk in the range. Add additional milk gradually just until the potatoes reach your desired creaminess.

↑

4. A ricer is a specialty tool made just for mashing potatoes. It produces very smooth, light, extra-fluffy potatoes. Press cooked, peeled potatoes through the ricer into a bowl. To maintain their lightness, be gentle when stirring additional ingredients into riced potatoes.

↑

5. A hand masher is the simplest tool for mashing potatoes, and you can mash them directly in the pan. It produces a coarse-texture mashed potato with a homemade appearance. Mashers with the grid plate (versus the traditional wavy wire) produce an even texture.

↑

6. A hand mixer requires less muscle than a masher. It produces fluffier potatoes and minimizes lumps, but you have to be careful. Beat just until fluffy or creamy. Overbeating will break the cell walls of the starch and give your potatoes a sticky, gluelike texture.

*Yukon gold*

*Russet*

*Red*

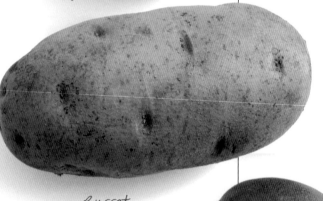

**FONTINA AND BASIL MASHED POTATOES**
Prepare as directed, except stir 6 oz. Fontina cheese, shredded (1½ cups), and ⅓ cup snipped fresh basil into mashed potatoes.

**TRUFFLE MASHED POTATOES** Prepare as directed, except cook 5 cloves garlic, halved, with the potatoes. Stir 1 Tbsp. truffle oil into mashed potatoes. Top with 1 to 2 oz. shaved Parmigiano Reggiano cheese and freshly ground black pepper.

**BACON AND LEEK MASHED POTATOES** Prepare as directed, except use the minimum amount of milk. Beat ½ cup sour cream in with the milk. In an extra-large skillet cook 8 slices applewood-smoked bacon over medium-high heat until crisp. Transfer bacon to paper towels to drain. Drain drippings from skillet, leaving 1 Tbsp. drippings in skillet. Add ¾ cup sliced leeks (white part only) to skillet. Cook over medium heat 4 minutes or until leeks are tender, stirring occasionally. Crumble bacon. Fold bacon and leeks into mashed potatoes.

# 065   HERBED LEEK GRATIN

TASTING COMMENTS: *Leek gratin is such a treat—rich, creamy, and crunchy all at the same time. To make sure this dish came out tender, I cut my leeks very thinly crosswise.—CC.*

**PREP** 20 MINUTES   **BAKE** 50 MINUTES AT 375°F   **STAND** 10 MINUTES

3 lb. slender leeks
½ cup heavy cream
2 Tbsp. chicken broth
2 Tbsp. snipped fresh marjoram or 1½ tsp. dried marjoram, crushed
½ tsp. salt
¼ to ½ tsp. freshly ground black pepper
1½ cups soft French or Italian bread crumbs
3 Tbsp. grated Parmesan cheese
3 Tbsp. butter, melted
Fresh marjoram leaves (optional)

*Fresh marjoram has pale, velvety green leaves with a delicate flavor that is similar to but sweeter and milder than oregano. Good substitutes include basil, thyme, and savory.*

**1.** Preheat oven to 375°F. Trim roots and wilted leaves from leeks. Cut leek pieces in half lengthwise; cut crosswise into ¼-inch-thick strips. Clean in cold water. Drain and dry leeks. Place in a 1½-qt. gratin dish or casserole.

**2.** In a small bowl combine cream and broth; pour over leeks in dish. Sprinkle with half the 2 Tbsp. fresh marjoram or 1½ tsp. dried marjoram, the salt, and pepper. Cover tightly with foil. Bake 20 minutes.

**3.** Meanwhile, in a small bowl stir together bread crumbs, Parmesan cheese, and remaining fresh or dried marjoram. Drizzle with melted butter; toss to coat. Sprinkle the partially baked leeks with bread crumb mixture. Bake, uncovered, 30 minutes more or until leeks are tender and crumbs are golden brown. Let stand 10 minutes before serving. If desired, top with fresh marjoram leaves.

PER SERVING *307 cal., 15 g fat (9 g sat. fat), 45 mg chol., 416 mg sodium, 40 g carb., 5 g fiber, 10 g sugars, 6 g pro.*

**ZUCCHINI AND SUMMER SQUASH GRATIN** Prepare Herbed Leek Gratin as directed, except omit leeks and chicken broth. Pat dry 3 cups ¼-inch-thick slices zucchini (about 1 lb.) and 3 cups ¼-inch-thick slices yellow summer squash (about 1 lb.). Alternately layer the slices in the gratin dish. Bake, covered, 10 minutes. Sprinkle with crumb mixture. Continue as directed.

*Slender leeks tend to be sweeter than large ones. Use just the white and light green parts and discard the tough dark green tops.*

## TESTING NOTES

1. Cut a thin slice from the root end of the leek. Remove any wilted outer leaves and cut off the dark green end of the remaining leek.

2. Slice the leeks in half lengthwise. Cut the halved leeks crosswise into very thin (about ¼-inch) strips.

3. Fill a large bowl with cold water; add sliced leeks. Swish them with your hands to separate the layers and remove any dirt and sand.

4. To dry leeks quickly, use a salad spinner. Or transfer leeks to a colander and pat dry with paper towels.

# 066   BAKED BEANS WITH BACON

TASTING COMMENTS:   *The sauce for these beans is thick and richly flavored. We know some people like their beans saucier. If you're one of them, stir in reserved cooking water until you achieve the consistency you like. —JH*

**PREP** 30 MINUTES   **STAND** 1 HOUR   **COOK** 1 HOUR   **BAKE** 1 HOUR 30 MINUTES AT 300°F

*Dry mustard has a stronger flavor than prepared mustard. If you need to swap, use 4½ tsp. yellow mustard.*

- 1 lb. dried navy beans or Great Northern beans (2⅓ cups)
- 16 cups water
- 4 oz. bacon or pancetta, chopped
- 1 cup chopped onion
- ¼ cup packed brown sugar
- ⅓ cup molasses or pure maple syrup
- ¼ cup Worcestershire sauce
- 1½ tsp. dry mustard
- ½ tsp. salt
- ¼ tsp. black pepper
- 4 oz. bacon or pancetta, chopped, crisp-cooked, drained, and crumbled (optional)

1. Rinse beans. In a 4- to 5-qt. oven-going Dutch oven combine beans and 8 cups of the water. Bring to boiling; reduce heat. Simmer, uncovered, 2 minutes. Remove from heat. Cover and let stand 1 hour. (Or place beans in water in Dutch oven. Cover and let soak in a cool place overnight.) Drain and rinse beans.

2. Return beans to Dutch oven. Stir in the remaining 8 cups fresh water. Bring to boiling; reduce heat. Cover and simmer 60 to 90 minutes or until beans are tender, stirring occasionally. Drain beans, reserving water.

3. Preheat oven to 300°F. In the same Dutch oven cook 4 oz. bacon and the onion over medium heat until bacon is slightly crisp and onion is tender, stirring occasionally. Add brown sugar; cook and stir until sugar is dissolved. Stir in the next five ingredients (through pepper). Stir in drained beans and 1¼ cups of the reserved water.

4. Bake, covered, 60 minutes. Uncover and bake 30 to 45 minutes more or until desired consistency, stirring occasionally. Beans will thicken slightly as they cool. If necessary, stir in additional reserved water. If desired, sprinkle with additional cooked bacon.

PER SERVING *267 cal., 6 g fat (2 g sat. fat), 8 mg chol., 282 mg sodium, 43 g carb., 11 g fiber, 0 g sugars, 12 g pro.*

**SWEET & SASSY** *Molasses and brown sugar are traditionally used to sweeten a pot of baked beans. Although they offer a sweet, almost smoky flavor, they are acidic ingredients. The calcium in each helps keep the beans firm, so while you are baking the beans to develop the flavor, they are not turning to mush. We added maple syrup as an option to molasses. It has less calcium, so watch more carefully and check the texture while baking.*

## TESTING NOTES

↑
1. Beans can be dirty. Sort through the package of beans and remove any twigs, pebbles, and broken or shriveled beans. Rinse thoroughly in a colander.

↑
2. Soaking dried beans helps the beans soften slightly, allowing them to cook quicker. Water starts to seep into the bean where it was attached to the plant. Soak beans overnight or use the quick-soak method in the recipe.

3. Beans will plump slightly after soaking. After you drain the beans, toss the soaking liquid. There's really no reason to keep it. (And your GI tract will thank you!)

4. Because the beans are pretty tender when the sauce ingredients are added, the first hour in the oven allows them to absorb that great molasses flavor

↑
5. How much time your beans spend in the oven for the last cooking time is up to you. Baking them with the lid off allows the excess liquid to evaporate and the sauce to thicken. When the beans are as saucy or as thick as you like, they're ready to serve!

*If bacon seems too ho-hum for you and pancetta isn't your thing, you can stir in 1 to 1½ cups of any variety of cooked smoked meats when you stir in the molasses and remaining ingredients.*

Ham

Turkey links

Smoked pork hocks

Kielbasa

# 067   FRIED RICE

**TASTING COMMENTS:** *Be sure your rice is cold! Warm or even room-temperature rice will clump when stir-fried. The grains of cold rice separate to blend easily with the other ingredients.—LB*

**START TO FINISH** 30 MINUTES

*To get the best flavor, use toasted sesame oil rather than the light-color, untoasted sesame oil. If you rarely use it, keep it in the fridge so it doesn't become rancid.*

2  eggs
1  tsp. soy sauce
1  tsp. toasted sesame oil or vegetable oil
1  clove garlic, minced
1  Tbsp. vegetable oil
½  cup thinly bias-sliced celery
¾  cup sliced fresh mushrooms
2  cups chilled cooked long grain white rice or one 8.5-oz. pouch cooked white rice
½  cup julienned carrots or packaged fresh julienned carrots
½  cup frozen peas
2  Tbsp. soy sauce
¼  cup sliced green onions

**1.** In a small bowl lightly beat eggs and the 1 tsp. soy sauce.

**2.** In a wok or large skillet heat sesame oil over medium heat. Add garlic and cook 30 seconds. Add egg mixture and cook, without stirring, until set. Turn egg and cook until just set. Turn egg out onto a cutting board, roll it up, and cut into thin slices.

**3.** Pour vegetable oil into the wok (add more oil as necessary during cooking). Heat over medium-high heat. Cook and stir celery in hot oil 1 minute. Add mushrooms; stir-fry 1 to 2 minutes or until vegetables are crisp-tender.

**4.** Add rice, carrots, peas, and the 2 Tbsp. and soy sauce to wok. Cook and stir 4 to 6 minutes or until heated through. Add sliced eggs and green onions; cook and stir 1 minute or until heated through.

PER SERVING *140 cal., 5 g fat (1 g sat. fat), 71 mg chol., 409 mg sodium, 18 g carb., 2 g fiber, 0 g sugars, 6 g pro.*

**SHRIMP FRIED RICE** Add 12 oz. peeled and deveined cooked shrimp when adding the rice. Makes 4 main-dish servings.

**TOFU FRIED RICE** Add 8 oz. extra-firm tofu, cut into ¾-inch cubes, when adding the rice. Makes 4 main-dish servings.

**PORK FRIED RICE** Add 12 oz. chopped cooked pork when adding the rice. Makes 4 main-dish servings.

**CHICKEN FRIED RICE** Add 12 oz. chopped cooked chicken when adding the rice. Makes 4 main-dish servings.

**WOK OR NOT** *The shape of a wok is designed to spread heat evenly while cooking over high heat for short periods of time. Round- and flat-bottom woks are available in aluminum, stainless steel, and carbon steel. If you don't own a wok, you can use a large skillet.*

## TESTING NOTES

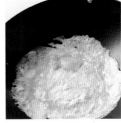

↑

1. Most restaurant-quality fried rice includes perfectly done eggs. Cook the eggs over medium-high heat, tilting the pan to spread the eggs in an even layer. Cook, without stirring, for 30 seconds until set.

4. Adding cold rice gives you the best-texture fried rice. Once rice is cooked and chilled, the long starch chains in rice (amylose) link tightly together and harden. You may have to break up larger clumps of rice to stir in the remaining ingredients.

5. After adding the veggies and the eggs, you really are just heating through. Don't get carried away and cook for longer than specified in the recipe.

↓

↑

2. Use a spatula to turn the egg and cook until just set. The egg will look dry and slightly shiny.

↑

3. Turn the egg out onto a cutting board, roll it up, and cut it into thin slices.

# 068   SUMMER PASTA SALAD

**TASTING COMMENTS:**   *One of our editors cooked her pasta ahead and tossed it with olive oil, lemon juice, salt, and garlic so it soaked up this mixture as it stood in refrigerator. When you toss it with the remaining ingredients, it's not dry and flavorless but yummy!—SM*

**PREP** 40 MINUTES   **CHILL** 12 HOURS

- 8 oz. dried lasagna noodles, broken into 3-inch pieces, or 3 cups dried bow tie or penne pasta
- 2 Tbsp. olive oil
- 1 Tbsp. lemon juice
- 1 tsp. salt
- 1 clove garlic, minced
- 1½ cups fresh green beans, trimmed
- 8 oz. cubed fresh mozzarella cheese or bite-size fresh mozzarella balls
- 1½ cups thinly sliced yellow summer squash and/or zucchini
- 1 cup chopped tomato, halved cherry tomatoes, and/or halved grape tomatoes
- 2 oz. thinly sliced prosciutto, torn into bite-size pieces, or salami, halved and sliced (optional)
- 1 cup arugula or fresh baby spinach
- ½ cup thinly sliced, halved red onion or sliced green onions
- ½ cup pitted ripe olives, halved pitted Kalamata olives, or sliced pimiento-stuffed green olives (optional)
- 2 to 3 Tbsp. slivered fresh basil
- 1 recipe Red Wine Vinaigrette

**1.** Cook pasta according to package directions; drain. Rinse with cold water; drain well. In an extra-large bowl whisk together the next four ingredients (through garlic). Add pasta; toss to coat. Cover; chill 8 to 24 hours.

**2.** In a large saucepan cook green beans in a large amount of boiling water 5 minutes; drain. Let cool. Add green beans and the next eight ingredients (through basil) to pasta. Add Red Wine Vinaigrette. Toss to coat. Cover; chill 4 to 24 hours.

**RED WINE VINAIGRETTE** In a screw-top jar combine 1 cup olive oil; ½ cup red wine vinegar, white wine vinegar, rice vinegar, or cider vinegar; ¼ cup shallots, finely chopped; 2 Tbsp. snipped fresh oregano, thyme, or basil, or 1 tsp. dried oregano, thyme, or basil, crushed; 1 Tbsp. Dijon-style mustard or ½ tsp. dry mustard; 2 tsp. sugar; 2 cloves garlic, minced; ¼ tsp. salt; and ¼ tsp. black pepper. Cover; shake well.

PER SERVING *245 cal., 19 g fat (4 g sat. fat), 10 mg chol., 290 mg sodium, 14 g carb., 1 g fiber, 2 g sugars, 5 g pro.*

**WINTER PASTA SALAD** Prepare Summer Pasta Salad as directed, except substitute 1½ cups fresh broccoli florets and 1½ cups cauliflower florets for the green beans and summer squash. Substitute Monterey Jack cheese for the mozzarella cheese. Substitute snipped fresh oregano or dill for the basil. Add ½ cup bottled roasted red sweet peppers, chopped, and ¼ cup oil-pack dried tomatoes, drained and chopped. Use the green olive option.

## TESTING NOTES

A bath of olive oil and lemon juice keeps pasta moist, preventing it from soaking up all the vinaigrette (which would dry out the rest of the salad).

SUMMER PASTA SALAD

WINTER PASTA SALAD

# 069   CLASSIC POTATO SALAD

TASTING COMMENTS:   *we love that with a few simple tweaks, this salad is transformed into four different flavor profiles (see pages 208-209). —SB*

**PREP** 40 MINUTES   **CHILL** 6 HOURS

- 2 lb. red and/or yellow new potatoes, quartered
- ¼ tsp. salt
- 1¼ cups mayonnaise or salad dressing
- 1 Tbsp. yellow mustard
- ½ tsp. salt
- ¼ tsp. black pepper
- 1 cup thinly sliced celery
- ⅓ cup chopped onion
- ½ cup chopped sweet or dill pickles or sweet or dill pickle relish
- 6 hard-cooked eggs, coarsely chopped
- Lettuce leaves (optional)
- Hard-cooked eggs, sliced (optional)
- Paprika (optional)

**1.** In a large saucepan combine potatoes, the ¼ tsp. salt, and enough water to cover. Bring to boiling; reduce heat. Simmer, covered, 15 minutes or just until potatoes are tender. Drain well; cool slightly.

**2.** Meanwhile, for dressing, in a large bowl stir together the next four ingredients (through pepper). Stir in celery, onion, and pickles. Fold in potatoes and chopped eggs. Cover and chill 6 to 24 hours.

**3.** If desired, line a salad bowl with lettuce leaves. Transfer the potato salad to the bowl. If desired, top with sliced eggs and/or sprinkle with paprika.

PER SERVING *252 cal., 20 g fat (3 g sat. fat), 102 mg chol., 360 mg sodium, 15 g carb., 2 g fiber, 3 g sugars, 5 g pro.*

*waxy potato varieties—reds such as Norland or Red La Soda; fingerlings such as La Ratte or French fingerling; and yellows such as Yukon gold—have a lower starch content and stay firm even after boiling, making them perfect for potato salad. They hold their shape but have a tender texture after cooking.*

## TESTING NOTES

1. Boil potatoes, skins on, about 15 minutes. Peeling the potatoes before cooking allows the starchy interior to absorb a lot of the liquid during boiling, resulting in a soggy, waterlogged salad.

2. Gently fold together ingredients until lightly coated. Folding together— as opposed to stirring—will keep the potato and egg pieces intact.

**SOUR CREAM AND DILL POTATO SALAD**  Prepare Classic Potato Salad as directed, except reduce mayonnaise to ¾ cup, use Dijon-style mustard instead of yellow mustard, and omit pickles. Stir ½ cup sour cream and 1 Tbsp. snipped fresh dill into dressing. If desired, top with fresh dill sprigs.

**TEX-MEX POTATO SALAD**  Prepare Classic Potato Salad as directed, except reduce mayonnaise to ¾ cup and omit yellow mustard, black pepper, and pickles. Stir ¾ cup bottled ranch salad dressing and 1 canned chipotle chile pepper in adobo sauce, finely chopped (tip, page 18), into dressing. Stir 1 cup rinsed and drained canned black beans and 1 cup frozen corn into salad with the potatoes. Just before serving, top salad with tortilla chips.

**HERB-ROASTED GARLIC POTATO SALAD** Prepare Classic Potato Salad as directed, except omit pickles and use coarse ground mustard instead of yellow mustard. Preheat oven to 400°F. Cut off the top ½ inch of a garlic bulb to expose ends of individual cloves. Leaving garlic bulb whole, remove any loose papery outer layers. Place garlic bulb in a custard cup. Drizzle with 1 tsp. olive oil. Roast, covered, 25 minutes or until garlic feels soft when squeezed; cool. Squeeze cloves from bulb into a bowl, mash with a fork, and stir into dressing. Stir 1 Tbsp. snipped fresh chives, parsley, or tarragon into the dressing. If desired, top salad with additional fresh herbs.

**BLT POTATO SALAD** Prepare Classic Potato Salad as directed, except use ½ cup sliced green onions instead of the ⅓ cup chopped onion. In a large skillet cook 6 slices bacon over medium heat until crisp. Remove bacon and drain on paper towels, reserving 1 Tbsp. drippings in skillet. Crumble bacon; set aside. Add 1 clove garlic, minced, to the reserved drippings; cook and stir 30 seconds. Stir garlic mixture into dressing. Stir crumbled bacon and 1 cup tomato pieces into salad with the potatoes. Serve in a lettuce-lined bowl or serve over shredded romaine lettuce.

# 070  CAESAR SALAD

TASTING COMMENTS: *With garlic, anchovies, and Dijon-style mustard, the dressing for this salad could easily be too sharp. We added just a tiny bit of sugar—½ tsp.—to soften and smooth out the flavor.—KB*

**PREP** 30 MINUTES  **BAKE** 20 MINUTES AT 300°F

3 cloves garlic
3 anchovy fillets
2 Tbsp. lemon juice
¼ cup olive oil
1 tsp. Dijon-style mustard
1 hard-cooked egg yolk
½ tsp. sugar
1 clove garlic, halved
10 cups torn romaine
¼ cup grated Parmesan cheese or ½ cup shaved Parmesan cheese
1 recipe Parmesan Croutons or 2 cups purchased garlic Parmesan croutons
Freshly ground black pepper
Grated Parmesan cheese (optional)
1 lemon, halved (optional)

*Don't skip the anchovies! They give the classic Caesar dressing its characteristic flavor. Once opened, anchovies can be stored in the refrigerator at least 2 months if covered with oil and sealed.*

**1.** For dressing, in a blender combine the 3 garlic cloves, anchovies, and lemon juice. Cover and blend until nearly smooth. Add the next four ingredients (through sugar). Cover and blend until smooth. Use immediately or cover and chill up to 24 hours.

**2.** Rub the inside of a wooden salad bowl with the cut edges of the halved garlic clove; discard halves. Add romaine to bowl. Drizzle dressing over salad; toss to coat. Sprinkle the ¼ cup grated or ½ cup shaved Parmesan cheese; toss gently. Top with Parmesan Croutons. Sprinkle with pepper. If desired, sprinkle with additional Parmesan cheese and serve with lemon halves.

**PARMESAN CROUTONS** Preheat oven to 300°F. Cut four ¾-inch-thick slices Italian bread or French bread into 1-inch pieces (about 3½ cups). In a small saucepan melt ¼ cup butter over medium heat. Transfer to a large bowl. Stir in 3 Tbsp. grated Parmesan cheese and 2 cloves garlic, minced. Add bread pieces; stir to coat. Spread bread pieces in a single layer in a shallow baking pan. Bake 20 minutes or until bread pieces are crisp and golden brown, stirring once. Cool completely. Store in an airtight container at room temperature up to 24 hours.

PER SERVING *261 cal., 20 g fat (8 g sat. fat), 62 mg chol., 362 mg sodium, 15 g carb., 2 g fiber, 2 g sugars, 6 g pro.*

**CHICKEN CAESAR SALAD** Prepare Caesar Salad as directed; add 2 cups chopped cooked chicken with the romaine. Makes 6 main-dish servings.

**SALMON CAESAR SALAD** Prepare Caesar Salad as directed; top each serving with one 4- to 6-oz. baked or grilled salmon fillet. Makes 6 main-dish servings.

*Grill chicken breasts over medium heat 12 to 15 minutes.*

*Grill salmon fillets 4 to 6 minutes per ½-inch thickness until flaky.*

## TESTING NOTES

1. Rinse romaine leaves and roll in kitchen towels to dry. Store leaves wrapped in the towel in the refrigerator until you assemble the salad. Or use a salad spinner to dry the leaves. Chill the leaves 30 minutes if you have time. Drying and chilling will crisp the leaves.

↓

2. If you like, you can remove the woody rib from the romaine by tearing away the outer leaves from the rib. If you like extra crunch, leave the rib and tear the whole leaf into pieces.

4. In traditional Caesar dressings, raw or coddled (partially cooked) egg serves as an emulsifier. Combining liquids that normally don't mix—here, olive oil and the water-base lemon juice mixture—requires an emulsifier to coat the molecules and allow them to combine. For our version, using a hard-cooked egg yolk avoids the risk of salmonella while preserving the taste and texture of a traditional Caesar. Don't worry about breaking up the yolk—the food processor will take care of the mixing.

5. Parmesan croutons are nearly as important as the rest of the salad! Toss bread cubes with melted butter and spread on a baking sheet for toasting. Tossing ensures each crusty cube gets a buttery coat.

↓

↑

3. For the most classic presentation, rub a raw halved garlic clove around the inside of a wooden bowl. The wood will soak up some of the oil from the garlic for a subtle tang. Of course, you can use any bowl, but you may want to add extra garlic to your dressing.

# 071 FRESH HERB VINAIGRETTE

TASTING COMMENTS: *This vinaigrette recipe is incredibly versatile. Really you could use any fresh herb you like. In addition to oregano, thyme, and basil, we like chives, parsley, and dill.—CW*

**START TO FINISH** 10 MINUTES

- 1 cup olive oil
- ⅓ cup red wine vinegar, white wine vinegar, rice vinegar, or cider vinegar
- ¼ cup finely chopped shallots
- 2 Tbsp. snipped fresh oregano, thyme, or basil, or 1 tsp. dried oregano, thyme, or basil, crushed
- 1 Tbsp. Dijon-style mustard or ½ tsp. dry mustard
- 2 to 3 tsp. sugar
- 2 cloves garlic, minced
- ¼ tsp. salt
- ¼ tsp. black pepper

**1.** In a screw-top jar combine all ingredients. Cover tightly and shake well. Serve immediately.

**TO STORE** If using fresh herbs, cover and store vinaigrette in the refrigerator up to 3 days. If using dried herbs, cover and store in the refrigerator up to 1 week. Olive oil will solidify when chilled, so let vinaigrette stand at room temperature 1 hour before using. Stir or shake well.

PER SERVING *72 cal., 8 g fat (1 g sat. fat), 0 mg chol., 34 mg sodium, 1 g carb., 0 g fiber, 0 g sugars, 0 g pro.*

**BALSAMIC VINAIGRETTE**
Prepare Fresh Herb Vinaigrette as directed, except use regular or white balsamic vinegar.

**RATIO IS KEY** *A classic vinaigrette is made from 3 parts oil to 1 part vinegar. This works if you like a mild dressing. But if your salad demands a stronger vinegar flavor, then 2 parts oil to 1 part vinegar may be better. In Summer Pasta Salad (page 204), we used a 2:1 ratio so the flavor of the vinegar is powerful enough to overcome the meat, cheese, and veggie flavors in the salad. Once you know the basic components of the dressing, you can change the ingredients based on what you like.*

*Cutting greens with a knife may cause them to oxidize and brown at the edges if you store them for any length of time. Tearing greens is usually preferred, but if you are preparing to serve them quickly, either method works fine. You could also use a plastic lettuce knife.*

*Washing and drying greens properly is key to a crisp, well-dressed salad. Dry greens allow dressing to cling to the leaves. Wet greens dilute the flavor of your dressing. Wash the leaves thoroughly in cool water. Tear the greens and dry in a spinner.*

**FRESH FLAVOR** Snip a combination of fresh herbs or use what you have on hand. This choice is entirely yours! If you don't have fresh herbs, use dried at one-third of the amount of fresh. Rule of thumb: 1 Tbsp. fresh = 1 tsp. dried.

**THE HEAVY LIFTER** Oil plays a big role in a vinaigrette, working to coat the greens with flavor. Any light, neutral oil will work. Olive oil is often the first choice, but a light safflower oil, canola oil, or vegetable oil is OK, too. If you want to try something new, substitute up to half of the oil (½ cup) with a nut oil such as hazelnut, walnut, or macadamia.

**OH, SWEETNESS** Honey, granulated sugar, or brown sugar will do. A small amount of sweetener helps to balance the acid in the dressing.

**A LITTLE TANGINESS** Every dressing cries out for that edgy, acidic bite. Although red or white wine vinegar is most commonly used, experiment with balsamic, rice, or cider vinegar, too.

**ESSENTIAL ONION** Shallots are a member of the onion family. Smaller than regular onions and shaped like garlic, shallots impart a mild onion flavor. You can trade these for chopped sweet onion or sliced green onions if you like.

**MUSTARD IS THE SECRET** This ingredient makes everyone get along, bind together, and hold the emulsion. If Dijon isn't your first choice, dry mustard or a whole-grain variety works, too.

**THE EXTRAS** The best part of do-it-yourself dressing is the little extras you can toss in. Try 1 to 2 Tbsp. of the following: dried tomatoes, grated fresh ginger, Parmesan cheese, crumbled feta or blue cheese, and/or chopped crisp-cooked bacon.

# 072 ROASTED BEET SALAD WITH SHREDDED GREENS, GOLDEN RAISINS, AND PINE NUTS

**TASTING COMMENTS:** *One of the marks of a really good recipe is a balance of flavors. When we tasted this, we all loved that it had sweetness from the beets and raisins, pleasant bitterness from the greens, tanginess from the vinegar, and a little saltiness from the cheese.—CC*

*Ricotta salata is simply a salted, aged version of the ricotta we know and love. It is firmer than regular ricotta and crumbles easily, like feta cheese.*

*To toast pine nuts, place them in a small skillet over low to medium heat, stirring constantly, for 4 to 5 minutes until golden.*

**PREP** 25 MINUTES    **ROAST** 55 MINUTES AT 450°F

- 2 lb. beets with leafy tops
- 2 sprigs fresh rosemary
- 3 Tbsp. olive oil
- ¾ cup balsamic vinegar
- Salt
- Black pepper
- 1 cup crumbled ricotta salata* or feta cheese (4 oz.)
- ⅓ cup golden raisins
- 2 Tbsp. pine nuts, toasted

**1.** Preheat oven to 450°F. Cut tops from beets; set aside. Place beets and rosemary on a large piece of heavy foil; drizzle with 1 Tbsp. of the oil. Bring up two opposite edges of foil; seal with a double fold. Fold in remaining edges to completely enclose, leaving space for steam to build. Roast 55 minutes or until tender. Carefully open packet to release steam. Set aside until cool enough to handle. Peel skins from beets and cut into wedges. Discard rosemary.

**2.** For balsamic reduction, pour balsamic vinegar into a small saucepan. Bring to boiling; reduce heat. Simmer 15 minutes or until reduced to ¼ cup. Cool. (Reduction will thicken as it cools.)

**3.** Meanwhile, remove stems from beet tops; discard stems. Cut tops into fine shreds. In a large bowl gently toss together roasted beets and beet tops with remaining 2 Tbsp. oil until greens are slightly wilted. Season to taste with salt and pepper.

**4.** Arrange salad on a platter and sprinkle with remaining ingredients. Drizzle with balsamic vinegar reduction.

**\*TIP** Look in large supermarkets or specialty cheese shops for ricotta salata.

PER SERVING *343 cal., 19 g fat (5 g sat. fat), 21 mg chol., 602 mg sodium, 36 g carb., 5 g fiber, 26 g sugars, 10 g pro.*

**BALSAMIC VINEGAR**
Balsamic vinegar is made when white grape pressings are boiled down to a dark syrup, then aged. The vinegars aged the longest under traditional restrictions are most expensive.

**BALSAMIC REDUCTION**
Reducing balsamic vinegar creates a more intensely flavored, almost syruplike consistency. Drizzle it over roasted meat or poultry, fresh berries, poached pears, and ice cream.

## TESTING NOTES

1. Because this salad uses the whole beet from root to stem, it's important to look for firm, brightly colored beets that are about 2 inches in diameter. The greens should be fresh without signs of wilting, and the taproot should still be attached to the beet.

↓

↑

2. Place the beets in heavy foil with rosemary and olive oil. Fold opposite edges together and seal with a double fold. Fold in the remaining edges to seal completely, but leave space for steam. This allows the beets to cook through completely and softens the skins for easy peeling.

↑

3. To remove the stems from the beet greens, hold the end of each stem with one hand and pull the leaf, from the bottom end of the stem, upward toward the top. It will slip right off.

4. Slicing the greens for the salad is much easier if you stack the leaves and roll them into a tube shape. Slice the greens, working all the way to the end of the rolled leaves. If you don't love beet greens, skip them and serve the roasted beets with another sturdy green, such as kale or a mesclun mix.

↓

Active dry yeast feeds on sugar in dough to make carbon dioxide. It works slowly and develops flavor in dough as the bread rises. Store any opened yeast in the refrigerator and use before the expiration date.

Salt adds flavor to bread and creates a stronger dough, but too much can inhibit yeast from doing its job.

MAKES: *12 servings* TESTED BY: *Juli H.*

# 073 ARTISAN BREAD

**TASTING COMMENTS:** *Most artisan-style breads require kneading to develop the gluten strands that give them their characteristic tuggy texture. We discovered that a long fermentation time—up to 24 hours—has the same effect. No kneading required!—JH*

**PREP** 25 MINUTES  **CHILL** 4 HOURS  **STAND** 30 MINUTES  **RISE** 1 HOUR  **BAKE** 25 MINUTES AT 400°F

¾ cup warm water (105°F to 115°F)
1 pkg. active dry yeast
½ cup milk
2 Tbsp. sugar
2 Tbsp. butter or olive oil
1½ tsp. salt
2¾ cups all-purpose flour
Nonstick cooking spray or olive oil
Cornmeal
1 egg
2 tsp. water

**1.** In a large bowl stir together the ¾ cup water and the yeast. Let stand 5 minutes. Meanwhile, in a small saucepan heat and stir milk, sugar, butter, and salt just until warm (120°F to 130°F) and butter, if using, almost melts. Stir milk mixture into yeast mixture until combined. Stir in flour (dough will be sticky). Place dough in a lightly greased bowl; turning to grease surface of dough. Cover and chill 4 to 24 hours.

**2.** Turn dough out onto a floured surface. Cover with greased plastic wrap. Let stand 30 minutes.

**3.** Lightly grease a baking sheet; sprinkle with cornmeal. Gently shape dough into a 6-inch round loaf. Place on the prepared baking sheet. Cover; let rise in a warm place until nearly double in size (about 1 hour).

**4.** Preheat oven to 400°F. In a bowl whisk together egg and the 2 tsp. water; brush over loaf. Bake 25 minutes or until bread sounds hollow when lightly tapped. (An instant-read thermometer should register at least 200°F when inserted in center of loaf.) If necessary, cover loosely with foil the last 5 minutes of baking to prevent overbrowning. Immediately remove from baking sheet; cool on a wire rack.

PER SERVING *199 cal., 7 g fat (3 g sat. fat), 29 mg chol., 469 mg sodium, 27 g carb., 2 g fiber, 3 g sugars, 7 g pro.*

**ARTISAN ROLLS** Prepare as directed, except shape dough into an 8-inch square. Cut into sixteen 2-inch squares, flouring the dough and knife as necessary. Place about 1 inch apart on a baking sheet. Bake about 15 minutes.

**STIR-INS** In Step 1, add any of these stir-ins in when you add the milk mixture to the yeast mixture.

**SMOKED GOUDA-BACON** ½ cup ground toasted almonds, ½ cup shredded smoked Gouda cheese (2 oz.), ¼ cup crisp-cooked and crumbled bacon, ¼ cup stone-ground mustard, and 2 tsp. toasted caraway seed

**RHUBARB-RAISIN** 1 cup chopped fresh or frozen rhubarb, ½ cup golden raisins, 2 Tbsp. finely chopped shallot (1 medium), 2 tsp. grated fresh ginger, and ½ tsp. ground coriander

**SWEET POTATO** ½ cup cooked mashed sweet potato and ½ tsp. pumpkin spice; reduce water in Step 1 to ½ cup

**CHEESE-OLIVE** ½ cup crumbled feta cheese (2 oz.); ½ cup grated Asiago cheese (2 oz.); ¼ cup chopped pitted Kalamata olives; ¼ cup thawed and well-drained chopped spinach; and 4 cloves garlic, minced

**APRICOT-SWISS** ½ cup cooked chopped onion, ½ cup finely snipped dried apricots, ½ cup shredded Swiss cheese (2 oz.), and 1 tsp. snipped fresh sage

1. This bread relies 100 percent on your yeast, so use a reliable instant-read thermometer to check the temperature of the water. It should be between 105°F and 115°F. Just as important, keep your milk mixture below 130°F before adding it to the yeast.

2. While the dough chills, magical things are happening. The yeast is working slowly, leavening the dough and altering the protein in the flour to allow for a more open, tuggier crumb and a tangy, yeasty flavor.

3. After chilling, use a dough scraper or rubber spatula to carefully and gently transfer the dough from the bowl, trying not to disturb the spongy texture. The dough will be sticky, but add as little excess flour as possible when you handle it.

↓

↑

4. Use wet hands and a little flour to help gently shape the dough before placing it on a cornmeal-covered baking sheet.

MAKES: *8 servings*   TESTED BY: *Linda B.*

# 074   SOFT PRETZELS

TASTING COMMENTS:   *We thought these were just the cutest—they had great color and flavor. At taste panel, we dipped half of them in melted butter but discovered they were so rich and delicious they didn't need it. These were the best soft pretzels we'd ever had—they disappeared after taste panel!—LB*

*Actual pretzel salt can be hard to find outside of gourmet markets, but it's readily available to order from online retailers. Try any kind of coarse salt to sprinkle on the pretzels, such as kosher or sea salt.*

**PREP** 35 MINUTES   **STAND** 5 MINUTES   **RISE** 1 HOUR   **BAKE** 10 MINUTES AT 450°F

- ¾ cup milk
- 1½ Tbsp. sugar
- ¼ cup water
- 1 pkg. active dry yeast
- 2⅓ to 2½ cups all-purpose flour
- 2 Tbsp. butter, softened
- 1¼ tsp. fine sea salt
- 3 cups hot water
- ½ cup baking soda
- 1 egg yolk, lightly beaten
- 1 Tbsp. cold water
- Coarse salt (optional)

**1.** In a small saucepan heat and stir milk, sugar, and the ¼ cup water over low heat until warm (110°F to 115°F). Pour into the large bowl of a mixer with a dough hook. Sprinkle with yeast; let stand 5 minutes or until foamy. Add 2⅓ cups of the flour, the butter, and the 1¼ tsp. salt. Beat on low 2 to 3 minutes or until combined, scraping sides occasionally. Beat on medium-low 8 to 10 minutes or until a soft dough forms. (The dough should pull away from the sides of the bowl but still be slightly sticky. If it is too sticky, beat in the additional flour.)

**2.** Turn out dough onto a clean, dry work surface. Knead a few times by folding and pressing dough, turning dough to knead uniformly; shape dough into a ball. Place in a lightly greased bowl, turning once to grease surface of dough. Cover and let rise in a warm place until double in size (about 1 hour).

**3.** Preheat oven to 450°F. Lightly grease a large baking sheet.

**4.** Punch dough down. Turn out onto a clean surface. Divide dough into eight portions. Roll and stretch each

portion into a 30-inch-long rope. (If the dough does not want to stretch, cover and let rest 10 minutes.)

**5.** To shape each pretzel, form each rope into a U shape. Cross the ends over each other twice, then lift the ends across to the bottom of the U shape; press to seal.

**6.** In a deep bowl or pot slightly larger than each pretzel, stir together the 3 cups hot water and the baking soda. Using a slotted spoon, lower pretzels, one at a time, into the water 10 seconds. Remove pretzels and place on paper towels. Arrange pretzels 2 inches apart on the prepared baking sheet.

**7.** In a small bowl combine egg yolk and the 1 Tbsp. cold water. Brush pretzels with egg yolk mixture. If desired, sprinkle with coarse salt. Bake 10 to 12 minutes or until deep golden brown. Cool slightly on a wire rack; serve warm.

PER SERVING *191 cal., 4 g fat (2 g sat. fat), 33 mg chol., 862 mg sodium, 32 g carb., 1 g fiber, 4 g sugars, 6 g pro.*

**BAKING SODA'S BIG ROLE** *Baking soda is an alkaline ingredient (the opposite of an acid) that, when used in a wash as it is here, will create an alkaline environment on the outside of the pretzel. During baking, a chemical reaction occurs that turns the pretzels a rich mahogany color in less time so the insides of the pretzels remain soft. Some bakers prefer using lye, a stronger alkaline ingredient, but it can be corrosive to skin and requires the use of safety goggles and gloves. (We'll take the baking soda instead, thank you very much!)*

## TESTING NOTES

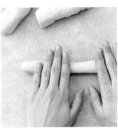

↑

**1.** Use a chef's knife to cut the dough into eight equal-size portions. (Start by cutting the dough in half, then cut each half in half. Continue halving the dough pieces until you end up with eight.) Moving your hands from one end to the other for evenness, roll each dough piece into a 30-inch rope.

↑

**2.** Holding one end of a rope in each hand, form the dough rope into a U shape. At the top of the U shape, overlap the two ends. Twist the overlapped ends once. (Work as quickly as you can to prevent dough from drying out.)

**3.** Fold the twisted ends down through the U shape and firmly press the two ends into the base of the U, leaving some overhang of the ends to create the traditional pretzel shape.

↓

↑

**4.** Here's the most important step: Use a slotted spoon to dip the uncooked pretzel into the hot water–baking soda mixture for 10 seconds. When you lift the pretzel out, let the water drain off before placing the pretzel on paper towels.

**MAKE-AHEAD DIRECTIONS** *Because of the hot water–baking soda dip, pretzels have more moisture than other baked goods and may get wrinkly during storage. Bake them long enough so the excess surface moisture evaporates, then cool completely before storing. Store at room temperature in a covered container up to 2 days or freeze up to 1 month.*

# SOUPS, STEWS & SAUCES

# 075   BONE BROTH

TASTING COMMENTS: *We wanted to see how the flavors were developing as the chicken broth bubbled away, so we tasted it at 4, 8, and 12 hours of cook time. We got great-tasting broth at 8 hours, but if you want even richer flavor, cook it for 10 to 12 hours. —CW*

## CHICKEN BROTH

**PREP** 25 MINUTES   **COOK** 8 HOURS

- 5 lb. bony chicken pieces (wings, backs, and/or necks)
- 6 stalks celery with leaves, cut up
- 4 medium carrots, unpeeled and cut up
- 2 large onions, unpeeled and cut up
- 8 sprigs fresh parsley
- 4 bay leaves
- 6 cloves garlic, unpeeled and halved
- 2 tsp. salt
- 2 tsp. dried thyme, sage, or basil, crushed
- 1 tsp. whole black peppercorns or ¼ tsp. black pepper
- 15 cups cold water
- 2 Tbsp. cider vinegar

*what's the cider vinegar for? The theory is that the extra acid pulls minerals from the bones, making the broth more nutritious.*

**1.** If using wings, cut each wing at joints into three pieces. Place chicken pieces in a 10- to 12-qt. pot; add remaining ingredients. Bring to boiling; reduce heat to low. Gently simmer, covered, 8 to 10 hours.

**2.** Remove chicken pieces from pot. Use a slotted spoon to remove as many vegetables as possible.

**3.** Strain broth into a large bowl through a colander lined with four layers of 100%-cotton cheesecloth. Discard vegetables and seasonings.

**4.** If using broth while hot, skim off fat. If storing, chill broth in a bowl 6 hours; lift off fat. Place broth in an airtight container. Cover and chill up to 3 days or freeze up to 6 months.

**SLOW COOKER DIRECTIONS**
Prepare as directed, except reduce all ingredients by half. Combine all ingredients in a 6-qt. slow cooker. Cover; cook on low 10 to 12 hours. Continue as directed in Step 2. Makes 9 cups.

PER SERVING *38 cal., 1 g fat (0 g sat. fat), 17 mg chol., 294 mg sodium, 2 g carb., 1 g fiber, 1 g sugars, 5 g pro.*

**SAVE YOUR SCRAPS** *Put your vegetable scraps to good use and save them for bone broth-making day. In addition to onions, celery, and carrots, you can save trimmings from mushrooms (such as shiitake stems), asparagus, leeks, and more. Place all your extras in resealable freezer bags and freeze up to 3 months.*

# BEEF BROTH

**PREP** 30 MINUTES  **ROAST** 45 MINUTES AT 450°F  **COOK** 8 HOURS

- 3 lb. beef soup bones (knuckle, neck, or marrow bones)
- 1 cup water
- 6 stalks celery with leaves, cut up
- 4 medium carrots, unpeeled and cut up
- 3 medium onions, unpeeled and cut up
- 2 Tbsp. dried basil or thyme, crushed
- 1 Tbsp. salt
- 20 whole black peppercorns
- 16 sprigs fresh parsley
- 4 bay leaves
- 6 cloves garlic, unpeeled and halved
- 18 cups cold water
- 2 Tbsp. cider vinegar

*Ask your butcher to cut the marrow bones into 2- to 3-inch lengths to expose more of the marrow, which infuses the broth with rich, beefy flavor.*

1. Preheat oven to 450°F. Place soup bones in a large shallow roasting pan. Roast 45 minutes or until browned, turning once.

2. Place soup bones in a 10- to 12-qt. stockpot. Pour the 1 cup water into the roasting pan and scrape up browned bits; add to stockpot. Add the remaining ingredients. Bring to boiling; reduce heat to low. Gently simmer, covered, 8 to 12 hours. Remove soup bones from broth.

3. Remove vegetables with a slotted spoon. Strain broth into a large bowl through a colander lined with four layers of 100%-cotton cheesecloth. Discard vegetables and seasonings.

4. If using the broth while hot, skim fat. If storing, chill broth in a bowl 6 hours; lift off fat. Place broth in airtight containers. Chill up to 3 days or freeze up to 6 months.

5. If desired, when bones are cool enough to handle, remove meat. Chop meat; discard bones. Place meat in airtight containers. Chill up to 3 days or freeze up to 3 months.

**SLOW COOKER DIRECTIONS**
Prepare as directed, except reduce all ingredients by half. Roast bones as directed in Step 1. Pour the 1 cup water into the roasting pan and scrape up browned bits. In a 6-qt. slow cooker combine the water and remaining ingredients. Cover and cook on low 10 to 12 hours. Remove soup bones from broth. Continue as directed in Step 3. Makes about 9 cups.

PER SERVING *36 cal., 1 g fat (0 g sat. fat), 11 mg chol., 170 mg sodium, 2 g carb., 0 g fiber, 0 g sugars, 5 g pro.*

**BONES, BONES, BONES** *The best way to get your hands on bones is to save the ones left over from roasts, steaks (think T-bone), and roasted chickens and turkeys. You can pack the bones in resealable plastic freezer bags and freeze up to 3 months. You can also buy beef bones from the butcher or at grocery stores that cut their own meat. Call ahead to see if the butcher can set aside soup bones such as marrow, knuckle, and neck bones for you.*

The color of your beef broth will be lighter than the canned variety you buy in the store. Why? Because it's all natural and free of caramel coloring.

# 076   FRESH TOMATO SOUP

**TASTING COMMENTS:** *If your fresh tomatoes are not perfectly ripe and juicy, roast them first. Roasting the tomatoes concentrates the sugars and intesifies the rich tomato flavor.—CC*

**START TO FINISH** 30 MINUTES

- 2 lb. tomatoes, cored and seeded
- 2 medium red sweet peppers, seeded and coarsely chopped (1½ cups)
- ½ of a sweet onion (such as Vidalia or Maui), chopped
- ¼ cup snipped fresh basil
- 1 cup reduced-sodium vegetable broth or chicken broth
- 2 Tbsp. heavy cream
- 1 Tbsp. honey

*Peak tomato season is typically July through September for most parts of the country. If fresh, in-season tomatoes aren't available, you can substitute canned. Any canned tomatoes will work, but opt for a higher-quality variety, such as San Marzano.*

**1.** In a blender or food processor combine half of the tomatoes, sweet peppers, onion, basil, and broth. Cover and blend or process until smooth. Transfer to a large saucepan. Repeat with the remaining tomatoes, sweet peppers, onion, basil, and broth. Cook over medium heat 5 to 6 minutes or until heated through. Stir in cream and honey. Serve warm.

**TIP** On hot summer days, serve this soup cold. Prepare as directed, except omit the cream. If desired, increase honey to 2 Tbsp. Cover and chill up to 24 hours before serving. If desired, top with cut-up cherry tomatoes, fresh basil leaves, and a drizzle of olive oil.

PER SERVING *69 cal., 2 g fat (1 g sat. fat), 7 mg chol., 105 mg sodium, 11 g carb., 3 g fiber, 8 g sugars, 2 g pro.*

**ROASTED TOMATO SOUP** Prepare Fresh Tomato Soup as directed, except line two 15×10-inch baking pans with foil. Preheat oven to 450°F. Cut tomatoes in half crosswise. Seed tomatoes; arrange halves, cut sides down, in one of the prepared pans. Cut the onion into ½-inch slices (rather than chopping it). Cut sweet peppers in half; remove stems, seeds, and membranes. Arrange onion slices and pepper halves, cut sides down, in the remaining prepared pan. Drizzle with 3 to 4 Tbsp. olive oil. Roast onions and peppers, uncovered, 20 minutes or until pepper skins are charred, turning onion slices once. Bring foil up around onions and peppers; fold edges together to enclose. Let stand 15 to 20 minutes or until cool enough to handle. Using a sharp knife, loosen edges of pepper skins; gently pull off skins in strips and discard. Preheat broiler. Broil tomatoes 4 inches from the heat 4 minutes or until skins are charred. Continue as directed in Step 1.

**TOMATO TALK** *Tomatoes come in many shapes, sizes, and colors. Small cherry and grape tomatoes are sweet and best for eating out of hand (it's too time-consuming to seed this type of tomato). Medium-size vine-ripened tomatoes are usually sweeter and more evenly ripened compared with other commercial tomatoes. Large, standard slicing varieties, such as Big Boy and beefsteak, are a good size and shape for efficient coring and seeding. Heirloom tomatoes are more flavorful and juicy than commercial varieties. Although tomatoes are available in a rainbow of colors, true red ones will give you the best color in this soup.*

## TESTING TIP

Roasting the tomatoes, peppers, and onions softens and breaks down the plant cells, allowing the water within to evaporate. This concentrates the vegetables for more intense flavor. In addition, roasting caramelizes the sugars on the surfaces of the vegetables, creating a rich and complex sweetness.

**GRILLED CHEESE CROUTONS** *Try these croutons for the perfect Fresh Tomato Soup topper. Just like preparing a grilled cheese sandwich, these little bites of melty goodness are easy to make and easier to customize. Sandwich together any type of bread and a good melting cheese. Brush the outsides of the bread with butter or oil and toast in a hot skillet or griddle until browned. Cut into bite-size croutons.*

# 077 OLD-FASHIONED CHICKEN NOODLE SOUP

TASTING COMMENTS: *This soup is chock-full of veggies, chunks of chicken, and chewy homemade noodles. We discovered that cutting up a whole chicken makes all the difference in getting the best rich, from-scratch flavor.—CW*

**PREP** 25 MINUTES   **COOK** 1½ HOURS + 10 MINUTES

- 1  3½- to 4-lb. broiler-fryer chicken, cut up, or 3 lb. meaty chicken pieces (breast halves, thighs, and/or drumsticks)
- ½  cup chopped onion (1 medium)
- 2  tsp. salt
- 1  tsp. dried thyme, sage, or basil, crushed
- ¼  tsp. black pepper
- 2  bay leaves
- 2  cloves garlic, peeled and halved
- 8  cups water
- 1  cup chopped carrots (2 medium)
- 1  cup chopped celery (2 stalks)
- 2  cups Homemade Egg Noodles (recipe, page 230) or 6 oz. dried egg noodles
- 1  Tbsp. snipped fresh thyme, sage, or basil (optional)

**1.** In a 6- to 8-qt. Dutch oven combine the first seven ingredients (through garlic). Pour the water over all in Dutch oven. Bring to boiling; reduce heat. Simmer, covered, about 1½ hours or until chicken is very tender.

**2.** Remove chicken from broth. When cool enough to handle, remove meat from bones. Discard bones and skin. Cut meat into bite-size pieces; set aside. Discard bay leaves. Skim fat from broth.

**3.** Bring broth to boiling. Stir in carrots and celery. Simmer, covered, 7 minutes. Add Homemade Egg Noodles, stirring to combine. Simmer, covered, 3 to 5 minutes more or until noodles are tender. Stir in chicken pieces and, if desired, fresh thyme; heat through.

PER SERVING *176 cal., 4 g fat (1 g sat. fat), 90 mg chol., 735 mg sodium, 12 g carb., 1 g fiber, 1 g sugars, 22 g pro.*

*Bay leaves add aromatic flavor to soups and other dishes, but they're bitter and fibrous—you don't want to eat them! Always remove before serving.*

*Fresh noodles can be delicate. Add them to the soup a handful at a time, stirring gently after each addition. Simmer dried noodles according to package directions.*

## TESTING NOTES

After removing cooked chicken pieces, use a large spoon to skim the fat (about ¼ cup total) from the surface of the broth. You can make the broth ahead of time and refrigerate several hours or overnight. Chilling congeals the fat and makes it easier to remove.

## CUTTING UP A WHOLE CHICKEN

↑

1. Place the whole chicken, breast side up, on a large, clean cutting board. Using a sharp chef's knife, make a deep incision between the two breast halves, putting pressure on the knife to cut though the breastbone.

↑

2. Flip the chicken over; place breast side down. Cut parallel on one side of the backbone, separating the chicken into two halves. You may need additional pressure as you reach the thigh area. Repeat down the other side of the backbone.

↑

3. Holding onto the end of a drumstick, use the knife to cut through the skin and muscle between the drumstick and the breast. This will expose the thigh joint. Cut firmly through that joint to separate the breast and leg. Repeat with the other breast and leg.

4. Place a leg, skin side down, on the cutting board. With your fingers, find the joint in the leg where the drumstick and thigh meet. Use the knife to cut firmly through that joint to separate the drumstick from the thigh. Repeat with the other leg.

↓

↑

5. Bend a wing away from the breast. With the knife, cut through the skin and muscle around the joint that connects the wing to the breast. Cut through that joint to separate the wing from the breast. Repeat with the other wing and breast.

# HOMEMADE EGG NOODLES

TASTING COMMENTS: *I made these noodles using both methods—by hand and in the food processor. Kneading the dough for the full 10 minutes is what really gives them their wonderfully chewy texture. The version made in the food processor doesn't require any kneading—the machine did it for me.—CW*

**PREP** 50 MINUTES **STAND** 30 MINUTES

- 2 **cups all-purpose flour**
- ½ **tsp. salt**
- 2 **egg yolks**
- 1 **egg**
- ⅓ **cup water**
- 1 **tsp. vegetable oil or olive oil**

   **All-purpose flour**

**1.** In a large bowl stir together 1¾ cups of the flour and the salt. Make a well in the center of the flour mixture. In a small bowl combine egg yolks, whole egg, the water, and the oil. Add egg mixture to flour mixture; stir until mixture forms a dough.

**2.** Sprinkle a clean kneading surface with the remaining ¼ cup flour. Turn dough out onto the floured surface. Knead until dough is smooth and elastic (10 minutes total kneading time). Cover and let the dough rest 10 minutes. Divide the dough into four equal portions.

**3.** On a lightly floured surface roll each dough portion into a 12-inch square (about ¹⁄₁₆ inch thick). Lightly dust both sides of the dough square with additional flour. Let stand, uncovered, about

20 minutes. (Or, using a pasta machine, pass each dough portion through machine according to manufacturer's directions until dough is ¹⁄₁₆ inch thick, dusting dough with flour as needed. Let stand, uncovered, 20 minutes.) Loosely roll dough square into a spiral; cut crosswise into ¼-inch-wide strips. Unroll strips to separate; cut strips into 2- to 3-inch-long pieces. Add to simmering soup and cook 3 minutes or until tender. If using noodles for another purpose, cook noodle pieces in a large amount of boiling lightly salted water 2 to 3 minutes or until tender; drain well. (Or place noodle pieces in a resealable plastic bag; store in the refrigerator up to 1 day before cooking.)

## EGG NOODLE POINTERS

1. Knead the pasta dough, adding flour as necessary to keep it from sticking, 10 minutes or until dough is smooth and slightly elastic. Kneading creates a gluten structure that binds the dough and gives the noodles their slightly chewy texture.

2. After the dough rests for 10 minutes, use a knife to cut it into four equal portions. This is the most manageable portion for both rolling the dough by hand and for using in a pasta machine.

3. A long rolling pin is helpful to roll each dough portion evenly. To begin, flatten each piece of dough from the center to the outer edge. As it starts to flatten, place one hand on the side of the dough and roll away from yourself, pushing down and stretching the dough slightly as you roll. If your dough snaps back into place as you roll, let it rest a bit longer. Then try again. Rotate occasionally and flip over once or twice. Dust with flour as necessary to keep it from sticking.

4. One at a time, loosely roll each square of dough into a spiral shape. Use a sharp knife to cut the spirals crosswise into ¼-inch strips.

5. Once each spiral has been completely sliced, unroll the ribbons of dough and use the knife to cut into 2- to 3-inch pieces.
↓

6. To dry noodles, don't cut into pieces. Spread uncut ribbons on a wire rack or hang them from a pasta-drying rack or clothes hanger. Let dry up to 2 hours; cut into desired lengths. Place in an airtight container and store in the refrigerator up to 3 days before cooking. Or dry the noodles at least 1 hour; cut into desired lengths. Place in a plastic freezer bag or freezer container. Seal and freeze up to 8 months before cooking. Add 1 to 2 minutes to cooking time for dried or frozen noodles.

**MAKE IT IN A FOOD PROCESSOR** *Place a steel blade in the food processor. Add all of the flour, salt, yolks, and egg to the food processor. Cover and process until the mixture forms fine crumbs, about the consistency of cornmeal. With the food processor running, slowly pour the water and oil through the feed tube. Continue processing just until the dough begins to form a ball (not all of the dough will clump). Transfer dough to a lightly floured surface; gather into a ball. Cover; let rest 10 minutes. Divide the dough into four equal portions. Continue with rolling out dough.*

*I filled a small fine-mesh sieve with 1 to 2 Tbsp. of flour as I worked with the dough. The sieve gives a light, even dusting without overflouring the dough, which can make it tough and dry.*

MAKES: *8 servings*   TESTED BY: *Juli H.*

# 078   VEGETARIAN CHILI

TASTING COMMENTS: *Umami—a pleasant savory flavor sensation—is lacking when you prepare chili without meat. To make up for its absence, we added layers of flavor in the form of beer, chili powder, fresh oregano, and ground cumin.—JH*

**START TO FINISH** 40 MINUTES

*Choose a beer that you like to drink. Remember, the stronger the flavor of the beer, the stronger it will be in the chili.*

*This recipe tastes delicious with regular chili powder only, but if you want to make the flavor more complex, try adding ancho and/or chipotle powders to your chili.*

- 1 cup chopped red, green, and/or yellow sweet peppers
- ½ cup chopped onion
- 3 cloves garlic, minced
- 1 Tbsp. vegetable oil
- 2 26-oz. cans diced tomatoes with chili spices or diced tomatoes, undrained
- 1 12-oz. can beer or one 14.5-oz. can vegetable broth
- 1 cup water
- 1 8-oz. can tomato sauce
- 3 to 4 tsp. chili powder
- 1 Tbsp. snipped fresh oregano or 1 tsp. dried oregano, crushed
- 1 tsp. ground cumin
- ½ tsp. black pepper
- Several dashes bottled hot pepper sauce (optional)

- 3 15-oz. cans pinto beans, black beans, cannellini beans (white kidney beans), and/or red kidney beans, rinsed and drained
- 2 cups fresh or frozen whole kernel corn
- 1 cup chopped zucchini and/or yellow summer squash
- 1 cup shredded cheddar cheese or Monterey Jack cheese (4 oz.) (optional)
- Fresh oregano leaves (optional)

**1.** In a 5- to 6-qt. Dutch oven cook sweet pepper, onion, and garlic in hot oil until tender, stirring occasionally. Stir in tomatoes, beer, the water, tomato sauce, chili powder, dried oregano (if using), cumin, black pepper, and hot pepper sauce (if using). Bring to boiling; reduce heat. Simmer, covered, 10 minutes.

**2.** Stir in beans, corn, and zucchini. Return to boiling; reduce heat. Simmer, uncovered, 10 minutes more. Stir in the 1 Tbsp. fresh oregano if using. If desired, top servings with 2 Tbsp. of the cheese and additional fresh oregano.

PER SERVING *276 cal., 5 g fat (1 g sat. fat), 0 mg chol., 1,268 mg sodium, 46 g carb., 11 g fiber, 12 g sugars, 12 g pro.*

**LOADED VEGGIE NACHOS** *Great game-day food! Top tortilla chips with shredded cheese and chili, then pop in a 350°F oven until cheese is melted.*

**1.** After peeling, cut the onion in half so you have a flat surface to rest it on. Cut slices toward the stem end but not through the stem. Then cut slices horizontally through the onion. Finish by cutting new slices perpendicular to the first cuts—chopped onion!

↓

**2.** Cut the four sides of the pepper away from the stem. Cut the sides into slices, then chop them. Discard the stem and core with the seeds.

↓

↑

**3.** Cooking the chopped sweet peppers, onion, and minced garlic in oil until tender but not browned is called sweating. This draws moisture from the veggies and weakens the cell walls. It's the first step to building a flavorful chili.

# 079  OLD-FASHIONED BEEF STEW

TASTING COMMENTS: *We tested this recipe side by side using both the stove-top and slow cooker methods. Both had great flavor but we got the best body from the stove-top version.—LB*

**PREP** 20 MINUTES  **COOK** 1 HOUR 30 MINUTES

- 2 lb. beef chuck roast or beef stew meat
- ¼ cup all-purpose flour
- ¼ tsp. black pepper
- 3 Tbsp. vegetable oil
- 3 cups vegetable juice
- 3 cups reduced-sodium beef broth
- 2 medium onions, cut into thin wedges
- 1 cup thinly sliced celery
- 2 Tbsp. Worcesershire sauce
- 1 tsp. dried oregano, crushed
- ½ tsp. dried marjoram, crushed
- 1 bay leaf
- 4 red potatoes, cut into 1-inch cubes
- 4 carrots, bias-sliced ¼ inch thick

*Beef chuck is a fatty cut. We start out with 2 lb. of meat because after trimming, you wind up with about 1½ lb. for the stew.*

**1.** Trim fat from meat; cut into ¾-inch pieces. In a large resealable plastic bag combine flour and pepper. Add meat to bag; shake until evenly coated. In a large pot or Dutch oven brown half the meat in half the oil over medium-high heat; remove meat from pot. Repeat with remaining meat and oil. Return all meat to pot. Stir in the next eight ingredients (through bay leaf). Bring to boiling; reduce heat. Simmer, covered, 1 hour.

**2.** Stir potatoes and carrots into stew. Return to boiling; reduce heat. Simmer, covered, 30 to 40 minutes more or until meat and vegetables are tender. Discard bay leaf.

PER SERVING *476 cal., 20 g fat (6 g sat. fat), 125 mg chol., 640 mg sodium, 30 g carb., 4 g fiber, 9 g sugars, 46 g pro.*

**SWITCH YOUR ROOTS** If you like, you can substitute fingerling potatoes and parsnips for the carrots and red potatoes. Peel and slice the parsnips as you would carrots and cut the fingerlings into 1-inch chunks.

**SLOW COOKER DIRECTIONS**
Prepare and brown meat as directed. In a 4- to 6-qt. slow cooker layer meat, onions, celery, potatoes, and carrots. Decrease vegetable juice to 2 cups. Combine vegetable juice, broth, Worcestershire sauce, oregano, marjoram, and bay leaf. Pour over meat and vegetables in slow cooker. Cover and cook on low 10 to 12 hours or high 5 to 6 hours or until meat and vegetables are tender. Discard bay leaf.

**PERSONAL PIES** *Make tasty individual beef pot pies with leftover beef stew. Ladle the stew into small casseroles or large ramekins. Top with squares of purchased piecrust or puff pastry and bake in a 400°F oven until stew is bubbly and pastry is golden brown, 20 to 25 minutes.*

## TESTING NOTES

1. Coating the meat cubes in seasoned flour accomplishes two things. The light coating of flour acts as a thickener for the stew as it cooks and the seasoning gives it flavor.

↓

2. Browning meat creates what is called the Maillard reaction—a chemical reaction between amino acids and reducing sugars that gives the meat its rich, beefy flavor. Brown just half of the meat at a time to achieve a deeply colored crust rather than overcrowding the pan and steaming it.

↓

**IT'S IN THE SAUCE** *Developed by the English in India but first bottled in Worcester, England, this thin, dark, piquant sauce is made from garlic, soy sauce, tamarind, onions, molasses, lime, anchovies, vinegar, and seasonings.*

# 080  VEGETABLE SOUP 8 WAYS

TASTING COMMENTS:  *When we have a good, solid base recipe—like this vegetable soup—we love to twist it in all sorts of ways to appeal to all kinds of tastes. These eight bowls hold something for everyone!—KB*

**PREP** 15 MINUTES  **COOK** 15 MINUTES

12 oz. ground beef

1 cup chopped carrots

1 cup chopped celery

½ cup chopped onion

1 32-oz. carton reduced-sodium beef broth

½ of a 6-oz. can tomato paste (⅓ cup)

1 1-oz. envelope onion soup mix

½ tsp. dried thyme, crushed

1 cup cooked medium shell pasta

4 Bread Bowls (opposite) (optional)

1. In a large saucepan cook beef, carrots, celery, and onion until meat is browned; drain off fat.

2. Stir in broth, tomato paste, onion soup mix, and thyme. Bring to boiling; reduce heat. Simmer, covered, 15 minutes. Stir in pasta; heat through. If desired, serve soup in Bread Bowls.

**CHICKEN AND WHITE BEAN SOUP** Prepare as directed, except substitute skinless, boneless chicken thighs, cut into 1-inch pieces, for ground beef and 1 cup each chopped zucchini, chopped potatoes, and whole kernel corn for the carrots, celery, and onion. Cook the chicken and vegetables in 1 Tbsp. vegetable oil. Substitute reduced-sodium chicken broth for the beef broth, one 1.4-oz. envelope vegetable soup mix for the onion soup mix, and one 15-oz. can cannellini (white kidney) beans, rinsed and drained, for the pasta.

**CHICKEN ALFREDO SOUP** Prepare as directed, except substitute skinless, boneless chicken thighs, cut into 1-inch cubes, for ground beef. Cook chicken in 1 Tbsp. vegetable oil until no longer pink; remove from pan. Cook vegetables in 1 Tbsp. vegetable oil until crisp-tender; return chicken to pan. Substitute 2 cups reduced-sodium chicken broth plus one 15-oz. jar Alfredo sauce for the carton of beef broth and one 1.4-oz. envelope vegetable soup mix for the onion soup mix. Omit the tomato paste. Substitute dried basil for thyme and use cooked broken spaghetti for the pasta.

## ASIAN PORK SOUP

Prepare as directed, except substitute boneless pork tenderloin, cut into 1-inch cubes, for ground beef. Cook the pork in 1 Tbsp. vegetable oil until desired doneness. Substitute 1½ cups each frozen stir-fry vegetables and frozen edamame for the carrots, celery, and onion; add to pork with broth. Omit the tomato paste, soup mix, and thyme. Add 2 Tbsp. reduced-sodium soy sauce with the broth. Substitute 3 oz. Asian noodles, cooked, for the pasta. Top each serving with Asian chili paste.

## BEEF STEAK AND MUSHROOM SOUP

Prepare as directed, except substitute beef sirloin steak, cut into strips, for ground beef and 2 cups sliced button or cremini mushrooms for the carrots and celery. Cook beef in 1 Tbsp. vegetable oil until desired doneness; remove from pan. Cook mushrooms and the onion in 1 Tbsp. butter until tender; return meat to pan. Substitute dried rosemary for thyme and cooked barley for the pasta.

## KALE AND BEAN SOUP

Prepare as directed, except omit beef. Cook vegetables in 1 Tbsp. vegetable oil until crisp-tender. Substitute vegetable broth for the beef broth. Add 4 cups chopped, trimmed kale with the broth. Substitute one 15-oz. can black beans, rinsed and drained, for the pasta.

## TURKEY, SWEET POTATO, AND RICE SOUP

Prepare as directed, except substitute turkey breast tenderloin, cut into strips, for ground beef and 2 cups peeled, chopped sweet potatoes for celery and carrots. Cook turkey in 1 Tbsp. vegetable oil until no longer pink; remove from pan. Cook onion in 1 Tbsp. vegetable oil until crisp-tender. Return turkey to pan; add sweet potatoes. Substitute reduced-sodium chicken broth for the beef broth, one 1.4-oz. envelope vegetable soup mix for onion soup mix, 1 Tbsp. snipped fresh basil for dried thyme, and 1 cup cooked rice for pasta.

## CHICKEN AND QUINOA SOUP

Prepare as directed, except substitute skinless, boneless chicken breast halves, cut into strips, for ground beef and chopped fennel for celery. Cook the chicken in 1 Tbsp. vegetable oil until no longer pink; remove from pan. Cook the vegetables in 1 Tbsp. vegetable oil until crisp-tender; return chicken to pan. Substitute reduced-sodium chicken broth for beef broth. Omit the tomato paste. Substitute one 1.4-oz. envelope vegetable soup mix for the onion soup mix and 1½ cups cooked quinoa for the pasta.

## SAUSAGE AND BEAN SOUP

Prepare as directed, except substitute bulk pork sausage for ground beef and one 15-oz. can red beans, rinsed and drained, for the pasta. Stir in 1 Tbsp. finely chopped chipotle peppers in adobo sauce (tip, page 18) with the beans. Top servings with snipped fresh cilantro.

## BREAD BOWLS

*Serve soup in a bowl you can eat. Edible vessels are easy to make when you start with frozen bread dough.*

Thaw two 1-lb. loaves frozen white or wheat bread dough. Cut each into thirds crosswise to make six pieces total. Shape each piece into a ball. Grease a large baking sheet and sprinkle lightly with cornmeal. Arrange the dough balls on the baking sheet. Cover and let rise in a warm place until nearly double (about 40 minutes). Preheat oven to 400°F. In a small bowl combine 1 egg and 1 Tbsp. water; brush dough balls with some of the egg mixture. Using a sharp knife, make two or three shallow cuts across the top of each ball. Bake 15 minutes. Brush again with egg mixture. Bake 8 to 10 minutes more or until golden and bread sounds hollow when lightly tapped. Remove and cool on a wire rack. To serve, cut a ½-inch-thick slice from the top of each bread round. Scoop out bread from the center of each round, leaving a ¾-inch shell. Fill bread bowls with hot soup; serve immediately.

# 081  FRESH TOMATO MARINARA SAUCE

TASTING COMMENTS:  *Peeling the tomatoes may be a little putzy, but the end result is so much better if you do. The meat of the tomatoes cooks down and softens, but the skins can be tough. —JH*

**PREP** 30 MINUTES  **COOK** 20 MINUTES

- 1 Tbsp. olive oil
- ⅓ cup finely chopped onion
- 4 cloves garlic, minced
- 2 lb. fresh roma tomatoes, peeled, seeded, and chopped (about 3 cups)
- ½ cup dry red wine
- 1 to 2 tsp. balsamic vinegar* (optional)
- ½ tsp. salt
- ½ tsp. black pepper
- ½ cup snipped fresh basil

*In the left margin:*

If good fresh tomatoes aren't available, substitute two 28-oz. cans whole peeled roma tomatoes, drained and chopped. You should have about 3 cups total. Reduce the salt to ¼ tsp.

The wine deepens the flavor of this sauce. If you prefer a nonwine option, substitute chicken broth.

**1.** In a large saucepan heat oil over medium heat. Add onion and garlic; cook 3 to 5 minutes or until onion is tender, stirring occasionally.

**2.** Stir in tomatoes, wine, vinegar (if using), salt, and pepper. Bring to boiling; reduce heat. Simmer, uncovered, 20 to 25 minutes or until sauce is slightly thickened, stirring occasionally. Stir in basil.

**\*TIP**  Add the balsamic vinegar if you want the sauce to be a little tangier.

**TO STORE**  Place sauce in an airtight container. Seal and chill in the refrigerator up to 3 days or freeze up to 3 months.

PER SERVING 69 cal., 3 g fat (0 g sat. fat), 0 mg chol., 202 mg sodium, 8 g carb., 2 g fiber, 4 g sugars, 2 g pro.

**ARRABBIATA MARINARA**  Prepare Fresh Tomato Marinara Sauce as directed, except cook 3 oz. finely diced pancetta or prosciutto with the onion. Stir ¼ tsp. crushed red pepper into the sauce with the salt and black pepper.

**CREAMY MARINARA**  Prepare Fresh Tomato Marinara Sauce as directed, except stir in ¾ cup whipping cream with the basil.

**PUTTANESCA SAUCE**  Prepare Fresh Tomato Marinara Sauce as directed, except mash 3 or 4 anchovy fillets (rinsed and patted dry) into the cooked onion mixture; cook about 30 seconds more or until anchovies are incorporated. Stir ½ cup sliced pitted ripe olives and 2 Tbsp. drained capers into the mixture after simmering; substitute snipped fresh Italian parsley for the basil.

**TOP TOMATO PICK**  *We specifically call for roma (or plum) tomatoes here because they have firmer flesh and contain less juice and seeds (which yields a richer, thicker sauce). Word to the wise: Tomatoes aren't fans of the fridge—cool temps cause them to lose flavor and become mealy.*

## TESTING NOTES

1. Use a small, sharp paring knife to cut a shallow X into the bottom of each tomato.

↓

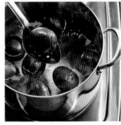

↑

2. Bring a large pot of water to boiling. Working in batches, immerse tomatoes into the boiling water to cover. Cook 30 to 60 seconds or until the skins begin to split open; remove with a slotted spoon.

3. Use the slotted spoon to transfer the tomatoes to a large bowl of ice water. This stops the cooking process and cools the tomatoes, making them easier to handle.

↑

4. When cool enough to handle, remove tomatoes from the water. Use a paring knife or your fingers to peel the skin away from the tomato. Start at the X where you scored the skin.

5. To remove the seeds, cut the tomato in half crosswise. Use the tip of a spoon to scoop out the seeds.

↓

6. Simmer the sauce, stirring occasionally to prevent burning, until the tomatoes just start to lose their shape and form a slightly chunky sauce. If you like a thicker sauce, cook it longer to evaporate more liquid. Stir in the fresh basil at the end of cooking to preserve its flavor.

# 082   BALSAMIC BBQ SAUCE

A bit of lager adds crisp, malty flavor to this sauce without overwhelming it.

TASTING COMMENTS: *We did a side-by-side test of three different barbeque sauces to choose one to include in this collection. This was the unanimous favorite. It's sweet, tangy, and acidic with a touch of heat. —LB*

**PREP** 10 MINUTES   **COOK** 45 MINUTES

- 1 cup lager beer
- 1 cup ketchup
- ½ cup packed brown sugar
- ⅓ cup white balsamic vinegar
- 6 cloves garlic, minced
- 1 Tbsp. honey
- 1 tsp. ground cumin
- 1 tsp. chili powder
- 1 tsp. sriracha sauce or sweet Asian chili sauce (optional)
- ½ tsp. freshly ground black pepper

The must (unfermented juice) of the grapes for regular balsamic is caramelized and aged for 12 years in wood-fired barrels. The must for white balsamic is not caramelized and is aged only a year in uncharred barrels. White balsamic has a lighter, cleaner taste than regular balsamic.

**1.** In a medium saucepan combine all ingredients. Bring to boiling; reduce heat. Simmer, uncovered, 45 minutes to 1 hour or until desired consistency, stirring frequently.

PER SERVING *86 cal., 0 g fat., 0 mg chol., 192 mg sodium, 21 g carb., 0 g fiber, 18 g sugars, 0 g pro.*

**CHILI SAUCE CHOICES** *There are many varieties of Asian chili sauce on the market. Sriracha may be the most familiar, but you can use other types as well. Just look for one that is made with chiles, vinegar, garlic, sugar, and salt.*

# BARBECUE SAUCE BASICS

**BROWN SUGAR** Brown sugar is a key component in the sweet flavor profile of barbecue sauce. Use dark brown sugar for a more intense molasses flavor.

**PAPRIKA** Paprika contributes a subtle smokiness to many barbecue sauce recipes. There are several varieties of Hungarian paprika, ranging from delicate to hot. Any paprika labeled as Hungarian is sure to contribute smoky flavor.

**ONION** In many recipes, cooking onions until softened is the first step to building the aromatic flavor of your sauce.

**BUTTER** Butter works as an emulsifier and stabilizer in barbecue sauce—it helps hold together the mixture. Butter also adds to the body and rich flavor of the sauce. If your meat is dry for any reason, the butter adds a velvety moisture back to the meat.

**GARLIC** Like the onion, garlic is an aromatic ingredient. Cook garlic just until it is light golden.

**CHICKEN BROTH** Water or chicken broth can serve as a sauce's base.

**BALSAMIC VINEGAR** A traditional barbecue sauce usually includes vinegar—most often cider vinegar. Balsamic vinegar adds the familiar punchy tang, but it offers a bold, complex sweetness, too.

**PEPPER** Freshly ground black pepper helps to round out the heat.

**CHILI POWDER** Chili powder—a seasoning mix of dried chiles, garlic, oregano, cumin, coriander, and cloves—adds smokiness and heat. Try ancho chile powder or chipotle chile powder for a more pronounced chile flavor.

**RED PEPPER FLAKES** Red pepper flakes add heat to barbecue sauce. Add a small amount of red pepper flakes, then taste after simmering. You can always add more!

**TOMATO PASTE OR KETCHUP** Tomato paste or ketchup adds a concentrated acidic flavor, as well as body, to the sauce.

**MOLASSES** Molasses, the syrupy by-product of refining sugar cane, adds sweetness to barbecue sauce. You can use either light or dark molasses—dark is slightly thicker with an earthier flavor.

**KEEP IT SAUCY** *Store any remaining sauce in an airtight container in your refrigerator up to 1 week. Looking for ways to use it? Brush barbecue sauce onto a homemade (or store-bought) pizza crust, then top with cheese, red onion, and pulled chicken or pork. Or mix some of the leftover sauce with shredded beef for quick and tasty barbecue quesadillas.*

# 083   BASIC WHITE SAUCE

TASTING COMMENTS:   *So many recipes start with a white sauce. To make sure you get it just right, you have to know the proportions of starch and liquid for the way you want to use the sauce.—CC*

**START TO FINISH** 15 MINUTES

1 Tbsp. butter

1 Tbsp. all-purpose flour

¼ tsp. salt

Dash black pepper

1 cup milk

**1.** In a small saucepan melt butter over medium heat. Stir in flour, salt, and pepper. Stir in milk. Cook and stir over medium heat until thickened and bubbly. Cook and stir 1 minute more.

PER SERVING *32 cal., 2 g fat (1 g sat. fat), 6 mg chol., 100 mg sodium, 2 g carb., 0 g fiber, 2 g sugars, 1 g pro.*

**MEDIUM WHITE SAUCE** Prepare as directed, except increase butter and flour to 2 Tbsp. each.

**CURRY SAUCE** Prepare as directed, except cook 1 tsp. curry powder in the melted butter 1 minute before adding the flour. Stir 2 Tbsp. snipped mango chutney into the cooked sauce. Serve with poultry and fish.

**HERB-GARLIC SAUCE** Prepare as directed, except cook 2 cloves garlic, minced, in the melted butter 30 seconds. Stir in ½ tsp. crushed dried basil with the flour, salt, and pepper. Serve with vegetables and poultry.

**LEMON-CHIVE SAUCE** Prepare as directed, except stir in 2 Tbsp. snipped fresh chives and 1 tsp. lemon zest with the flour, salt, and pepper. Serve with vegetables, poultry, and fish.

**CHEESE SAUCE** Prepare as directed, except stir 2 oz. cheddar cheese, shredded, and 2 oz. (3 slices) American cheese, torn, into sauce after thickening.

*Try the Curry Sauce variation as the base for a creamy curry cauliflower soup.*

*Double the Cheese Sauce recipe and toss with 6 cups cooked elbow macaroni (8 oz. or 2 cups dried elbow macaroni).*

## TESTING NOTES

↑
1. Flour coated with fat (butter) is called a roux. Melting the butter so it coats the flour particles prevents lumps from forming when milk is added. Cook and stir until the roux is just golden—not brown.

↑
3. A whisk is your best tool because it makes multiple points of contact as you stir the sauce. A whisk will also quickly get rid of any lumps if you see them begin to form. As the sauce thickens, whisk gently. You don't want to break down the starch particles at this point.

↑
2. Add cold milk to the roux, whisking constantly. Whisking in cold milk allows the flour particles to stay suspended—again preventing lumps. Warm milk may warm the flour particles quicker, potentially promoting formation of lumps.

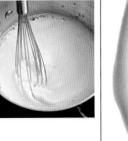

↑
4. Cook until the white sauce shows bubbles across the entire surface. Thickening results when heat expands the starch particles in the flour. Cook 1 minute more to ensure the flour is fully cooked. Add cheeses or other flavors at this point.

**THIN SAUCE** *Our Basic White Sauce is made with a low proportion of flour and butter to milk and can be poured rapidly. Most often thin white sauces are the base for creamed soups and cheese sauces for pasta.*

**MEDIUM SAUCE** *A medium white sauce is made with a higher proportion of flour and butter to milk. It will flow smoothly but should have more body to it. This sauce is the base for scalloped dishes and also makes a great dipping sauce.*

*Try the lemon–chive variation, using the Medium White Sauce formula, to serve with vegetables and as a topper for fish and seafood.*

*Try the herb–garlic variation, using the medium white Sauce formula, in scalloped potatoes.*

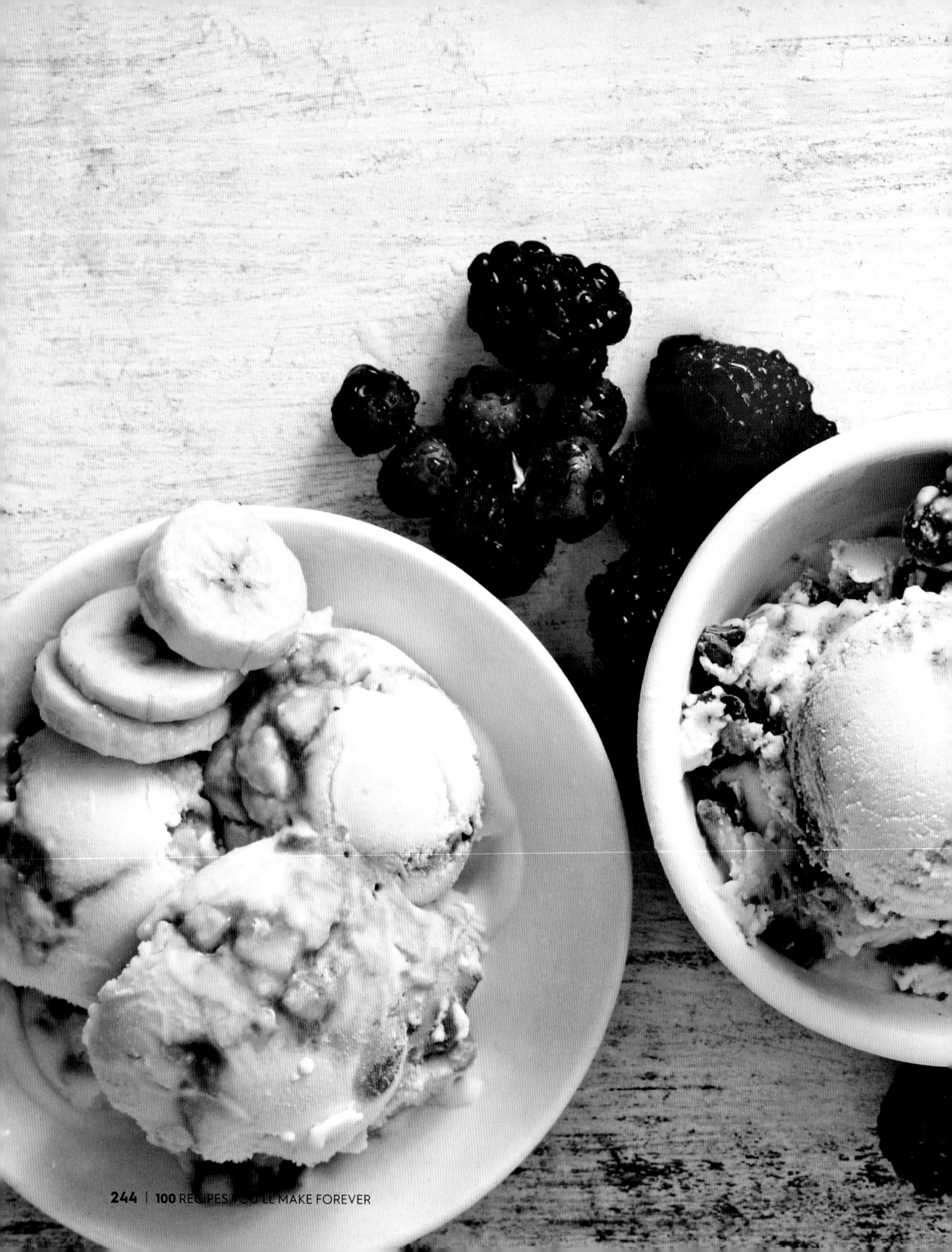

# ANYTIME SWEETS

MAKES: *48 servings*    TESTED BY: *Sarah B.*

# 084   CHOCOLATE CHIP COOKIES

TASTING COMMENTS: *This recipe creates a classic puffy, slightly chewy cookie—but with just a few tweaks, you can make cookies that are soft and cakelike or thin and crispy. The secret to getting the cookie you love is to know how each ingredient works: butter for crispness, cake flour for a finer texture, brown sugar for chewiness. —SB*

**PREP** 30 MINUTES   **BAKE** 6 MINUTES PER BATCH AT 375°F   **COOL** 2 MINUTES

½ cup butter, softened

½ cup shortening*

1 cup packed brown sugar

½ cup granulated sugar

1 tsp. baking soda

¾ tsp. salt

2 eggs

2 Tbsp. light-color corn syrup**

1 Tbsp. vanilla

2¾ cups all-purpose flour

1 12-oz. pkg. semisweet chocolate baking pieces or miniature candy-coated semisweet chocolate pieces (2 cups)

1½ cups chopped walnuts, pecans, or hazelnuts, toasted (optional) (tip, page 248)

**1.** Preheat oven to 375°F. In a large bowl beat butter and shortening on medium to high 30 seconds. Add sugars, baking soda, and salt. Beat on medium 2 minutes, scraping sides of bowl occasionally. Beat in eggs, corn syrup, and vanilla until combined. Beat in as much of the flour as you can. Stir in any remaining flour. Stir in chocolate pieces.

**2.** Drop dough by rounded teaspoons 2 inches apart onto ungreased cookie sheets. Bake 6 to 8 minutes or just until edges are lightly browned (cookies may not appear set). Cool on cookie sheets 2 minutes. Transfer to wire racks and let cool.

***TIP** To substitute ½ cup vegetable oil for the shortening, prepare as directed, except beat butter on medium to high 30 seconds, then gradually beat in oil.

****TIP** The corn syrup ensures chewy, tender cookies that stay fresh for days.

PER SERVING *128 cal., 6 g fat (3 g sat. fat), 13 mg chol., 85 mg sodium, 17 g carb., 1 g fiber, 11 g sugars, 1 g pro.*

**SOFT-AND-CAKELIKE CHOCOLATE CHIP COOKIES** Prepare as directed, except omit butter, use 1½ cups packed brown sugar, omit granulated sugar, add ½ tsp. baking powder with the brown sugar, beat in one 8-oz. carton sour cream after beating in eggs and vanilla, and substitute cake flour for the all-purpose flour. Bake on parchment paper-lined cookie sheets 10 minutes or just until edges are lightly browned (cookies may not appear set).

**THIN-AND-CRISPY CHOCOLATE CHIP COOKIES** Prepare as directed, except use 1 cup butter, omit shortening, use ¾ cup each packed brown sugar and granulated sugar, and reduce flour to 2¼ cups.

**WHOLE WHEAT CHOCOLATE CHIP COOKIES** Prepare as directed, except substitute 1 cup whole wheat flour for 1 cup of the all-purpose flour.

## ESSENTIAL COOKIE INGREDIENTS

### FATS

Fats influence the cookie's flavor and how much the batter will spread while baking.

**SHORTENING** doesn't melt as quickly as butter during baking, so cookies keep their shape and won't be too crisp.

**BUTTER** adds a richer flavor to the baked cookies than shortening. Butter also melts faster during baking, so the batter spreads more, resulting in thinner cookies.

### FLOURS

Different types of flour contain different amounts of protein. The protein content may influence the shape, tenderness, and color of the final cookies.

**CAKE FLOUR** is low in protein, so baked cookies are tender and light in texture and color.

**BREAD FLOUR** is a high-protein flour, so the final cookies will be chewier.

**ALL-PURPOSE FLOUR** has a moderate amount of protein and falls in the middle of the two.

### LEAVENERS

**BAKING SODA** is a chemical leavener that activates when it comes in contact with an acidic ingredient. Additional baking soda may contribute to browning.

**BAKING POWDER** is another chemical leavener. Most is double-acting, so it first reacts when it comes in contact with liquid and then again with heat.

### SUGARS

**GRANULATED SUGAR** has a low moisture content, so the sugars crystallize when baked, creating a crisp texture.

**BROWN SUGAR** has a higher moisture content because it contains molasses. This moisture makes the cookies softer and well suited for cakelike or chewy cookies.

## TESTING NOTES

↑

1. Softened butter is the perfect consistency to cream with sugar. To soften, leave butter on the counter at room temperature 30 minutes or microwave on 50% power for 15-second intervals until you can press into it easily. Don't melt the butter; it won't behave the same way in the batter.

↑

2. Creaming the butter and sugar together traps tiny air bubbles, helping to leaven the cookies. Beat the butter and sugar together until the mixture is light in color and resembles whipped butter.

↑

3. Although you can use two teaspoons to drop cookie dough, a cookie scoop makes consistently shaped cookies. Look for a 1¼-inch scoop for these cookies.

**CHEWY BASIC** *This cookie formula is made with a combination of butter and shortening, which gives the cookies a buttery flavor without spreading too thin. It has more brown than granulated sugar, and that makes these cookies just-right chewy.*

**SOFT + CAKELIKE** *To make this cookie light with a cakelike texture, cake flour is used instead of all-purpose flour. Shortening helps the tender cookies hold their shape. Sour cream adds extra moisture. Brown sugar is used exclusively to make the cookies extra tender.*

**THIN + CRISPY** *This cookie is made with only butter, which produces rich, thin, and crisp baked cookies. There is more granulated sugar in this recipe than the basic formula, which also adds to the crispness. Extra baking soda boosts the browning.*

**TOASTING NUTS** *Why toast nuts when they are on their way into a hot oven? The cookie batter insulates the nuts, preventing them from getting hot enough to be toasted. Toasting nuts before baking brings out their nutty flavor and helps to keep them crisp in the finished cookies.*

*To toast nuts, preheat the oven to 350°F. Spread nuts in an even layer in a shallow baking pan. Bake 5 to 10 minutes or until toasted, stirring once or twice.*

*If you're toasting hazelnuts, place the warm nuts on a clean kitchen towel. Rub the nuts with the towel to remove the loose skins.*

**CHOOSE YOUR CHIPS** *All chocolate is made from the nut of the cacao (kuh-KOW) tree. The difference between chocolates is the percentage of cacao included in each kind, which is usually indicated on the package. The rest of the chocolate is sugar, so the higher the percentage of cacao, the more pronounced the chocolate flavor will be.*

To jazz up even the best chocolate chip cookies, try one of these add-ins:

**DARK CHOCOLATE CHIPS** Dark chocolate can be either semisweet or bittersweet.

**SEMISWEET CHOCOLATE CHIPS** Technically considered a dark chocolate, semisweet chocolate usually contains 52–62% cacao, resulting in a smooth, dark chocolate flavor.

*2 cups chopped mini peanut butter cups*

*1½ cups chopped nuts*

*1 cup snipped dried fruit*

**MILK CHOCOLATE CHIPS** Milk chocolate contains 36–46% cacao and has the addition of milk, which makes the chocolate creamier.

**CHOCOLATE CHUNKS** These could be any percentage of cacao, but the larger chunks will make the chocolate in the cookies stand out even more.

*2 cups rolled oats (reduce flour to 2½ cups)*

# 085   PUMPKIN BARS

TASTING COMMENTS: *Oil is the key to the moist tenderness of these bars. Unlike melted butter, oil does not firm up when combined with the other ingredients, so it coats the flour granules for a more evenly textured bar. —SM*

In the left margin:

*Unlike butter, the mild flavor of oil allows strong feature flavors, such as pumpkin and spices, to shine through in bars and cakes. Butter is better in recipes with mild feature flavors, such as yellow cake.*

**PREP** 25 MINUTES   **BAKE** 25 MINUTES AT 350°F   **COOL** 2 HOURS

- 2 cups all-purpose flour
- 1½ cups granulated sugar
- 2 tsp. baking powder
- 2 tsp. ground cinnamon
- 1 tsp. baking soda
- ½ tsp. salt
- ¼ tsp. ground cloves
- 4 eggs, lightly beaten
- 1 15-oz. can pumpkin
- 1 cup vegetable oil
- 1 recipe Browned Butter Frosting or Cream Cheese Frosting (page 276)

**1.** Preheat oven to 350°F. In a large bowl stir together the first seven ingredients (through cloves). Add eggs, pumpkin, and oil; stir until combined. Spread batter in an ungreased 15×10-inch baking pan.

**2.** Bake 25 to 30 minutes or until a wooden toothpick inserted near the center comes out clean. Cool in pan on a wire rack 2 hours.

**3.** Spread with Browned Butter Frosting. Cut into bars. Cover and store bars in the refrigerator up to 3 days.

**BROWNED BUTTER FROSTING** In a small saucepan heat ⅓ cup butter over low heat until melted. Continue heating until butter turns a light golden brown, stirring occasionally. Remove from heat. In a large mixing bowl combine 3 cups powdered sugar, 2 Tbsp. milk, and 1 tsp. vanilla. Add browned butter. Beat with a mixer on medium until spreading consistency, adding additional milk if necessary. Makes about 1½ cups.

PER SERVING *178 cal., 8 g fat (2 g sat. fat), 28 mg chol., 109 mg sodium, 25 g carb., 1 g fiber, 19 g sugars, 2 g pro.*

**APPLESAUCE-CRANBERRY BARS** Prepare Pumpkin Bars as directed, except substitute ½ cup honey for ½ cup of the granulated sugar, substitute one 15-oz. jar (1¾ cups) applesauce for the pumpkin, and stir 1 cup dried cranberries and/or dried tart cherries into the batter. Lightly sprinkle frosted bars with ground cinnamon.

**CREAM CHEESE SWIRL-PUMPKIN BARS** Prepare as directed in Step 1. In a medium bowl combine half of an 8-oz. pkg. cream cheese, softened, and ¼ cup granulated sugar. Beat on medium until combined. Beat in 1 egg and 1 Tbsp. milk. Drizzle cream cheese mixture over pumpkin batter. Using a table knife or thin metal spatula, gently cut through batters to swirl them (do not overmix). Sprinkle batter with ½ cup miniature semisweet chocolate baking pieces. Continue as directed in Steps 2 and 3, except omit Browned Butter Frosting.

**NUTTY CARAMEL-PUMPKIN BARS** Prepare Pumpkin Bars as directed in Step 1. In a small bowl stir together 1½ cups chopped pecans, toasted (tip, page 248), and ⅓ cup caramel ice cream topping. Spoon nut mixture over batter. Continue as directed in Steps 2 and 3, except use only half of the Browned Butter Frosting (chill or freeze the remaining frosting and use it to frost your favorite cupcakes). Stir milk into frosting to make drizzling consistency. Drizzle over cooled bars.

## TESTING NOTES

1. It sounds fancy, but browned butter is simply butter melted on the stove top until the milk solids begin to turn a lovely golden brown color. Once it starts to brown, it can go from just right to burned quickly, so pull the pan off the heat as soon as it gets to the right color.

↓

↑

2. Your frosting should be smooth, spreadable, and soft enough that it doesn't pull up the top of the bars as you apply the frosting. If your frosting seems too stiff, just add additional milk, 1 Tbsp. at a time, to reach the desired consistency.

# 086   SHORTBREAD

TASTING COMMENTS:   *The dough for these cookies will look crumbly when you are done mixing it. Resist the urge to add any liquid—this will only make the cookies tough!—CW*

**PREP** 15 MINUTES   **BAKE** 25 MINUTES AT 325°F

1¼  cups all-purpose flour

3  Tbsp. granulated sugar

½  cup butter, cut-up

*A stick of cold butter is easier to cut into pieces than softened butter, so cut while it's fresh out of the fridge. Set the pieces aside to warm up a little while you measure the other two ingredients, but expect the butter to still be firm and chilled when you start cutting it into the flour mixture.*

**1.** Preheat oven to 325°F. In a medium bowl combine flour and sugar. Add butter. Using a pastry blender, cut in butter until the mixture resembles fine crumbs and starts to cling together. Form mixture into a ball and knead until smooth.

**2.** To make shortbread wedges, on an ungreased cookie sheet pat or roll the dough into an 8-inch circle. If desired, make a scalloped edge. Cut circle into 16 wedges; leave wedges in the circle.

**3.** Bake 25 to 30 minutes or just until bottom starts to brown and center is set. Cut circle into wedges again while warm. Cool on cookie sheet 5 minutes. Transfer to a wire rack and let cool.

**NOTE** To make different shortbread shapes, on a lightly floured surface roll or pat dough until ½ inch thick. Use cookie cutters or a knife to cut desired shapes. Place 1 inch apart on an ungreased cookie sheet. Bake 20 to 25 minutes.

PER SERVING *96 cal., 6 g fat (4 g sat. fat), 15 mg chol., 51 mg sodium, 10 g carb., 0 g fiber, 2 g sugars, 1 g pro.*

**VANILLA BEAN ICING** If you'd like to frost your shortbread, make an icing that's a little more special. Prepare Powdered Sugar Icing on page 258, except omit the vanilla. Instead stir in ½ to 1 tsp. vanilla bean paste. (Vanilla bean paste is a thickened extract that contains real vanilla bean seeds for exceptional flavor. Look for it at specialty cooking stores or online.)

## TESTING NOTES

↑

**1.** Pastry blenders (available where cooking supplies are sold) are used to cut the pieces of butter into the flour until your mixture has a fine-crumb texture. This process coats all sides of the tiny butter pieces with flour. As you go, you may have to use a table knife to scrape large chunks of butter and flour from the sides and blades of the blender. When it's ready, the mixture will start to clump and hold together more, but it will still be crumbly and dry-looking.

↑

**2.** As you knead the dough (keep it brief!), the heat from your hands will continue to soften the butter, which will help the crumbly-looking mixture come together into a smooth ball.

↑

**3.** Use your hands to pat the dough into an 8-inch circle. To make the circle nicely rounded, while using one hand to press dough out, use the other hand to press in and shape the outside edge so it doesn't become lopsided or cracked. You can also use a rolling pin to roll out the dough, but it can be more difficult to form a perfect circle.

**4.** To make a scalloped edge as shown, gently press one thumb into the dough while using the thumb and forefinger from your other hand to press the dough from the outside into the other thumb.

↓

**CHERRY-PISTACHIO SHORTBREAD** Prepare as directed, except after cutting in butter, stir in 2 Tbsp. each snipped dried cherries and chopped pistachios. Drizzle cooled cookies with melted white chocolate. Sprinkle with more chopped pistachios.

**SPICED SHORTBREAD** Prepare as directed, except substitute brown sugar for the granulated sugar and stir 1 tsp. apple pie spice into the flour mixture. Brush with egg white and sprinkle with coarse sugar before baking.

**HOLIDAY SHORTBREAD** Prepare as directed, except after cutting in butter, stir in ¼ cup finely chopped candied cherries. Dip one end of each cooled cookie into melted white chocolate, then in red and/or green candy sprinkles.

**CHOCOLATE-ORANGE SHORTBREAD** Prepare as directed, except add 1½ tsp. finely shredded orange peel with the butter. After cutting in butter, stir in ⅓ cup miniature semisweet chocolate baking pieces.

**BUTTER-PECAN SHORTBREAD** Prepare as directed, except substitute brown sugar for the granulated sugar. After cutting in butter, stir in 2 Tbsp. finely chopped pecans. Press pecan halves into wedges before baking.

**TOFFEE-ALMOND SHORTBREAD** Prepare as directed, except substitute brown sugar for the granulated sugar. After cutting in butter, stir in 2 Tbsp. each chopped almonds and crushed toffee pieces. Drizzle cooled cookies with melted chocolate.

**LEMON-POPPY SEED SHORTBREAD** Prepare as directed, except stir in 1 Tbsp. poppy seeds with the flour mixture and add 1 tsp. finely shredded lemon peel with the butter. Before serving, sprinkle with powdered sugar.

**ROSEMARY-CRANBERRY SHORTBREAD** Prepare as directed, except substitute ¼ cup cornmeal for ¼ cup of the all-purpose flour and stir in 1 tsp. snipped fresh rosemary. After cutting in butter, stir in 2 Tbsp. snipped dried cranberries.

# 087 LEMON BARS DELUXE

TASTING COMMENTS: *Freshly squeezed lemon juice is absolutely essential to the flavor success of this recipe. When baking, never substitute bottled lemon juice for real—the flavor just can't compare.—CC*

**PREP** 20 MINUTES  **BAKE** 45 MINUTES AT 350°F

- 2 **cups all-purpose flour**
- ½ **cup powdered sugar**
- 1 **cup butter, softened**
- 1 **lemon**
- 4 **eggs, lightly beaten**
- 1½ **cups granulated sugar**
- ¼ **cup all-purpose flour**
- **Powdered sugar**

1. Preheat oven to 350°F. Line a 13×9-inch baking pan with foil, extending the foil over edges of pan. For crust, in a large bowl stir together the 2 cups flour and the ½ cup powdered sugar; add butter. Beat on low to medium just until mixture begins to cling together. Press into the prepared baking pan. Bake 25 minutes or until light brown.

2. Meanwhile, remove 1 Tbsp. zest and ⅓ cup juice from lemon. In a medium bowl whisk together the eggs, granulated sugar, and lemon juice. Whisk in the ¼ cup flour and lemon zest. Pour over hot crust.

3. Bake 20 minutes more or until edges begin to brown and center is set. Cool in pan on a wire rack. Using the edges of the foil, lift uncut bars out of pan. Cut into bars. Just before serving, sprinkle with additional powdered sugar. Cover and store in the refrigerator up to 3 days.

**TO STORE** Place bars in a single layer in an airtight container; cover. Store in the refrigerator up to 2 days.

PER SERVING *182 cal., 9 g fat (5 g sat. fat), 51 mg chol., 80 mg sodium, 24 g carb., 0 g fiber, 15 g sugars, 2 g pro.*

**LEMON-ORANGE BARS** Prepare Lemon Bars Deluxe as directed, except reduce lemon juice to 3 Tbsp. and reduce finely shredded lemon peel to 1 tsp. Add 3 Tbsp. orange juice and 1 tsp. orange zest. If desired, for a glaze, combine 1¼ cups powdered sugar, ½ tsp. orange zest, and 1 Tbsp. orange juice. Stir in enough additional orange juice to make icing drizzling consistency. Drizzle over baked bars just before cutting.

*There are three ways to juice citrus: with a reamer (left), with a juicer (middle), or simply by piercing the flesh in several places with a fork and squeezing.*

↑

1. The crust mixture will be crumbly (like piecrust dough before the water is added), but don't worry! Once you start pressing it into the pan, it will come together to create a solid base for the filling. Use your fingers and/or the flat bottom of a dry measuring cup to press crumbs evenly into the bottom of the pan. Bake as directed.

2. The juice inside the lemon is locked up in the pulpy membranes. To get the most juice possible, let the lemon stand at room temperature at least 30 minutes. Firmly roll the lemon on the countertop under your palm to break up the pulp inside and free the juice. Cut the lemon in half crosswise; pick a juicing method (opposite).

3. A Microplane grater is a must-have tool (found in kitchen supply stores) for effortlessly removing the zest of citrus fruits—it's definitely earned a top spot on our kitchen-tools list. Take care, though, as it also effortlessly removes the bitter white pith just below the peel. Continually turn and rotate the lemon as you go until no yellow zest remains.

↓

4. While the crust is baking, you should make the filling. When you finish the filling, the crust should be coming out of the oven. Immediately pour filling over the hot crust. This allows the crust and filling to adhere to one another and prevents the crust from absorbing the filling and becoming soggy.

↓

*1 medium lemon = about 3 Tbsp. juice and 2 tsp. zest*

MAKES: *52 cookies*   TESTED BY: *Juli H.*

# 088   SUGAR COOKIE CUTOUTS

TASTING COMMENTS:   *We tasted these side by side with a recipe from a 1960s edition of the New Cook Book made with all shortening. Everyone liked this one better—the cookies had a fuller flavor—but there were varying opinions on how done we liked our sugar cookies.—JH*

**PREP** 40 MINUTES   **CHILL** 1 HOUR   **BAKE** 7 MINUTES PER BATCH AT 375°F

1 cup butter, softened

1¼ cups granulated sugar

1½ tsp. baking powder

½ tsp. salt

2 eggs

2 tsp. vanilla

3 cups all-purpose flour

1 recipe Powdered Sugar Icing, Creamy White Frosting, or Royal Icing (page 260) (optional)

*Baking powder is a mixture of baking soda and the exact amount of acid—such as cream of tartar—needed to activate it. If you want to make your own, for each 1 tsp. baking powder, substitute a combination of ½ tsp. cream of tartar and ¼ tsp. baking soda.*

**1.** In a large bowl beat butter with a mixer on medium to high 30 seconds. Add sugar, baking powder, and salt. Beat until combined, scraping sides of bowl occasionally. Beat in eggs and vanilla until combined. Beat in as much of the flour as you can with the mixer. Stir in any remaining flour. Divide dough in half. Cover and chill 30 minutes or until easy to handle.

**2.** Preheat oven to 375°F. On a lightly floured surface roll out half the dough at a time to ⅛- to ¼-inch thickness. Using 2½-inch cookie cutters, cut dough into desired shapes. (Dip cutters in flour to prevent sticking.) Place cutouts 1 inch apart on ungreased cookie sheets. Repeat with the remaining dough.

**3.** Bake 7 to 10 minutes or until edges are firm and bottoms are very light brown. Transfer cookies to a wire rack; let cool. If desired, frost cookies. Let stand until icing is set.

**TO STORE** Layer uniced cookies between sheets of waxed paper in an airtight container. Store at room temperature up to 3 days or freeze up to 3 months.

PER SERVING *74 cal., 4 g fat (2 g sat. fat), 15 mg chol., 59 mg sodium, 10 g carb., 0 g fiber, 4 g sugars, 1 g pro.*

**POWDERED SUGAR ICING** In a bowl combine 1½ cups powdered sugar, ¼ tsp. vanilla or almond extract, and enough milk (3 to 4 tsp. total) to make drizzling consistency.

**CREAMY WHITE FROSTING** In a large bowl beat 1 cup shortening, 1½ tsp. vanilla, and, if desired, ½ tsp. almond extract on medium 30 seconds. Gradually add 2 cups powdered sugar, beating well. Beat in 2 Tbsp. milk. Gradually beat in 2 cups powdered sugar and 1 to 2 Tbsp. milk to reach spreading consistency.

**CHOCOLATE CUTOUTS** Prepare Sugar Cookie Cutouts as directed, except substitute ⅓ cup unsweetened cocoa powder or unsweetened dark Dutch-process cocoa powder for ⅓ cup of the flour.

**CITRUS CUTOUTS** Prepare Sugar Cookie Cutouts as directed, except beat in 2 tsp. lemon or orange zest with the egg and substitute lemon juice or orange juice for the milk.

**NUTTY CUTOUTS** Prepare Sugar Cookie Cutouts as directed, except add ⅓ cup finely chopped toasted pecans or walnuts (tip, page 248) with the flour.

**PEPPERMINT CUTOUTS** Prepare as directed, except substitute 1 tsp. peppermint extract for the vanilla and add ¼ cup finely crushed striped round peppermint candies with the flour.

**SPICE CUTOUTS** Prepare Sugar Cookie Cutouts as directed, except add 1 to 2 tsp. apple pie spice or pumpkin pie spice with the sugar. If desired, substitute eggnog for the milk.

# ROYAL ICING

TASTING COMMENTS: *When thinning the icing, add the least amount of water possible to create a thick, spoonable consistency. If the icing is too watery, it will develop a pitted appearance as it dries.—JH*

**START TO FINISH** 10 MINUTES

- 1 16-oz. pkg. powdered sugar (4 cups)
- 3 Tbsp. meringue powder (tip, opposite)
- ½ tsp. cream of tartar
- ½ cup warm water
- ½ tsp. vanilla
  Paste food coloring (optional)

**1.** In a large bowl stir together powdered sugar, meringue powder, and cream of tartar. Add warm water and vanilla.

**2.** Beat on low until combined; beat on high 7 to 10 minutes or until icing is very stiff. If desired, tint with food coloring. Use immediately.

**TO STORE** Cover bowl with a damp paper towel; cover with plastic wrap. Chill up to 48 hours before using.

## TESTING NOTES

1. Flour requires a light hand when measuring. Start by gently stirring the flour in the bag or canister with a fork to aerate it. Lightly spoon the flour into a dry measuring cup until it is overflowing. Use the back of a table knife to level off the top. Packing flour into the cup will increase the amount of flour in your recipe and result in tough, dry cookies.

↓

2. For better blending, let butter stand at room temperature 30 minutes before beating it. Or microwave it on the defrost setting 15 seconds at a time just until spreadable.

3. We soften the butter so it blends better, but this creates a soft dough that sticks to surfaces and is hard to work with. So here's the trick: Divide the dough in half, flatten each half slightly, and wrap separately in plastic wrap. Chill them in the fridge 2 hours to let the butter harden. That makes rolling dough and transferring cookies easier.

↓

4. To roll out each dough half, start with rolling pin in the middle of the dough and roll to the edge. Continue rolling from middle to edge, giving the rolling pin a quarter turn with each stroke. This creates an even thickness across the dough.

↑

5. It's up to you whether you want your cookies thin (⅛ inch) or thicker (¼ inch). Thicker cookies will be softer, and thinner cookies will be crispier. (Keep a close eye on thinner cookies because they will bake quicker.) Position cookie cutters as close as possible on dough to maximize the number of cookies you get from the first rolling. The dough can be rerolled once to make more cutouts, but cookies will be less tender as you continue to work and handle the dough.

↑

6. To apply the icing so it dries smooth, use a disposable plastic pastry bag or a resealable plastic bag with a very small hole snipped in one corner. Pipe an outline around the edge of the cookie. Pipe thinned icing inside the outline and spread to the edges with the back of a spoon, a thin metal spatula, or a clean small artist's paintbrush.

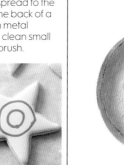

↑

7. To create an embedded web design, pipe a second color of icing in concentric circles over the base coat while it is still wet. Use a toothpick to drag lines through the two colors from the center toward the points of the star. Between star points, drag the toothpick from the outside toward the center. You can create several different looks by piping dots or lines of different colors and using a toothpick to drag the icing in a variety of patterns.

**MERINGUE POWDER** *Meringue powder is a mixture of pasteurized egg whites, sugar, and edible gums. It is the secret ingredient to making Royal Icing dry quickly with a smooth, hard finish. Look for it in the baking aisle of large supermarkets or in the cake decorating department of hobby and crafts stores.*

**PASTE FOOD COLORING** *Paste food coloring is perfect for creating bright colors. There are many colors to choose from and it doesn't thin the icing like liquid coloring. Use a clean toothpick to add the coloring to the icing a little at a time until you reach the desired color.*

MAKES: *16 servings*  TESTED BY: *Linda B.*

# 089  FUDGY BROWNIES

TASTING COMMENTS: *Varying the amounts of chocolate, butter, sugar, and flour in a brownie recipe makes them cakey or fudgy. With just ²/₃ cup flour in this recipe, these are super chocolaty and decadent! —LB*

**PREP** 20 MINUTES  **BAKE** 30 MINUTES AT 350°F

½ cup butter

3 oz. unsweetened chocolate, coarsely chopped

1 cup sugar

2 eggs

1 tsp. vanilla

²/₃ cup all-purpose flour

¼ tsp. baking soda

½ cup chopped nuts (optional)

1 recipe Chocolate-Cream Cheese Frosting (optional)

**CHOCOLATE-CREAM CHEESE FROSTING** *In a small saucepan melt 1 cup semisweet chocolate pieces over low heat, stirring occasionally; cool. In a medium bowl stir together two 3-oz. pkg. softened cream cheese and ½ cup powdered sugar. Stir in melted chocolate until smooth.*

**1.** In a medium saucepan melt butter and unsweetened chocolate over low heat, stirring occasionally until smooth; set aside to cool. Preheat oven to 350°F. Line an 8×8-inch baking pan with foil, extending foil over pan edges. Grease foil.

**2.** Stir sugar into the cooled chocolate mixture. Add eggs, one at a time, stirring just until combined. Stir in vanilla. In a small bowl stir together flour and baking soda. Add flour mixture to chocolate mixture; stir just until combined. If desired, stir in nuts. Spread batter in the prepared pan.

**3.** Bake 30 minutes. Cool in pan on a wire rack. If desired, spread Chocolate-Cream Cheese Frosting over cooled brownies. Using foil, lift uncut brownies out of pan. Cut into bars.

PER SERVING *157 cal., 10 g fat (6 g sat. fat), 43 mg chol., 90 mg sodium, 18 g carb., 1 g fiber, 12 g sugars, 2 g pro.*

**CARAMEL-PECAN** Use pecans for the nuts. In a bowl melt 16 to 18 vanilla caramels with 1 tbsp. milk in the microwave on high about 1 minute or until melted, stirring once. Drizzle caramel on batter. Continue as directed. If desired, frost and/or drizzle with additional caramel.

**BANANA SPLIT** Prepare brownies as directed. Frost. In a bowl combine ⅓ cup sliced fresh strawberries and ⅓ cup sliced banana. Sprinkle fruit on frosting. Sprinkle with ¼ cup chopped peanuts. Top each brownie with some whipped cream. If desired, top with additional fruit and nuts.

**COFFEE** Dissolve 1 tsp. instant espresso coffee powder in 2 tsp. hot water. Add coffee mixture and ½ tsp. ground cinnamon with the eggs. Continue as directed. For the frosting, stir ½ tsp. instant espresso powder into the melted chocolate. Top with chopped chocolate-covered espresso beans.

**MALTED** Stir ¼ cup malted milk powder in with the flour. Continue as directed. Frost and sprinkle with ½ cup coarsely chopped malted milk balls.

**MARSHMALLOW-WALNUT** Sprinkle frosted brownies with ½ cup chopped walnuts and ¾ cup tiny marshmallows.

**COCONUT-ALMOND** Use almonds for the nuts. Sprinkle frosting with ½ cup chopped soft coconut macaroon cookies.

**RASPBERRY** Spread ²/₃ cup raspberry preserves over baked brownies. Cool. Frost as directed. Top with fresh raspberries.

**MINT** Stir ½ tsp. mint extract in with the vanilla. Frost and sprinkle with 1 cup chopped layered chocolate-mint candy.

**PEANUT BUTTER CUP** Fold ¾ cup chopped bite-size chocolate-covered peanut butter cups into batter. Bake as directed. Sprinkle frosting with an additional ½ cup chopped peanut butter cups.

**WHITE CHOCOLATE** Fold ¾ cup white chocolate baking pieces into batter. Continue as directed. Frost. If desired, sprinkle frosting with chocolate curls and/or shavings.

MAKES: *16 servings*   TESTED BY: *Colleen W.*

# 090 **GREEK FROZEN YOGURT**

TASTING COMMENTS: *Although your frozen yogurt may look ready right from the ice cream maker, ripening it in the freezer for at least 2 hours deepens the flavor and improves the finished texture.—CW*

**PREP** 15 MINUTES   **FREEZE** PER MANUFACTURER'S DIRECTIONS + 2 TO 4 HOURS   **STAND** 5 MINUTES

3 cups plain low-fat (2%) Greek yogurt

1 cup sugar

¼ cup fresh lemon juice

2 tsp. vanilla

⅛ tsp. salt

**1.** In a bowl stir together all ingredients. Whisk until smooth.

**2.** Freeze the yogurt mixture in a 1½- or 2-qt. ice cream maker according to the manufacturer's directions. Transfer to an airtight container and freeze 2 to 4 hours or until firm. Keep frozen up to 1 week. Let stand at room temperature 5 to 15 minutes before serving.

PER SERVING *84 cal., 1 g fat (1 g sat. fat), 3 mg chol., 35 mg sodium, 15 g carb., 0 g fiber, 15 g sugars, 4 g pro.*

**FROZEN YOGURT SANDWICHES**
Prepare as directed. Spread frozen yogurt on flat sides of oatmeal cookies; top with additional oatmeal cookies, flat sides down. If desired, roll sides in chopped pistachio nuts.

**STRAWBERRY FROZEN YOGURT**
Prepare as directed, except add 1 cup sliced strawberries the last minute of freezing in ice cream maker.

**BERRY FROZEN YOGURT** Prepare as directed, except add 1 cup blueberries, blackberries, and/or raspberries the last minute of freezing in the ice cream maker.

## ALMOND CHOCOLATE CHUNK FROZEN YOGURT

Prepare as directed, except omit the lemon juice and increase the vanilla to 1 Tbsp. before freezing in the ice cream maker. Stir in 1 cup chocolate chunks and ½ cup chopped toasted almonds (tip, page 248) before placing in airtight container and freezing.

## MINT FROZEN YOGURT

Prepare as directed, except stir 2 Tbsp. snipped fresh mint into frozen yogurt before placing in airtight container and freezing.

## BANANA FROZEN YOGURT

Prepare as directed, except omit the lemon juice and increase the vanilla to 1 Tbsp. before freezing in the ice cream maker. In a bowl combine 1 sliced banana and ½ cup caramel ice cream topping. Swirl into frozen yogurt before placing in airtight container and freezing.

## RASPBERRY FUDGE FROZEN YOGURT

Prepare as directed, except swirl ¼ cup raspberry preserves and ¼ cup chocolate-flavor syrup into frozen yogurt before placing in airtight container and freezing. Serve with shaved chocolate and/or fresh red raspberries.

## DOUBLE VANILLA FROZEN YOGURT

Prepare as directed, except omit lemon juice. Split 1 or 2 vanilla beans lengthwise; scrape seeds from beans. Stir the seeds into yogurt before freezing in the ice cream maker.

## PEACH FROZEN YOGURT

Prepare as directed, except puree 2 cups fresh or frozen (thawed) sliced peaches; swirl into yogurt before placing in airtight container and freezing.

## TESTING NOTES

1. Ice cream makers work by churning a dairy mixture to incorporate air and prevent large ice crystals from forming during the freezing process (small ice crystals = smooth texture). This recipe calls for a small countertop ice cream freezer, which is widely available.

↑

2. When adequately frozen in the ice cream maker, the Greek yogurt mixture will be thick, rich, and creamy. At this point, you'll transfer the mixture to a freezer-safe container with a tight-fitting lid.

↑

3. Sneak a couple of spoonfuls of the finished Greek Frozen Yogurt before you put it in a freezer container, but then let the mixture ripen in the freezer 2 to 4 hours to improve its consistency and flavor.

# DESSERTS

# 091 CHOCOLATE SOUR CREAM CAKE WITH FUDGY FROSTING

TASTING COMMENTS: *No one likes a dry cake. The goal was to make a moist AND tender version. The sour cream helped with the moisture, but the key to tenderness was beating the sugar and shortening together at least 3 minutes. I set a timer to make sure I didn't skimp on the time!—SM*

**PREP** 45 MINUTES   **STAND** 30 MINUTES   **BAKE** 25 MINUTES AT 350°F   **COOL** 2 HOURS

*Chop the chocolate and heat it in a small heavy saucepan over low, stirring constantly, just until it begins to melt. Take it off the heat and keep stirring until smooth. Be sure all of your equipment is dry—just a drop of water can cause the chocolate to seize up!*

- 1½ cups all-purpose flour, plus more for pan
- ⅓ cup unsweetened cocoa powder, plus more for pan
- 1 tsp. baking powder
- ½ tsp. baking soda
- ½ tsp. salt
- ½ cup shortening
- 1¼ cups sugar
- 2 eggs, room temperature
- 1 tsp. vanilla
- 3 oz. bittersweet chocolate, melted and cooled
- 1 8-oz. carton sour cream
- 1 cup milk
- 1 recipe Fudgy Frosting (page 271)

1. Grease and flour two 9-inch round cake pans or grease and coat with cocoa powder. Set aside.

2. Preheat oven to 350°F. In a small bowl combine flour, cocoa powder, baking powder, baking soda, and salt. In a large mixing bowl beat shortening and sugar with mixer on medium until light, about 3 to 5 minutes. Add eggs and vanilla; beat until combined. Beat in melted chocolate and sour cream. Add about one-third of the flour mixture; beat on low speed just until combined. Add half of the milk; beat just until combined. Repeat to add the remaining flour mixture and milk, ending with the flour mixture. Divide batter evenly between the prepared pans. Using a small offset metal spatula or a rubber spatula, smooth top of batter in each pan.

3. Bake about 25 minutes or until a wooden pick inserted near centers comes out clean. Cool cake layers in pans on wire racks 10 minutes. Using a small metal spatula, loosen sides of each cake layer. Place a wire rack on top of one pan; carefully invert pan with rack (use pot holders to protect your hands). Lift pan off cake layer. Repeat with the remaining cake layer. Cool cake layers on wire racks about 2 hours or until completely cool.

4. To assemble cake, place one cake layer, flat side down, on a serving plate. Spread top of this cake layer with 1 cup of the Fudgy Frosting. Place second cake layer, flat side down, on top of the frosting. Spread top and sides with the remaining Fudgy Frosting.

PER SERVING *555 cal., 27 g fat (14 g sat. fat), 56 mg chol., 201 mg sodium, 77 g carb., 2 g fiber, 63 g sugars, 4 g pro.*

## TESTING NOTES

↑

**1.** Grease two 9-inch cake pans with butter or shortening. Sprinkle about 1 Tbsp. cocoa powder or flour into each pan. While holding a pan with one hand, use the other to tap the pan and move the flour or cocoa powder around until it covers the bottom and sides.

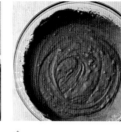

↑

**3.** Beat on low only as long as it takes to combine each addition of wet and dry ingredients. Overmixing will pop the bubbles and leave you with a flat, dense cake. It will also start to develop the gluten in the flour, leaving you with a tough, rubbery cake.

↑

**2.** Beat the shortening and sugar on medium speed until light, about 5 minutes. It's the most important step when making a shortened (or creamed) cake. Tiny air bubbles are created and trapped in the mixture, acting as a leavener along with the baking powder and baking soda. Preserving these bubbles is essential to having a light and fluffy crumb after baking.

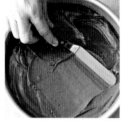

↑

**4.** Measure the finished amount of batter. This will tell you exactly how much to put in each pan. An even amount in each pan results in even layers for the finished cake. A small offset spatula is the best tool for spreading the batter in each pan and for smoothing the tops of the cakes. This helps the cakes bake evenly.

**5.** To test the doneness of the cake, at the minimum baking time poke a toothpick into the center of each cake. If it comes out clean, the cakes are finished. When gently touched with your finger, the top of the cake should spring back.

**MAKE A CAKE ANY SIZE YOU WANT** *This recipe is super versatile. We tested different sizes of cake for accurate bake times. You can make one large cake or your favorite-size cupcakes. Grease the pans and dust with cocoa powder or add paper cupcake liners to the cupcake pan.*

2½-inch cupcakes, 16 to 18 minutes

13×9-inch baking pan, 20 to 25 minutes

Jumbo 3½-inch cupcakes, 22 to 25 minutes

Fluted tube pan, 35 to 40 minutes

*If you want a very even layer cake, trim the rounded top of the bottom layer with a serrated knife so it will sit level when stacked.*

9-inch round pans, 25 minutes

MAKES: *4 cups*  TESTED BY: *Sammy M.*

# FUDGY FROSTING

TASTING COMMENTS: *Cooling the melted chocolate before adding the sour cream is the key to velvety frosting. I occasionally stirred the melted chocolate to speed up cooling.—SM*

**START TO FINISH** 10 MINUTES

1 12-oz. pkg. semisweet chocolate baking pieces

½ cup butter

1 8-oz. carton sour cream

4½ cups powdered sugar (1 lb.)

**1.** In a large saucepan combine chocolate and butter. Heat over low heat until melted and smooth, stirring constantly. Remove from heat; cool 10 minutes. Stir in sour cream. Gradually add powdered sugar, beating vigorously swith a wooden spoon until smooth.

## INGREDIENTS TO KNOW

*Natural unsweetened cocoa powder gives you the most intense chocolate flavor!*

**BITTERSWEET CHOCOLATE**
Bittersweet chocolate is considered a dark chocolate and contains as much as 85% cacao. Bittersweet chocolate is an excellent choice for this cake batter, which contains the right amount of sugar to balance out the strong flavor of the chocolate.

**COCOA POWDER**
Because cocoa powder is slightly acidic, this recipe includes baking soda (in addition to baking powder) as a leavener.

**SOUR CREAM**
Sour cream helps to make the cake moist and tender. This acidic ingredient reacts with the baking soda, releasing gas bubbles to help leaven your cake.

## TESTING NOTES

↑
1. A heavy-bottom pan is essential to melt the butter and chocolate for this frosting. It helps to prevent burning or scalding on the bottom of the pan. After the mixture is melted, take the pan off the heat and let it cool 10 minutes.

↑
2. After adding the sour cream and powdered sugar, the end consistency of the frosting should be silky and smooth. For tips on how to frost a cake, see page 275.

MAKES: *12 servings*  TESTED BY: *Juli H.*

# 092  WHITE CAKE

TASTING COMMENTS:  *Separate the whites from the yolks when the eggs are cold—it's easier—then let them stand at room temperature for 30 minutes. They'll beat up fluffier, which means a lighter cake!—JH*

**PREP** 55 MINUTES   **BAKE** 30 MINUTES AT 350°F   **COOL** 1 HOUR

- 2 cups all-purpose flour
- 1 tsp. baking powder
- ½ tsp. baking soda
- ½ tsp. salt
- ½ cup butter or shortening, softened
- 1¾ cups sugar
- 1 tsp. vanilla
- 4 egg whites, room temperature
- 1⅓ cups buttermilk or sour milk (see tip, page 53)
- 1 recipe Butter Frosting (page 274)

**1.** Preheat oven to 350°F. Grease and lightly flour two 9-inch or 8-inch round cake pans or grease one 13×9-inch baking pan; set pan(s) aside. In a medium bowl stir together the first four ingredients (through salt).

**2.** In a large bowl beat butter with a mixer on medium to high 30 seconds. Add sugar and vanilla; beat 3 to 5 minutes or until light. Add egg whites, one at a time, beating well after each addition. Alternately add flour mixture and buttermilk, beating on low after each addition just until combined. (Begin and end with flour mixture.) Spread batter into prepared pan(s).

**3.** Bake 30 to 35 minutes or until a wooden toothpick inserted near center(s) comes out clean. Cool cake layers in pans on wire racks 10 minutes. Remove layers from pans; cool on racks. Or cool 13×9-inch cake in pan on a wire rack. Frost with desired flavor of Butter Frosting.

PER SERVING *275 cal., 8 g fat (5 g sat. fat), 21 mg chol., 271 mg sodium, 47 g carb., 1 g fiber, 31 g sugars, 4 g pro.*

## REMOVING CAKES FROM PANS STEP-BY-STEP

**1.** Once cake layers have cooled for 10 minutes only, run a thin metal spatula or knife around the edges of the cake pan. Place a cooling rack over top.

**2.** Invert the pan with the rack so the pan ends up on top. Shake gently to loosen cake layer from the pan.

**3.** If you lined the bottom of the cake layer with paper, carefully remove the paper, pulling slowly and gently.

## TESTING NOTES

**1.** This is the most important step when making a "shortened" (or creamed) cake. Beat the fat and sugar together for 3 to 5 minutes. Don't cut this short. Tiny air bubbles are created and trapped in the mixture, acting as a leavener along with the baking powder and soda in this recipe. Preserving these bubbles is essential to having a light and fluffy crumb texture.

↓

↑

**2.** Add egg whites, one at a time, beating after each until integrated. The protein in the egg whites helps create structure around the air bubbles to reinforce the texture.

↑

**3.** When adding milk and the dry ingredients alternately, gluten can develop. Too much gluten makes for a tough cake. If you add more of the flour first, it will be coated with the butter and protected from gluten development. Once you add milk, gluten might form. Beat on low speed and try not to overmix at this point. Batter may look curdled at certain times through this step.

**4.** Plan to end with the last of your milk instead of the last of your flour, beating on low just until combined.

↓

↑

**5.** Pour batter evenly between prepared pans. Using a metal spatula, smooth tops before baking.

MAKES: *12 servings*  TESTED BY: *Juli H.*

# BUTTER FROSTING

TASTING COMMENTS: *Always do a crumb coat—a very thin layer of frosting over the entire cake that you let dry before frosting more thickly—to prevent crumbs in your frosting and tears in your cake layers.—JH*

**START TO FINISH** 20 MINUTES

¾ cup butter, softened

8 cups powdered sugar
(about 2 lb.)

⅓ cup milk

2 tsp. vanilla

Milk

Food coloring
(optional)

1. In an extra-large bowl beat butter with a mixer on medium until smooth. Gradually add 2 cups of the powdered sugar, beating well. Slowly beat in the ⅓ cup milk and the vanilla. Gradually beat in remaining powdered sugar. Beat in enough additional milk to reach spreading consistency. If desired, tint with food coloring. (This frosts the tops and sides of two 8- or 9-inch layers. Halve the recipe to frost a 13×9-inch cake.)

PER SERVING *401 cal., 12 g fat (7 g sat. fat), 31 mg chol., 85 mg sodium, 76 g carb., 0 g fiber, 74 g sugars, 0 g pro.*

**CITRUS** Substitute lemon or orange juice for the milk; add ½ tsp. lemon or orange zest. Top frosted cake with additional zest.

**DARK CHOCOLATE** Substitute ½ cup unsweetened cocoa powder for ½ cup of the powdered sugar.

**COFFEE** Add 1 Tbsp. instant espresso coffee powder or instant coffee crystals or substitute strong brewed coffee for the milk. Top frosted cake with chocolate-covered coffee beans.

**PEPPERMINT** Substitute ½ tsp. peppermint extract for the vanilla; if desired, tint pink with red food coloring. Sprinkle top of frosted cake with crushed peppermint candies; press additional candies on sides of cake.

**ALMOND** Substitute ½ tsp. almond extract for the vanilla. Top frosted cake with toasted sliced almonds.

**MILK CHOCOLATE** Melt 1 cup milk chocolate baking pieces and beat into the butter before adding powdered sugar. Top frosted cake with chocolate curls.

**PEANUT BUTTER** Beat ½ cup peanut butter into butter before adding powdered sugar. Top frosted cake with chopped peanuts.

**STRAWBERRY** Beat ⅓ cup strawberry jam into butter before adding powdered sugar. Top frosted cake with fresh strawberries.

## TESTING NOTES

1. Place the first cake layer on a pedestal or cake plate. If necessary, use a serrated knife to trim the rounded surface off the cake layer so it sits flat (see below). For quick cleanup, tuck small pieces of waxed paper around and under the cake. Spread ½ cup frosting evenly over surface to ¼ inch of the edge.

2. Place the second cake layer on top of the frosting. Trim surface of cake if desired. Center the cake, aligning the edges of the layers.

3. Spread a very thin coat of frosting over the entire cake to seal in crumbs and fill in imperfections. Allow the crumb coat to dry before finishing frosting the cake. Using the thin metal spatula, frost cake with the remaining frosting. Push the frosting onto the sides of the cake without moving the spatula back and forth.

## FINISH IT!

**STRIPES** Using a straight metal spatula and starting at the base of the cake, pull the spatula straight up toward the top of the cake. Repeat until you've covered the entire cake.

**ROSES** Place your remaining frosting in a pastry bag fitted with a large star tip and pipe rose circles around the cake. You can decide how large or small and how closely spaced they are.

↓

↑

**PETALS** Place your remaining frosting in a pastry bag fitted with an open tip or transfer frosting to a gallon resealable plastisc bag and cut off a corner. Pipe three dots of frosting of similar size in a row from top to bottom. Using a rounded knife or thin metal spatula, place the tip in the center of the frosting dot and pull the frosting horizontally to one side; repeat.

**FILLING FLAVORS** *Add a little flavor surprise to your layer cake. Instead of using frosting between the two cake layers, spread approximately ½ to ⅔ cup jam or preserves; lemon, orange, or lime curd; or chocolate-hazelnut spread.*

**FROSTING TOOLS** *Two of the best tools to have are a thin straight or offset metal spatula and a long serrated knife. The thin metal spatula comes in many sizes; if you don't feel like a pro, choose a smaller spatula. A LONG serrated knife is best for making cake layers even and trimming when necessary.*

# 093   CARROT CAKE

TASTING COMMENTS: *While shredded carrots add moisture and natural sweetness to this cake, you don't want to bite into a big chunk of carrot in your dessert. Use a fine box grater or a food processor for the ideal size.—CC*

**PREP** 30 MINUTES   **BAKE** 35 MINUTES AT 350°F   **COOL** 2 HOURS

- 2 cups all-purpose flour
- 2 cups sugar
- 2 tsp. baking powder
- 1 tsp. ground cinnamon
- ½ tsp. salt
- ½ tsp. baking soda
- 4 eggs, room temperature
- 3 cups finely shredded carrots, lightly packed
- ¾ cup vegetable oil
- 1 recipe Cream Cheese Frosting
  Chopped pecans and/or pecan halves, toasted (tip, page 248) (optional)

*Lightly beating the eggs incorporates air, which, when coupled with baking powder, serves as a leavening agent for this cake.*

**1.** Preheat oven to 350°F. Grease and flour two 8-inch round cake pans. In a large bowl stir together the first six ingredients (through baking soda).

**2.** In another bowl lightly beat eggs; add carrots and oil. Add egg mixture to flour mixture. Stir until combined. Pour batter into prepared pans.

**3.** Bake 35 to 40 minutes or until a wooden pick inserted near centers comes out clean. Cool cake layers in pans on wire racks 10 minutes. Remove layers from pans. Cool on wire racks.

**4.** Frost cake with Cream Cheese Frosting. If desired, lightly press chopped pecans onto sides of cake and pipe additional frosting around top edge of cake. Cover cake and store in the refrigerator up to 3 days.

**CREAM CHEESE FROSTING** In a large bowl combine one 8-oz. pkg. cream cheese, softened; ½ cup butter, softened; and 2 tsp. vanilla. Beat with an electric mixer on medium speed until light and fluffy. Using 5½ to 6 cups powdered sugar, gradually beat in enough powdered sugar to reach spreading consistency. (This frosting complements most cakes. The recipe makes enough to frost the tops and sides of two 8- or 9-inch layers. Halve the recipe to frost a 13×9-inch cake.)

PER SERVING *705 cal., 30 g fat (11 g sat. fat), 103 mg chol., 394 mg sodium, 107 g carb., 1 g fiber, 89 g sugars, 6 g pro.*

**SWEET POTATO CAKE** Prepare as directed, except substitute 3 cups (about 1 lb.) peeled, finely shredded orange-flesh sweet potatoes for the carrots.

**CONFETTI CARROT CAKE** Prepare as directed, except use only 1 cup finely shredded carrot and add 1 cup finely shredded zucchini and 1 cup finely shredded yellow summer squash.

*1 carrot = ½ cup finely shredded; you will need about 6 carrots for this recipe*

## TESTING NOTES

**1.** Use the fine shredding surface of a box grater to shred your carrots. They will stay evenly distributed in the cake and won't sink.

↓

↑

**2.** For cakes that slip right out of the pan, combine ¼ cup vegetable oil, ¼ cup shortening, and ⅓ cup flour. Brush on the mixture when a recipe calls for greasing the pan. You can store the mixture in the fridge up to 3 days.

↑

**3.** Oil-base cakes are usually moist with a dense crumb. The oil coats the flour proteins, which helps prevent gluten from developing. Too much gluten makes a tough cake! When mixing an oil-base cake, stir together wet ingredients, then stir them into the dry ingredients just until combined. The batter will be lumpy.

↑

**4.** To make cleanup easy, tuck parchment or waxed paper under the bottom layer of cake before frosting. When you are finished, gently pull the paper from under the cake and discard.

**5.** After letting your cakes cool about 10 minutes in pans and then 2 hours on wire racks, spread about ½ cup of the frosting over the first layer. Top with the second layer.

↓

↑

**6.** An offset spatula makes frosting a two-layer cake a breeze! Using this perfect tool, spread a paper-thin coating of frosting onto the cake to seal in crumbs and fill in imperfections. Allow the crumb coat to dry before frosting the rest of the cake. Then use the same great little spatula held vertically against the cake to push the frosting onto the sides, turning the cake to apply an even coat.

# 094  CLASSIC NEW YORK–STYLE CHEESECAKE

TASTING COMMENTS: *The key to a smooth, crack-free cheesecake is lightly stirring the beaten eggs into the batter. Overbeating the filling once the eggs are added whips in too much air. This causes the cheesecake to puff in the oven, then fall and crack when it cools. —LB*

**PREP** 40 MINUTES   **BAKE** 45 MINUTES AT 350°F   **COOL** 45 MINUTES
**CHILL** 4 HOURS   **STAND** 15 MINUTES

*Change up your crust by swapping an equal amount of crushed vanilla wafers, chocolate wafers, or gingersnaps for the graham cracker crumbs.*

2¼ cups finely crushed graham crackers
1 Tbsp. sugar
½ tsp. ground cinnamon (optional)
⅔ cup butter, melted
4 8-oz. pkg. cream cheese, room temperature
1¼ cups sugar
¼ cup all-purpose flour
3 eggs, room temperature
4 tsp. vanilla
2 8-oz. cartons sour cream
¼ cup sugar

1. Preheat oven to 350°F. For crust, in a large bowl combine crushed graham crackers, the 1 Tbsp. sugar, and, if desired, the cinnamon. Stir in melted butter. Press crumb mixture onto the bottom and about 2 inches up the sides of a 10-inch springform pan.

2. In a large bowl combine cream cheese and the 1¼ cups sugar; beat with a mixer on medium to high until fluffy. Add flour; beat on low until smooth. Using a fork, lightly beat the eggs. Add eggs and 3 tsp. of the vanilla all at once to the cream cheese mixture; stir just until combined. Stir in ½ cup of the sour cream. Pour filling into crust-lined pan. Place pan in a shallow baking pan in oven.

3. Bake 40 minutes or until a 2½-inch area around the outside edge appears set when gently shaken. Remove from oven. In a medium bowl stir together the remaining sour cream, the ¼ cup sugar, and the remaining 1 tsp. vanilla. Gently spread sour cream mixture on top of cheesecake. Return to oven; bake 5 minutes more.

4. Cool in pan on a wire rack 15 minutes. Using a small sharp knife, loosen crust from sides of springform pan. Cool 30 minutes. Remove sides of pan; cool on rack. Cover and chill at least 4 hours or overnight before serving. Let stand at room temperature 15 minutes before cutting. Store, covered, in the refrigerator up to 5 days.

**MAKE-AHEAD DIRECTIONS** Bake and cool cheesecake as directed. Place cheesecake in a freezer bag or freezer container and freeze up to 1 month. Thaw cheesecake in refrigerator 24 hours (or thaw individual pieces 30 minutes at room temperature).

PER SERVING *466 cal., 35 g fat (20 g sat. fat), 132 mg chol., 342 mg sodium, 34 g carb., 0 g fiber, 26 g sugars, 6 g pro.*

**PUMPKIN CHEESECAKE** Prepare crust as directed, except omit New York–Style Cheesecake filling and topping. In a large bowl beat four 8-oz. pkg. softened cream cheese and 1 cup sugar on medium until fluffy and combined, scraping bowl occasionally. Add one 15-oz. can pumpkin, 1 Tbsp. pumpkin pie spice, and 1 tsp. vanilla; beat until well combined. In a bowl lightly beat 4 eggs; stir into the pumpkin mixture until combined. Pour filling into crust. Bake 45 minutes or until a 2½-inch area around the outside edge appears set when gently shaken. Remove from oven. Cool as directed. If desired, garnish with pomegranate seeds before serving.

## TESTING NOTES

↑

1. Use your hands to press crumbs evenly into the bottom of the pan and about 2 inches up the sides. To smooth out the crust, run a small measuring cup firmly across the crumbs.

2. Softened cream cheese is easier to beat into other ingredients (and doesn't leave big pieces in your otherwise silky batter). Soften the cream cheese by letting it stand at room temperature on the countertop 30 minutes. In a pinch, microwave the unwrapped cream cheese on the defrost setting for 10 seconds at a time, checking after each interval.

↑

3. Cheesecakes are thickened with lightly beaten eggs, which give a cheesecake its light and airy texture. Gently fold in the eggs—overbeating will incorporate too much air, which causes the cheesecake to puff up too high during baking. When it falls during cooling, it will create cracks in the filling.

4. New York cheesecake consists of three layers: crust, filling, and a sweetened sour cream topping. The sour cream topping is added near the end of the baking time so the layers stay separate and intact. When the filling is set, remove cheesecake from the oven and gently spread the sour cream mixture evenly over the top. The cheesecake is then baked 5 more minutes just to set the topping.

↓

*Overbeating the eggs or filling incorporates excess air, which causes the filling to puff too much in the oven, then fall and crack as it cools.*

*Overbaking makes the filling dry and crumbly—nothing like the delicate, creamy texture cheesecakes are known for.*

**IS IT DONE YET?** *The hardest part of making cheesecake is knowing when it's done baking. For most cheesecakes, there will be a small area in the center that is still wobbly when gently shaken, while 2½ inches around the outside edges will be set. No worries! The jiggly portion in the center will firm up during chilling. For the New York-Style Cheesecake, the sour cream topping is added at this doneness point, then returned to the oven for just 5 more minutes of baking.*

**THE WATER BATH METHOD** *A water bath will help your cheesecake bake slowly and evenly, protecting and insulating the delicate filling so the outer edge of the cake won't bake faster than the center. Place your crust-lined springform pan on a double layer of heavy-duty foil. Bring edges of foil up and mold around sides of pan to form a watertight seal. Place springform pan into a roasting pan. After adding the cheesecake filling, pour enough boiling water into the roasting pan to reach halfway up the sides of the springform pan (keep water level below the foil). Bake 60 minutes. Turn off oven; let stand in oven 60 minutes. Promptly remove from water bath; cool as directed.*

**SPRINGFORM PAN** *Cheesecakes are baked in a springform pan—a round pan with straight sides that expand with the help of a clamp. The separate bottom can be removed from the sides to make serving the cheesecake a breeze. Springform pans are ideal for the soft texture of traditional cheesecake—removing a cheesecake from any other type of pan is nearly impossible.*

*Store cheesecake, covered, in the refrigerator up to 5 days. Make sure not to let the plastic wrap touch the surface of the cheesecake.*

MAKES: *8 servings*   TESTED BY: *Kelsey B.*

# 095   DOUBLE-CRUST FRUIT PIE

TASTING COMMENTS: *Always roll each pastry half from the center to the edge, working to create uniform circles. Achieving two nicely shaped circles makes trimming and crimping that much easier!—KB*

**PREP** 30 MINUTES   **BAKE** 1 HOUR 5 MINUTES AT 375°F

1 recipe Pastry for a
   Double-Crust Pie
1 recipe filling
   (recipes, right)
   Milk (optional)
   Sugar (optional)

**1.** Preheat oven to 375°F. Prepare and roll out Pastry for a Double-Crust Pie. Transfer half the pastry to a 9-inch pie plate, being careful not to stretch pastry.

**2.** For filling, in an extra-large bowl combine ingredients.* Transfer filling to the pastry-lined pie plate. Trim pastry to edge of pie plate. Cut slits in remaining pastry; place on filling. Crimp edge as desired.

**3.** If desired, brush pastry with milk and sprinkle with additional sugar. To prevent overbrowning, cover edge of pie with foil. Place a foil-lined baking sheet on the rack below the pie in oven. Bake 30 minutes (50 minutes for frozen fruit). Remove foil. Bake 35 to 40 minutes more or until fruit is tender and filling is bubbly. Cool on a wire rack.

*****TIP** For added flavor, add one of the following to filling with the flour: ½ tsp. lemon zest, ¼ to ½ tsp. ground cinnamon or ground ginger, ¼ tsp. ground allspice, or ⅛ tsp. ground nutmeg; or add ¼ tsp. almond extract with the fruit.

**PASTRY FOR A DOUBLE-CRUST PIE**
In a large bowl stir together 2½ cups all-purpose flour and 1 tsp. salt. Using a pastry blender, cut in ½ cup shortening and ¼ cup cut-up butter until pieces are pea size. Sprinkle 1 Tbsp. ice water over part of the flour mixture; toss gently with a fork. Push moistened dough to side of bowl. Repeat with additional ice water, 1 Tbsp. at a time (½ to ⅔ cup total), until all of the flour mixture is moistened. Gather mixture into a ball, kneading gently until it holds together. Divide dough in half. Shape each portion into a ball.

**PEACH OR NECTARINE** 6 cups peaches or nectarines, pitted and thinly sliced; ½ to 1 cup sugar; 3 Tbsp. all-purpose flour or 1½ Tbsp. quick-cooking tapioca or cornstarch

**PEAR** 6 cups pears, peeled, cored, and thinly sliced; ⅓ to ½ cup sugar; 3 Tbsp. all-purpose flour

**RASPBERRY** 6 cups raspberries; ¾ to 1 cup sugar; ¼ cup all-purpose flour or 2 Tbsp. quick-cooking tapioca or cornstarch

**RHUBARB** 6 cups 1-inch pieces rhubarb; 1¼ to 1½ cups sugar; ½ cup all-purpose flour or ¼ cup quick-cooking tapioca or cornstarch

**APPLE** 6 cups peeled, cored, and thinly sliced apples; ½ to ¾ cup sugar; 2 Tbsp. all-purpose flour

**BLACKBERRY** 6 cups blackberries; 1 to 1¼ cups sugar; ⅓ cup all-purpose flour or 3 Tbsp. quick-cooking tapioca or cornstarch

**BLUEBERRY** 6 cups blueberries; 1 to 1¼ cups sugar; ¼ cup all-purpose flour or 2 Tbsp. quick-cooking tapioca or cornstarch

**CHERRY** 6 cups tart cherries, pitted; 1¼ to 1½ cups sugar; ⅓ cup all-purpose flour or 3 Tbsp. quick-cooking tapioca or cornstarch

**GOOSEBERRY** 6 cups gooseberries, stemmed; 1¼ to 1½ cups sugar; ⅓ cup all-purpose flour or 3 Tbsp. quick-cooking tapioca or cornstarch

## TESTING NOTES

↑
1. After filling the pastry-lined pie plate, use kitchen shears or a sharp knife to trim the bottom pastry even with the plate's edge.

↑
3. Gently fold the pastry in half and carefully place it on top of the filling, making sure to cover half of the filling. Unfold the pastry to cover other half of filling.

↑
2. Roll out remaining pie pastry. Use a sharp knife to cut slits in the pastry to allow steam to escape (or use small cutters for a decorative look).

↑
4. Using kitchen shears, trim the top pastry ½ inch beyond the edge of the plate. Fold the top pastry under the bottom pastry edge and crimp as desired.

**FRESH OR FROZEN?** *For the best pies, take advantage of fruit that is fresh and in season. If you have a craving for rhubarb pie in the winter, you can use frozen fruit. Don't thaw the fruit before measuring. Measure it frozen and let it stand at least 30 minutes once it is tossed with the sugar mixuture.*

## LATTICE

For a lattice top, cut half the pastry into ½-inch-wide strips. Lay half of the strips on top of the filling about 1 inch apart. Fold alternating pastry strips back halfway. Place a strip in the center of the pie across the strips already in place. Unfold the folded strips. Place another strip across the first set of strips parallel to the strip in the center. Repeat until lattice covers filling.

## PRETTY PIECRUSTS

**CHEVRON CRUST** Prepare Pastry for a Double-Crust Pie as directed; roll out bottom pastry and fill as directed. Trim to ½ inch beyond edge of pie plate. Roll remaining dough as directed. Cut zigzag strips from the dough. Arrange strips on pie, spacing about 1 inch apart. Trim strips so they're even with the edge of the pie plate. Fold extra ½ inch bottom pastry over the strips; crimp as desired. If desired, sprinkle with sugar. Bake pie as directed.

**POINSETTIA CRUST** Prepare Pastry for a Double-Crust Pie as directed; roll out bottom pastry and fill as directed. Trim to ½ inch beyond edge of pie plate. Roll remaining ball of dough as directed. Use a small pizza cutter or knife to cut pastry into strips of various lengths and widths. Lay strips on filled, unbaked pie from the center to the edge, allowing them to overlap and hang over the edge slightly to create a flower shape. Cut a 2-inch circle from the dough and place in the center; roll scraps of dough into small balls and arrange in the center of the circle, brushing with lightly beaten egg to help balls adhere. Brush petals with beaten egg. Sprinkle with sugar. Bake pie as directed.

**LEAF CRUST** Prepare Pastry for a Double-Crust Pie as directed; roll out bottom pastry and fill as directed. Trim to ½ inch beyond edge of pie plate. Crimp bottom pastry as desired. Bake pie as directed. Meanwhile, roll remaining ball of dough as directed. Use a leaf-shape cutter to cut shapes; arrange on a parchment paper-lined baking sheet. If desired, use a small knife to make indentations in leaves for veins. Brush lightly with beaten egg; sprinkle with sugar. Bake until golden and crisp; cool. Arrange leaves on pie as desired. You can add a bit of desired frosting to help them adhere.

**DIAMOND CRUST** Prepare Pastry for a Double-Crust Pie as directed; roll out bottom pastry. Trim to ½ inch beyond edge of pie plate; fold under extra pastry. Crimp as desired. Add pie filling as directed. Roll remaining ball of dough as directed. Cut pastry into 1½-inch-wide strips. Cut each strip crosswise to create diamond shapes. Arrange pastry diamonds over the top of pie as desired. Brush diamonds with milk. Bake pie as directed.

**TIP** *Give some of the leaf cutouts dimension and curves by baking them on small rolls or balls of foil.*

MAKES: *6 servings* TESTED BY: *Juli H.*

# 096 MIXED-BERRY CROSTATA

TASTING COMMENTS: *This is a hybrid between a fresh berry tart and a fruit-filled pie. It starts with a baked berry filling and finishes with juicy fresh berries tossed in sugar and lemon juice. We held the amount of sugar in both to a minimum to allow the flavor of the fruit to really shine through. —JH*

**PREP** 25 MINUTES  **BAKE** 45 MINUTES AT 375°F  **COOL** 45 MINUTES  **STAND** 1 HOUR

1 recipe Crostata Pastry

⅓ cup granulated sugar

3 Tbsp. cornstarch

2 cups cut-up fresh strawberries

2 cups fresh blueberries

2 cups fresh raspberries

1 egg

1 Tbsp. water

1 tsp. coarse sugar

3 Tbsp. granulated sugar

2 Tbsp. lemon juice

**1.** Preheat oven to 375°F. On a lightly floured sheet of parchment paper roll Crostata Pastry to a 16×12-inch oval. Transfer pastry on parchment paper to a baking sheet.

**2.** For filling, in a medium bowl stir together the ⅓ cup sugar and the cornstarch. Add 1½ cups of the strawberries, 1½ cups of the blueberries, and 1½ cups of the raspberries; toss to coat. Spread filling on pastry, leaving a 2-inch border. Fold crust over filling. In a bowl whisk together egg and the water; brush over edges of pastry; sprinkle pastry with coarse sugar. Bake 25 minutes. Cut an oval out of foil to cover exposed filling. Bake 20 minutes more or until filling is bubbly and pastry is golden brown. Cool crostata on baking sheet on a wire rack 45 minutes.

**3.** Meanwhile, for berry topping, in a bowl stir together the remaining berries, the 3 Tbsp. sugar, and the lemon juice. Let stand at room temperature at least 1 hour. Spread topping over the fruit filling.

**CROSTATA PASTRY** In a medium bowl stir together 1½ cups flour, 2 Tbsp. sugar, and ½ tsp. salt. Cut ⅓ cup cold butter into pieces. Using a pastry blender or two knives, cut butter pieces into flour mixture until pieces are pea size. In a small bowl whisk together ⅓ cup cold water and 1 egg yolk. Sprinkle 1 Tbsp. of the water mixture over part of the flour mixture; toss with a fork. Push moistened pastry to sides of bowl. Repeat moistening flour mixture, using 1 Tbsp. of the water mixture at a time, until all of the flour mixture is moistened. Using your fingers, gently knead the dough just until a ball forms.

PER SERVING *393 cal., 13 g fat (7 g sat. fat), 89 mg chol., 300 mg sodium, 66 g carb., 6 g fiber, 32 g sugars, 6 g pro.*

**FRESH BERRIES MAKE ALL THE DIFFERENCE!** *When the crostata first goes into the oven, toss together the fresh berry topper, which needs to stand at least an hour before it goes on the crostata. The standing time will allow the sugar and lemon juice to draw out the natural juices in the berries to create a sweet-tart sauce.*

## TESTING NOTES

1. For an easy transfer to the baking sheet, roll out the pastry dough on a lightly floured piece of parchment paper, then simply slide the whole thing onto the pan—paper and all! The light-color parchment paper is oven-safe up to 425°F.

↓

↑

2. Heap the berry filling onto the center of the pastry oval, leaving a 2-inch border of pastry around the outside. This extra pastry will be folded up to partially hug the filling, holding it in place during baking.

3. Using the parchment paper as a guide, fold one part of the pastry up and over the filling. This will keep the pastry from tearing or ripping as you work with it.

↓

↑

4. Continue folding the pastry up and over the filling in sections, overlapping to create pleats. Continue folding and pleating all around the pastry oval. There is no right or wrong way to do this. Just nestle the pastry against the filling.

↑

5. Brushing the pastry with egg wash does double duty—first, it gives the sugar something to stick to so it doesn't just fall off; second, it turns the crust a golden brown during baking.

↑

6. To prevent the berries from getting dry or crispy during the last part of the baking time, cut or fold a piece of foil to fit just over the exposed filling in the center. Don't let the foil cover the crostata beyond the filling or the pastry won't brown evenly.

# 097   LEMON MERINGUE PIE

TASTING COMMENTS: *Getting a piece of meringue pie that holds a nice edge depends on ensuring that the filling doesn't squish out of the crust when it's sliced. The secret: Don't cut the cooking time short. That last 2 minutes is a make-or-break step!—LB*

**PREP** 40 MINUTES   **BAKE** 30 MINUTES AT 325°F   **COOL** 1 HOUR   **CHILL** 5 HOURS

1 recipe Baked
  Pastry Shell

5 eggs

2 cups sugar

→ ⅓ cup cornstarch

2 tsp. lemon zest
  (optional)

1 cup water

¾ cup lemon juice

⅓ cup butter, cut up

1 recipe Five-Egg
  White Meringue

*Cornstarch must be added to a cold liquid and then heated for it to lose its starchy flavor and start the thickening process. Closely follow the timings in the recipe for perfectly thickened filling.*

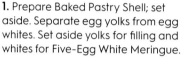

*1 medium lemon = about 3 Tbsp. juice and 2 tsp. zest*

**1.** Prepare Baked Pastry Shell; set aside. Separate egg yolks from egg whites. Set aside yolks for filling and whites for Five-Egg White Meringue.

**2.** Preheat oven to 325°F. For filling, in a medium saucepan stir together sugar and cornstarch. Stir in lemon zest (if desired), the water, and lemon juice. Cook and stir over medium heat until thickened and bubbly. Remove from heat.

**3.** Lightly beat egg yolks with a whisk. Gradually whisk half of the hot lemon mixture into the egg yolks. Return egg yolk mixture to saucepan. Bring to a gentle boil; reduce heat. Cook and whisk 2 minutes more. Remove from heat. Add butter pieces, whisking until melted. Cover filling with plastic wrap and keep warm.

**4.** Prepare Five-Egg White Meringue. Pour warm filling into Baked Pastry Shell. Immediately spoon meringue over filling; spread meringue evenly, sealing it to the edges of the pastry shell. Using the back of a spoon, swirl meringue to form high, decorative peaks. Bake 30 minutes. Cool 1 hour on a wire rack. Chill 5 to 6 hours before serving; cover pie for longer storage.

**BAKED PASTRY SHELL** Preheat oven to 450°F. In a medium bowl stir together 1½ cups all-purpose flour and ½ tsp. salt. Using a pastry blender, cut in ¼ cup shortening and ¼ cup butter, cut up, until pieces are pea size. Sprinkle 1 Tbsp. ice water over part of the flour mixture; toss gently with a fork. Push

moistened dough to side of bowl. Repeat with additional ice water, 1 Tbsp. at a time (¼ to ⅓ cup ice water total), until all of the flour mixture is moistened. Gather mixture into a ball, kneading gently until it holds together. On a lightly floured surface use your hands to slightly flatten pastry. Roll pastry from center to edge into a 12-inch circle. Wrap pastry circle around rolling pin; unroll into a 9-inch pie plate. Ease pastry into pie plate without stretching it. Trim pastry to ½ inch beyond edge of pie plate. Fold under extra pastry to make even with edge of pie plate. Crimp edge as desired. With a fork, prick side and bottom of pastry. Line pastry with double thickness of foil. Bake 8 minutes. Remove foil. Bake 6 to 8 minutes more or until pastry is golden brown. Cool on a wire rack.

**FIVE-EGG WHITE MERINGUE** Allow 5 egg whites to stand at room temperature 30 minutes. In a large bowl combine the egg whites, 1 tsp. vanilla, and ½ tsp. cream of tartar. Beat with a mixer on medium about 1 minute or until soft peaks form (tips curl). Add 1 cup sugar, 1 Tbsp. at a time, beating on high 6 minutes or until mixture forms stiff, glossy peaks (tips stand straight) and sugar dissolves (rub a small amount between two fingers; it should feel completely smooth).

PER SERVING *623 cal., 23 g fat (11 g sat. fat), 167 mg chol., 283 mg sodium, 101 g carb., 1 g fiber, 76 g sugars, 7 g pro.*

## TESTING NOTES

1. Even a little fat will hinder your meringue. Beat room-temperature egg whites, vanilla, and cream of tartar just until the tips curl over. The whites will move less like liquid in the bowl once you hit soft-peak stage.

↓

↑

2. Add the sugar to the egg white mixture, 1 Tbsp. at a time, beating continuously. Occasionally rub a small amount of meringue between your fingers. It should feel smooth if the sugar is dissolved. If not, keep beating before you add more.

↑

3. The meringue is ready when the mixture forms stiff, glossy peaks (the tips will stand straight) and all of the sugar has dissolved.

↑

4. To test the texture of the meringue for doneness, rub a small amount between two fingers. It should feel completely smooth.

↑

5. Spread the meringue over the filling while it is still hot to prevent the meringue from weeping (forming a watery layer between the meringue and filling) after baking.

↑

6. Make sure the meringue completely covers the hot filling right up to the edge of the crust. This helps the bottom of the meringue cook and stick to the filling so it won't slide off the pie when it is cut. Use a small spoon or spatula to make high peaks and decorative swirls in the meringue before baking.

MAKES: *6 servings*   TESTED BY: *Kelsey B.*

# 098 STRAWBERRY SHORTCAKE

TASTING COMMENTS: *A high oven temp produces a flaky shortcake that's light and fluffy inside. The heat turns the liquid in the batter to steam, which lightens the texture.—KB*

**PREP** 25 MINUTES   **BAKE** 18 MINUTES AT 400°F

1½ cups all-purpose flour

¼ cup sugar

1 tsp. baking powder

¼ tsp. salt

¼ tsp. baking soda

⅓ cup cold butter

1 egg, lightly beaten

½ cup sour cream or plain yogurt

3 Tbsp. milk

5 cups sliced fresh strawberries

3 Tbsp. sugar

1 recipe Sweetened Whipped Cream

**1.** Preheat oven to 400°F. Grease an 8-inch round baking pan. In a bowl combine the first five ingredients (through baking soda). Using a pastry blender, cut in butter until mixture resembles coarse crumbs. Using the back of a spoon, make a well in the center of the flour mixture. In another bowl stir together egg, sour cream, and milk; add to flour mixture all at once, stirring with a fork just until moistened.

**2.** Using a small offset metal spatula, spread dough in the prepared pan. Bake 18 to 20 minutes or until a wooden pick inserted near center comes out clean. Cool in pan on a wire rack 10 minutes. Using a small metal spatula, loosen sides of shortcake. Invert pan onto the wire rack; lift pan off shortcake. Cool on rack.

**3.** Meanwhile, combine 4 cups of the strawberries and the 3 Tbsp. sugar. If desired, mash berries slightly.

**4.** Transfer shortcake to a plate. Cut shortcake in half horizontally. Spoon Sweetened Whipped Cream and half of the strawberry mixture over shortcake bottom. Replace the top. Top with the remaining sliced strawberries.

**SWEETENED WHIPPED CREAM**
In a chilled bowl combine 1 cup whipping cream, 2 Tbsp. sugar, and ½ tsp. vanilla. Beat with a mixer on medium until soft peaks form (tips curl).

PER SERVING *502 cal., 30 g fat (18 g sat. fat), 122 mg chol., 366 mg sodium, 54 g carb., 3 g fiber, 26 g sugars, 7 g pro.*

**MAKE SAVORY SHORTCAKES** *Shortcake isn't just for dessert. Try serving savory biscuits as a side dish or appetizer. Just prepare the dough as directed, except decrease sugar from ¼ cup to 1 Tbsp. in Step 1. Stir in the sour cream mixture, then stir in one of the following mixtures. Bake as directed for Individual Shortcakes.*

**BACON + BLUE**
2 slices bacon, crisp-cooked and crumbled, and ¼ cup crumbled blue cheese (1 oz.)

**CHIPOTLE + CHEDDAR**
¼ cup finely shredded cheddar cheese (1 oz.) and 2 tsp. chopped canned chipotle chile peppers in adobo sauce (tip, page 18)

**CHEDDAR + ONION**
¼ cup finely shredded white cheddar cheese (1 oz.) and 3 Tbsp. thinly sliced green onions

**MEDITERRANEAN**
2 Tbsp. pitted and finely chopped Kalamata olives, 2 Tbsp. snipped dried tomatoes, and 2 Tbsp. crumbled feta cheese

**INDIVIDUAL SHORTCAKES** Prepare as directed, except drop dough into eight mounds on a greased baking sheet. Bake 12 to 15 minutes or until golden brown. Transfer to wire rack; cool completely. Cut each shortcake in half horizontally. Spoon strawberry mixture and Sweetened Whipped Cream over shortcake bottoms. Replace shortcake tops. Top with the remaining sliced strawberries. Makes 8 servings.

**STRAWBERRY LEMON-POPPY SEED SHORTCAKE** Prepare as directed, except stir 1 Tbsp. poppy seeds and 1 tsp. lemon zest into flour mixture after cutting in butter.

**MIXED-BERRY OR MIXED-FRUIT SHORTCAKE** Prepare as directed, except substitute 5 cups mixed fresh berries (blueberries, raspberries, and/or blackberries) or 5 cups mixed fresh fruit (sliced peaches, nectarines, bananas, strawberries, raspberries, and/or halved grapes) for the 5 cups sliced strawberries. Do not mash fruit. If desired, drizzle fruit with honey.

**STRAWBERRY-NUT SHORTCAKE** Prepare as directed, except stir ½ cup chopped walnuts into flour mixture after cutting in butter.

MAKES: *6 servings*   TESTED BY: *Carla C.*

# 099  WHITE CHOCOLATE CRÈME BRÛLÉE

**TASTING COMMENTS:** *We bake these custards in a water bath—a pan with very hot water in it—to insulate the fragile cream-and-egg mixture from the dry heat of the oven. This method keeps the texture smooth, rich, and creamy.—CC*

*In traditional crème brûlée (which means "burnt sugar" in French), the chilled custards are sprinkled with sugar, which is then browned quickly under a special broiler or with a culinary torch. No need for a torch—this version is practical for any kitchen.*

**PREP** 20 MINUTES   **BAKE** 30 MINUTES AT 325°F   **CHILL** 1 HOUR   **STAND** 20 MINUTES

1³/₄ cups half-and-half

4 oz. white chocolate (with cocoa butter), chopped

5 egg yolks, lightly beaten

¹/₃ cup sugar

1 tsp. vanilla

¹/₈ tsp. salt

2 Tbsp. sugar

**1.** Preheat oven to 325°F. In a small heavy saucepan combine ½ cup of the half-and-half and the white chocolate; cook and stir over low heat just until chocolate is melted. Gradually whisk in the remaining 1¼ cups half-and-half. Bring to simmering. Remove from heat.

**2.** Meanwhile, in a medium bowl whisk together egg yolks, the ¹/₃ cup sugar, the vanilla, and salt just until combined. Slowly whisk hot white chocolate mixture into egg yolk mixture.

**3.** Place six 4-oz. ramekins or 6-oz. custard cups in a 3-qt. rectangular baking dish. Divide custard among ramekins. Place baking dish on oven rack. Pour enough boiling water into dish to reach halfway up sides of ramekins.

**4.** Bake 30 to 40 minutes or until a knife inserted near the centers comes out clean (centers will shake slightly). Remove ramekins from water; cool on a wire rack. Cover and chill 1 to 8 hours.

**5.** Before serving, let custards stand at room temperature 20 minutes. Meanwhile, for caramelized sugar, in a medium heavy skillet heat the 2 Tbsp. sugar over medium-high heat until sugar begins to melt, shaking skillet occasionally to heat sugar evenly. Do not stir. Once the sugar starts to melt, reduce heat to low and cook 3 minutes or until all of the sugar is melted and golden brown, stirring as needed with a wooden spoon.

**6.** Quickly drizzle caramelized sugar over custards. (If sugar hardens in the skillet, return to heat and stir until melted.) Serve immediately.

PER SERVING *307 cal., 18 g fat (10 g sat. fat), 180 mg chol., 98 mg sodium, 31 g carb., 0 g fiber, 28 g sugars, 6 g pro.*

**THE RIGHT WHITE CHOCOLATE** *This is important! Don't mistake those little white baking pieces (available next to chocolate baking pieces) for real white chocolate (which is found next to packaged chocolate bars). The difference lies in the type of fat used in each—white baking pieces are made with waxy hydrogenated oils; white chocolate is made with real cocoa butter (extracted from cocoa beans). The flavor, consistency, and texture of white chocolate is far superior, so make sure your package's ingredients include cocoa butter.*

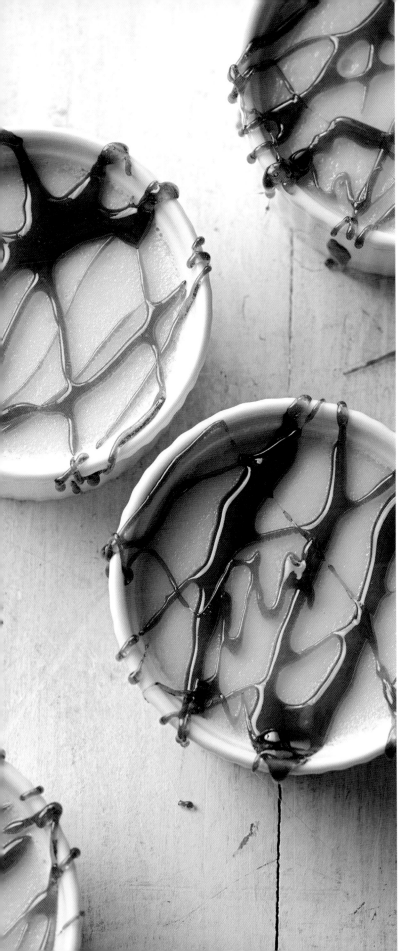

## TESTING NOTES

↑

1. Gradually whisk the hot half-and-half mixture into the beaten egg yolks (a process called tempering), which will slowly heat them through and won't cause a sudden temperature shock. If eggs are exposed to too much heat too quickly, the egg proteins will cook and coagulate, which will leave you with pieces resembling scrambled eggs instead of a smooth custardy mixture.

↑

2. Baked egg-thickened custards that don't contain either flour or cornstarch (like this crème brûlée) need to be baked in a water bath for temperature protection. This will prevent overbaking and separating, which leaves behind tunnels of watery liquid in your dessert.

3. When it's done, the center of the custard will jiggle slightly when gently shaken, which makes it appear undercooked. However, if a thin-blade knife inserted in the center of the custard comes out clean, it is fully baked. Immediately remove the ramekins from the water so the custard doesn't continue to bake.

4. In a heavy skillet (because of sugar's high melting temperature, avoid nonstick skillets), heat the sugar until it begins to melt and turn syrupy. Avoid stirring; occasionally shake the pan lightly to move the sugar around and heat it evenly until it starts to look syrupy around the edges.

↓

↑

5. Start stirring the sugar once it begins to melt so it cooks and browns evenly. When the mixture becomes golden brown, immediately remove from the heat so it doesn't continue to get darker.

↑

6. Immediately drizzle the hot caramelized sugar in thin strings over the custard. Although you can reheat the sugar to resoften, it will continue to get darker.

MAKES: *12 servings*   TESTED BY: *Colleen W.*

# 100   CREAM PUFFS

TASTING COMMENTS: *These are the perfect puffs. When we tested them, we pricked some of the baked puffs with a fork to see if releasing the steam made any difference in texture. It didn't. We also made a batch using refrigerated egg product, but they weren't nearly as crisp or golden. They did not make the grade!—CW*

**PREP** 25 MINUTES   **COOL** 10 MINUTES   **BAKE** 30 MINUTES AT 400°F

1 cup water
½ cup butter
⅛ tsp. salt
1 cup all-purpose flour
4 large eggs
3 cups Sweetened Whipped Cream (page 290), vanilla or chocolate pudding, or ice cream

**1.** Preheat oven to 400°F. Grease a baking sheet. In a saucepan combine the water, butter, and salt. Bring to boiling. Immediately add flour all at once; stir vigorously. Cook and stir until mixture forms a ball. Remove from heat. Cool 10 minutes. Add eggs, one at a time, beating well after each addition.

**2.** Drop dough into 12 mounds on baking sheet. Bake 30 to 35 minutes or until golden brown and firm. Transfer to a wire rack; let cool.

**3.** Just before serving, cut tops from puffs; remove soft dough from inside. Fill with Sweetened Whipped Cream. Replace tops.

PER SERVING *233 cal., 21 g fat (12 g sat. fat), 132 mg chol., 114 mg sodium, 9 g carb., 0 g fiber, 0 g sugars, 4 g pro.*

**MINI PUFFS** Prepare as directed through Step 1. In Step 2 drop dough by rounded teaspoons 2 inches apart onto greased baking sheets. Bake, one sheet at a time, 25 minutes (keep remaining dough covered while first batch bakes). Continue with Step 3. Makes about 30 mini puffs.

## TESTING NOTES

1. After adding the flour, vigorous stirring will get the dough to pull away from the pan sides and come together in a ball or mass. Once the dough ball forms, pull the pan from the heat and let the dough stand to cool. Slight cooling will prevent pieces of the eggs from cooking when you start stirring them in.

2. Add one egg to the warm dough and stir well with the mixing spoon until the egg is mixed in and the dough is smooth. Continue stirring in one egg at a time until four of the eggs are used.

3. After adding all the eggs, the dough will be beautifully smooth and shiny, but also quite sticky and pasty to work with.

↑

1. Drop the heaping tablespoons of dough onto the prepared baking sheet far enough apart to allow for expansion and for hot air to adequately circulate around them during baking to ensure even doneness.

↑

2. Wait until right before serving the puffs to pull the soft interior out and fill them. If you fill your puffs too far ahead, they'll get soggy.

↑

3. There are many wonderful ways to fill a cream puff. Good options include Sweetened Whipped Cream, vanilla or chocolate pudding, and your favorite ice cream.

# INDEX

# A